IS CAPITALISM SUSTAINABLE?

MICHAEL MUNGER

AMERICAN INSTITUTE FOR ECONOMIC RESEARCH

Is Capitalism Sustainable?
By Michael Munger

ISBN 978-1-63-069173-8

Cover design: Vanessa Mendozzi

IS CAPITALISM SUSTAINABLE?

MICHAEL MUNGER

AIER | AMERICAN INSTITUTE *for* ECONOMIC RESEARCH

Contents

GENERAL INTRODUCTION

I have been thinking about markets, and problems with managing human cooperation, for nearly 40 years. In graduate school I was lucky enough to study with Yoram Barzel, Lee Benham, Harold Demsetz, Arthur Denzau, Douglass North, William Riker, Kenneth Shepsle, Murray Weidenbaum, and Barry Weingast. Early in my career I became interested in the work of James Buchanan, Ronald Coase, Friedrich Hayek, Elinor Ostrom, and Gordon Tullock.

When you are young, everything is complicated and each thing seems to have its own separate logic. As you think more about things, common themes and shared, universal explanations start to emerge. For me, the common themes that matter most were those elaborated by James Buchanan and Douglass North. In their work I found the unifying fabric that wove together all the separate threads I had found interesting.

The way Doug North "taught" me the single most important feature of cooperation and failure to cooperate was memorable. In 1984, I was preparing to defend my doctoral thesis, a daunting prospect, because success or failure implied such different futures. At the actual defense, Doug asked me a question, which had several parts, and which I frankly didn't understand. I did what economists always do when they don't understand a question: I went to the blackboard and started drawing equations.

To be fair, economists also do this when they do understand a question, so no one thought much of it. But it quickly became clear I was just spinning my wheels and wasting time. Finally after what seemed like a long time, Doug North raised his hand, gave it a sad but patient shake, and then told me, in a voice you might use to address a beloved but not-very-bright child, "Michael, the answer I was looking for was 'transaction costs.' That's all, just transaction costs."

Within a few years, I realized that this was the unifying theme. For North, the answer was always transaction costs, regardless of the question. It took me another decade to realize that North was right, and that starting with transaction costs would crack almost all the analytical nuts I cared about.

Still, I wondered: Why it had taken me so long to understand something so simple? After thinking about it for a decade, I concluded that the answer was obvious, if ironic: the way that the best analysts and scholars had written about transaction costs was so theoretical, and so opaque to the general public, that it was inaccessible. Yes, the transaction costs of learning about transaction costs was too high. (I told you it was the answer to every question, didn't I?)

So I resolved to devote much of my effort as a scholar to describing and explaining how markets function, what justifies capitalism as a system of social cooperation, and why there are some worrisome tendencies--not inevitable, but worrisome nonetheless--toward political and economic outcomes that none of us want. The result was more than 200 short and medium-length essays. Some of them focused directly on transaction costs; some examined the implications of the failure to take the problem of transaction costs seriously.

The essays were published, in various forms, at the "Econlib" page of the Liberty Fund, headquartered in Indianapolis, IN; at the "Learn Liberty" page of the Institute for Humane Studies, headquartered in Arlington, VA; and at the American Institute for Economic Research, headquartered in Great Barrington, MA.[1] The last, of course, is also the publisher of this book. My thanks to all three organizations for supporting the work over the past fifteen years. In particular, I want to acknowledge the editorial help and comments of David Henderson, Mike Reid, Russ Roberts, Daniel WInchester, and of course Jeffrey Tucker. Chloe Anagnos, Laurie Rice, and the team at AIER did all the work of making mess into manuscript. FInally, my wife, Donna Gingerella put up with all my sullen pouting over the years when I was trying to figure out what I thought, and how to say all that in writing.

Plan of the Book

My goals in these essays are (1) to explain the benefits, and in fact the necessity, of capitalism in organizing human cooperation at scale, and (2) to consider some problems inherent in capitalism.

Karl Marx called some of these problems "contradictions," and while he was wrong about many things, including a value theory based on embodied labor, his perceptions of capitalism were very accurate. The problem for Marxists is simple: every flaw in markets is worse under socialism. At the micro level, every flaw in consumers is worse, and in fact much worse, in voters. Unless you are willing to advocate monarchism, or actual communist dictatorship, markets

1 libertyfund.org, theihs.org, and aier.org, respectively.

and democracy are the only two mechanisms we have for organizing society. So while Marx's theory about the flaws of capitalism has some merit, he was utterly blind to the problems of democracy. Looking back now, with the benefit of the contributions of the Public Choice branch of political economy, we are in a position to evaluate markets and democracy on an even playing field.

And most of the time, for most purposes, capitalism wins. The insight is ancient, actually. You can find it in Cicero (1991, emphasis added), who recognized the possible tension between self interest and the public good. Cicero called "mischievous" the claim that *goodness* (virtue) and *wisdom* (business) are incompatible:

> [A] good man will neither pretend nor conceal anything for the sake of buying or selling on better terms… All falsehood, then, must be removed from contracts. The seller must not employ a sham purchaser, nor the buyer one to depreciate the article on sale by too low a bid. Let either party, if it comes to naming the price, say once for all what he will give or take. Quintus Scaevola, the son of Publius, when he asked to have the price of an estate that he was buying named once for all, and the seller had complied with his request, said that he thought it worth more, and added a hundred thousand sesterces.
>
> There is no one who would say that this was not the act of a good man; *but men in general would not regard it as the act of a wise man, any more than if he had sold an estate for less than it would bring. This, then, is the mischievous doctrine, — regarding some men as good, others as wise…*

> I see, indeed, that Hecato of Rhodes, a disciple of Panaetius, says, in the books on Duties which he dedicated to Quintus Tubero: *"It is a wise man's duty, while he does nothing contrary to morals, laws, and customs, to have regard to his private fortune. For we desire to be rich, not for ourselves alone, but for children, kindred, friends, and most of all for the state, — considering that the means and resources of individual citizens are the wealth of the state."* (Book 3, Chapter 15)

That's pretty big stuff. So long as you obey the laws and norms of exchange, profits are yours to keep. And this conception of profits actually strengthens the nation. It is "mischievous" to claim that some people are good, and others are wise. Capitalism, operating under a rule of law protecting property rights, is the means by which the actions of the "wise" are also "good" for the entire society.

Capitalism is the essential organizing system for large societies. Full stop. Period. There are no other contenders. There are three arguments for why this is true, and each is explored in some depth in this book. But the key thing to start out with is the fact that humans, with very few exceptions, are by nature cooperative and happy to give mutual aid. Adam Smith (1991; Book I, Chapter 2) famously called this the tendency to "truck, barter, and exchange." Smith was surprisingly self-aware—and frankly, egalitarian—in his view of basic human abilities. Smith compares the "philosopher," the person held in highest esteem by the Enlightenment, and the "street porter," a person among the most "lumpen" (ragged, slow-witted) of what Marx would later call the "lumpenproletariat." Smith noted that, while the philosopher might like to think of his/herself as being innately superior in some way, much of the apparent differences are simply the result of extended application of study and practice, made possible by division of labor.

> The difference of natural talents in different men, is, in reality, much less than we are aware of; and the very different genius which appears to distinguish men of different professions, when grown up to maturity, is not upon many occasions so much the cause, as the effect of the division of labour. The difference between the most dissimilar characters, between a philosopher and a common street porter, for example, seems to arise not so much from nature, as from habit, custom, and education. When they came in to the world, and for the first six or eight years of their existence, they were, perhaps, very much alike, and neither their parents nor play-fellows could perceive any remarkable difference. About that age, or soon after, they come to be employed in very different occupations. The difference of talents comes then to be taken notice of, and widens by degrees, till at last the vanity of the philosopher is willing to acknowledge scarce any resemblance. *But without the disposition to truck, barter, and exchange, every man must have procured to himself every necessary and conveniency of life which he wanted.* All must have had the same duties to perform, and the same work to do, and there could have been no such difference of employment as could alone give occasion to any great difference of talents.
>
> As it is this disposition which forms that difference of talents, so remarkable among men of different professions, so it is this same disposition which renders that difference useful. Many

tribes of animals, acknowledged to be all of the same species, derive from nature a much more remarkable distinction of genius, than what, antecedent to custom and education, appears to take place among men. By nature a philosopher is not in genius and disposition half so different from a street porter, as a mastiff is from a grey-hound, or a grey-hound from a spaniel, or this last from a shepherd's dog. Those different tribes of animals, however, though all of the same species are of scarce any use to one another. The strength of the mastiff is not in the least supported either by the swiftness of the greyhound, or by the sagacity of the spaniel, or by the docility of the shepherd's dog. The effects of those different geniuses and talents, for want of the power or disposition to barter and exchange, cannot be brought into a common stock, and do not in the least contribute to the better accommodation and conveniency of the species. Each animal is still obliged to support and defend itself, separately and independently, and derives no sort of advantage from that variety of talents with which nature has distinguished its fellows. Among men, on the contrary, the most dissimilar geniuses are of use to one another; the different produces of their respective talents, by the general disposition to truck, barter, and exchange, being brought, as it were, into a common stock, where every man may purchase whatever part of the produce of other men's talents he has occasion for.

In other words, the mastiff's muscle does not depend on the spaniel's sagacity; they are just genetically different and that's that. But the people who are now the philosopher and street

> porter were once very similar, and in fact nearly indistinguishable. One developed the talent of "being a philosopher." That development depended on a system where others did all the other things—making food and clothing, providing housing and security, and so on—that made it possible for the philosopher to study for decades. (Smith, 1991; Book I)

In other words, our ability to cooperate is not based on genetic differences. Instead, specialization is the result of a system--capitalism--that allows each of us to invest in highly differentiated skills and knowledge. We can be confident of two things: other people will specialize in all the other things, the things we need but won't be able to make for ourselves. And we will be entitled to the increase in consumption opportunities, or "profits," that result from our specialization.

There are two key mechanisms operating within a capitalist system. Each is important. Together they are indispensable.

A. Capitalism gives individuals the incentive, and also the means, of acting to advance the interests of others. It is a moral mistake for me to use something that is valued more highly by someone else. But without capitalism there are two problems, both species of transaction costs. First, I have no way of knowing whether someone else values my widget, my tool, or my medicinal herb more than I do. Capitalism solves this problem by using prices as low cost signals of the desire other people have to use what I own. Second, I have no easy way of sharing the useful thing, without harming myself. A good person would give it to the needier party, perhaps, but a wise person would not. Capitalism solves this problem by allowing transactions or mutually beneficial voluntary exchange. If I value something more than you, I can pay you more than you value it but less than I value it. You can take that value, or money, and use it for something you want more. I actually *benefit* from ensuring that the widget is delivered to someone who values it more. The wise action and the good action are the same. It's the first miracle of capitalism.

B. Capitalism rewards investment, whether it be in specialized tools and capital for the producer or specialized skills and talents by the artisan. If I can create new products or services, or deliver existing products or services at a lower price, I am creating value for the society. The constant search for profit by entrepreneurs, where thousands of people are independently seeking along every conceivable avenue a means of serving others, is a remarkable achievement of capitalism. Innovation and the discovery of what people want face very high transaction costs, because no one has enough information to be able to foresee how new products will be evaluated by consumers. In fact, consumers themselves may not know. As Henry Ford (may have) said, "If I had asked customers what they wanted, they would have said 'faster horses.'" Profits are the reward that society offers for the enormous deliveries of "consumer surplus" that capitalism provides daily to participants in the market.

The book is organized into sections, with each section arguing a particular theme. The argument and style is informal, but I have tried to give references and sources where I can. If the source is academic or "published" in the traditional fashion, I have used the convention of giving an in-line citation, with the references listed at the end of the book. The references that are web sites or blogs are usually given in footnotes; I'm afraid it's the nature of the interwebs that some of those are likely dead, or will be non-functional by the time you read this.

Further, the book is a collection of essays. I hope that they build on each other. But some of the references and examples are repetitive, because that's how I think of the subject in each separate essay. The book is meant to be read episodically, essay by essay, rather than like a textbook with a unidirectional organization. (It worked for David Hume, so….)

The first section of the book is an overview of capitalism, and the potential problem of sustainability of capitalism in a democracy. This was, and is, the most important Marxist or leftist critique of capitalism, and it is important to address it at the outset.

The second section takes a step back and looks at the problem of rules, and the way groups of people organize themselves. There are two very different conceptions of rules, those that emerge from practice and experience (like language) and those that are the product of conscious choice and intentional wording (like constitutions). Both have their place. But it turns out that the transaction costs of getting rules right is very high, and "paving the muddy paths" that have emerged over time is more useful than you might think.

The third section makes the argument for capitalism. Surprisingly few people know the core arguments for capitalism; I try to cover several, from different perspectives. For one thing, capitalism makes racism and bigotry a lot more expensive; in a competitive system, in fact, racism is impossible. Further, the real argument for capitalism, as I pointed out above, rests on the benefits to consumers. The creation of consumer surplus is hard to measure, but the past 100 years have seen an unprecedented increase in benefits, in terms of the type, variety, quality, and declining prices of most products and services. We don't notice any of this, though, because our ticket to capitalism is free.

Section four discusses key concepts, including division of labor, public goods, rent-seeking, opportunity costs, and externalities. Section five zeroes in on a particularly interesting, but controversial, topic: profits. Profits, because of their role in increasing inequality, in the view of many observers at least, are often misunderstood and frankly misrepresented. I try to work out some of the problems with how profits are perceived, and offer at least a qualified defense of profits in the absence of rent-seeking.

Sections six and seven switch the focus from markets to the state. I am an ex-president of the Public Choice Society, and was a long-time editor of the journal *Public Choice*. So the approach that I take to understanding the state, and democratic processes, derives from that view. Public Choice has three essential elements: the notion of politics as "exchange," methodological individualism, and motivational symmetry. More simply, it takes as the objective of politics the mutual and collective benefits that come from cooperation, but it also assumes that people act on their own and that it is not sufficient simply to assume that people will act in the public interest in politics. Public Choice is concerned with the study of rules and in the problem of aggregation.

The final section looks to the future. I am concerned about the future of the economy, but also about the future of how we conceive the nature of politics. I argue for a "directional," rather than "destinationist," conception of political action. Many people, across the ideological and political spectrums, have a particular conception of "the good," and they are obdurate about rejecting any proposal or policy that does not fully and immediately achieve their utopia. There are two problems with this view, as I see it. First, politics doesn't work that way: there are short term movements, and compromises, with piecemeal implementation of some portions of one program laid on top of older, possibly contradictory, programs. Second, we don't know enough to be able to plan out full systems of political organization; the best we can hope is to direct marginal change in the right direction. My concern is that we have been going in the wrong directions, on many dimensions, for some time. And this book is my effort to reduce some of the transaction costs of rethinking those directions.

I

INTRODUCTION: IS CAPITALISM SUSTAINABLE?

1. Capitalism is Fragile

Folks on the political left claim they believe capitalism doesn't work.

The real problem is exactly the opposite: the political left thinks that capitalism is robust, and in fact indestructible. Government can tack on taxes, social policy requirements like required leave or generous benefits, and aggressive and highly restrictive regulation, and capitalism will just keep motoring along.

An example: I have a good friend, a university professor and committed leftist, who is absolutely convinced that capitalism is full of "contradictions." Because Marx said so.

My friend was set to retire, in 2009. Everything was scheduled, the papers were signed in 2007 in preparation, he was on the glide path. Except that the stock market started to turn sour. And then it turned rancid.

As a fan of capitalism, I knew that it often punished bad decision-making. I hate to brag (okay, that's not true), but at my suggestion my wife and I put all our assets, including retirement and savings, into money market funds or very short bonds. We did this in August, 2007, and stayed in cash until March 2009. Since cash returns about zero, that means we made about a 40% return compared to having invested in stocks, which started vibrating badly in October, and went completely off the rails in late November of 2007. (When I do something dumb, and my wife Donna is mad at me, I still bring up the "armadillo strategy" of August 2007. This defense is fading in effectiveness, but I'll probably keep using it).

In early 2009, I noticed my leftist friend was looking kind of glum. He asked to talk. As the department chair, I was the administrator he reported to, the one he needed to talk to about changing his retirement plans. When we met, he said that he couldn't afford to retire. Turned out he had had 100% of his retirement funds (he was more than 70 in 2007) in stocks. He had lost nearly half of his retirement money in the period between November 2007 and December 2008. So, he asked to have his employment extended and retirement delayed.

He was a good teacher and a productive scholar, so I was happy to agree. Still, I was curious: why had he changed his mind?

His answer was that capitalism had killed his dreams. He actually said that there ought to be regulation to prevent stocks from declining in value, now that it had turned out that it could go down and people could lose money. He was old, so I pointed out he surely knew that already, having seen it happen in '74, '87, and '01 (at a minimum). I asked why, if he knew stocks were risky, he had put all his retirement funds in stock. Looking sheepish, he said, "I thought I could make a higher return that way."

This story illustrates two ways that capitalism is fragile. First, taxes, regulations and government actions can hammer the expectations of investors and the plans of entrepreneurs. Uncertainty about politics and the direction of monetary policy is extremely toxic to growth. Second, because investors and entrepreneurs recognize the first fact, it is very tempting to seek state "help," seeking subsidies and regulatory protection instead of seeking honest profits. And even if most entrepreneurs and CEOs steadfastly refuse the blandishments of the state, that siren's song of subsidy, some entrepreneurs are likely to succumb. And the state itself benefits, at least in terms of power and aggrandizement of political leadership, from centralizing and regulating industry.

Let's think a little more deeply about this problem.

Tyranny, Rent-Seeking, and the False Promise of "Next Time, All We Need is Good People!"

Tyranny is unchecked power, concentrated in a few hands. The only hope for people who live in tyranny is the naïve hope that the tyrant will be wise and benevolent.

In many cases, the form this naïve hope takes is expressed through the institution of elections. But majority rule, or for that matter any voting system, is at best a partial solution. Without constitutional protections for individual rights, elections are simply the "freedom" to choose a tyrant.

Advocates for capitalism claim that — unlike in politics — markets "work" even if people are self-interested, because the dynamics of competition limit bad actions. As economists, we have long accepted this claim. But political events, and the tendencies of market economies around the world, have led me to question whether capitalism is really sustainable.

Sustainability, according to the U.S. Environmental Protection Agency, is "meeting the needs of the present without compromising the ability of future generations to meet their own needs." We have always thought of sustainability in terms of the environment, or use of resources, but systems like capitalism face some of the same problems.

One reason that we tolerate the instability and inconveniences of capitalism is that this "creative destruction" is the mechanism that enables entrepreneurs find ways to produce new products, new services, or new ways of making things that make consumers better off. Many of us would pay far more than the store price for clean water, wholesome food, cars that run for 200,000 miles, or cell phones that connect us to the entire world. Entrepreneurs think up the new goods or services, and competition drives down the price. The result is that many products not available even to the very wealthy in 1900 are now owned by all but the poorest among us.

The word that capitalism uses to identify the rewards for entrepreneurial creativity is "profit," or what's left over after the entrepreneur pays all workers and suppliers who make the product. The only way that there can be profits, under capitalism, is if consumers are willing to pay a lot more for the product than it costs to make. Lots of profits, lots of benefits to consumers, rapid increase in the wealth of the society. Sure, that increase may not be equally shared, but it makes sense that the people who take risks and find the right new way to make consumers better off should win big, right?

Maybe. The problem is that even if you believe that, there is another way to make what look like "profits," in the accounting sense of revenues exceeding costs. Economists call that "rent-seeking," or the use of state-created privileges, favorable government rules and regulations to attract taxpayer-funded subsidies, or protection from competition. Those government programs allow producers to charge much higher prices, because competition is kept out by regulation. Or the government may take money from taxpayers and simply give it to companies. Either way, no value is created for consumers. In fact, consumers are likely harmed because they are denied choices and have to pay higher prices.

Markets to Government

There's nothing illegal about rent-seeking, mind you, because the government is making up the rules. In fact, from the perspective of the participants, rent seeking is rational. Imagine that you are a corporate CEO, and you want to do some hiring. You could hire engineers, the kind of folks who make new products or make existing products more cheaply. Or, you could hire lawyers and lobbyists, folks who work with government officials to pass new laws that keep out competition or pay you subsidies.

The problem is that if you want to earn honest profits, you have to sell to consumers, who want quality and low prices. That's hard, especially for mature products in industries that have been around a while. At some level, even the most independent-minded entrepreneurs realize that it's easier to sell a sad story to the state than it is to sell real products to consumers. In fact, you can't blame the corporate leaders who succumb to this temptation: there's nothing illegal about making government your source of revenue.

But rent seeking is not capitalism, which involves the pursuit of profit through selling willing consumers better and cheaper products. And that's why we wonder if capitalism is sustainable: we are asking our business leaders to have enough scruples that they leave money on the table. Rent-seeking is immoral, but not illegal, so when we ask corporate leaders to refuse to participate in cronyism we are invoking the idea of "the system will only work if we can ensure that people are good."

Remember, the argument for capitalism is based on the claim that even self-interested business leaders will benefit the whole system. But if self-interest leads toward cronyism, there's a problem. Of course, we could just move one step up the chain, and hope for "good" political leaders. After all, politicians get to design the system of incentives, and in principle that system could deny opportunities for rent-seeking. But why would a politician want to do that? Forcing businesses to line up to beg for favors is a big help at fundraising time.

The problem, then, is that we are on the "road to cronyism," and it's hard to see how we can turn off. I recently wrote (Munger and Villarreal-Diaz, 2019) about this problem at greater length, with my very smart coauthor Mario Villarreal-Diaz at the University of Texas. Here's the difficulty, as succinctly as I can manage it: corporate leaders benefit, monetarily and in the short run, from negotiating favorable legislation and protection from politicians.

Even if business leaders behave "irrationally" and leave that money on the table — remember, it's legal to lobby, even if it's immoral — it's still true that politicians benefit from making businesses dependent on taxpayer handouts. Businesses that don't play along will be singled out for "special" attention, either by extra taxes or unwelcome regulation.

Money for the Taking

Worse, if some modern Commodore Vanderbilt--as Folsom (1987) pointed out, the original was famously opposed to rent-seeking--tried to refuse subsidies, it's likely he or she would be fired and replaced by someone who was less principled and more willing to deliver short-run profits from taking subsidies. Or some outside firm might buy up the stock of the principled company, because the equity would be underpriced compared to its value if managers sought government rents and handouts.

It comes down to this: as a company grows, it has fewer opportunities to make new investments that have high returns. At some point, the last dollar invested in honest profits is going to return less than the first dollar to be spent on cronyism. After that, the firm becomes dependent on the state. And that's crony capitalism. Independent capitalism may not be sustainable, in the face of such incentives.

2. Is Capitalism Worth Saving?

Any social system must coordinate production and cooperation, and must also implement a system of distribution that participants perceive as sustainable, which often means morally fair. As Nobelist Elinor Ostrom (1990; 2000) demonstrated, there are many and widely varied social systems that can be found in settings where there are small groups and long-term, indefinitely repeated interactions.

But at scale—meaning in groups of 10,000 or more—there are only three social systems available:

1. Some form of authoritarianism, sometimes with a legitimating creation myth based on religion or tradition, and sometimes simply based on the threat of violence. In these systems, production and distribution are idiosyncratic. In some, such as Singapore, the results may be pretty good. In others, such as Zimbabwe or North Korea, the results are catastrophic.
2. Capitalism, using markets for production and input prices, asset prices, and profits and losses for distribution. To the extent that the violent powers of the state are put up for sale, distribution may be skewed toward wealthy elites.
3. Democratic Socialism, where the means of production and most prices are decided by majority rule, or by some technocracy to whom authority is delegated by law. The system of distribution is often egalitarian in concept, but skewed in practice toward those who have political power.

I will say no more of authoritarianism because it is hard to be systematic about idiosyncrasy. And I will note that zealous defenders of capitalism, or socialism, might object to my characterizations of their "tendencies." But there is a tradition, dating back at least to Aristotle, to mention both the ideal system and its corrupted form. And it is clear that in capitalist systems there is the possibility for wealth to metastasize into political power, and that in socialist systems there is the possibility that political power expands to command unearned material wealth. This problem, of placing constitutional limits on power, is the core of the "limiting Leviathan" approach of "constitutional political economy," an offshoot of public choice pioneered by James Buchanan.

The reason to include both the ideal types and their corrupted forms is to avoid a common mistake, a kind of ideal type bias. We all want to compare the actual form, and pathologies, of systems we dislike with the ideal form, as we can imagine it, of systems we admire.

The Pretty Pig

I call this the "pretty pig" problem. The snag is that while some pigs may be less ugly than others, no adult pigs are pretty. Nonetheless, imagine that there is a beauty contest of adult pigs.[2] The judges were ready, and the first pig was brought out.

---

2 The reader may recognize what James Buchanan and Gordon Tullock called, at least in lectures, the "Emperor Problem." In their version, it played out with minstrels, singing for the emperor. The first was so awful that the contest was ended and the prize given to the unheard second minstrel. A version of the story is told by Peter Boettke (2013) at about minute 1:00.

"Holy smokes! What an ugly pig!" The judges gag in disgust. The old boar is muddy, smelly, fat, and hairy; it grunts and blows snot as it walks.

The judges conferred, and announce their decision: That first pig is so ugly that they will simply give the second pig the prize. Members of the audience protest, saying that they hadn't even seen the second pig. "Yes, that's true. But we have seen the first pig. And it is not pretty. The second pig wins!"

This real/ideal comparison is common for almost everyone. People on the left note the problems with market processes, and then conclude "therefore the state should step in." But that's not obvious, unless the actual actions of the state are an improvement. The reverse is also true: highlighting (legitimate) problems with democracy or the state does not automatically imply "and therefore the market is the best option."

The Argument for Capitalism

But then, what *is* the argument for capitalism? It is simple: wealth and prosperity is the result of the division of labor. If a group of people can cooperate by carrying out different specialized functions, then everyone can have more. In fact, they can have a lot more, of almost everything.

The difficulty is that the division of labor makes each of us dependent on the delivery of all the many things we need, in exchange for the very small number of things we know how to make, or do. This kind of specialization is reflected in many of our last names: Coopers made barrels, Smiths made iron items, Bakers were bread makers, Mongers sold things, and so on.

Adam Smith (1976) illustrated the benefits of the division of labor using his "pin factory" example: 18 people making pins as artisans could make only a few pins per day. But if the 18 people divide up the tasks in what we would now call a production line, those same 18 workers could make thousands of pins.

Of course, that's a lot more pins than they could use. As Smith pointed out, the division of labor is limited by the "extent of the market." This is great for consumers, but it can be hard on workers.

Smith gives a clever example: the woolen coat. For centuries, artisans had made a living by making crude clothing out of skins and rough fabrics. Even quite early in the Industrial Revolution these thousands of artisans were replaced by processes that were far more efficient and also produced better quality clothing. A few dozen people working on a production line could produce a coat that was of such high quality that only royalty could have obtained such an item just a few decades earlier.

Capitalism, in short, is about consumer sovereignty, not about creating jobs. Capitalism finds ways to create new products, better versions of existing products, and cheaper prices for products that are also much more widely available. Capitalism creates a complex, voluntary mutual dependence, and the only way one person can consume things is by creating things other people want to consume. It's actually a kind of sharing, except that we don't need to know much about the people we are depending on.

The creation of this huge amount of wealth—and notice that wealth is stuff, things to consume and use, not money or gold—went a long way toward curing poverty, in much of the world. But some people would say that curing poverty came at a price: a big increase in inequality.

At least, that's the most sensible form of the argument. For the least sensible opponents of capitalism, the only consideration is inequality. But poverty and inequality are completely different things. And they have very different solutions: The way to end poverty is to enable the poor to enrich themselves, so there are no poor people. The way to end inequality is to destroy wealth, so there are no rich people.

It is tempting to think, "Why not both?" The problem is that it appears doing both at the same time is not easy. Since the pro-market reforms of Deng Xiaoping, beginning in 1978, China has seen two enormous changes.

1. The largest decline in poverty in history. More than 500 million people were lifted out of extreme poverty as China's poverty rate fell from 88 percent in 1981 to 6.5 percent in 2012. Poverty defined as living on the equivalent of US$2.00 or less per day in 2011 purchasing price parity terms.
2. An enormous increase in income inequality. China has by far the greatest income inequality of any nation or region in the world.

If you ask the poor people of China who have seen a dramatic increase in their living standard, in many cases an increase of 1,000 percent or more in PPP terms, many are likely to say that the increased inequality from using market systems was easily worth it, because of the dramatic decline in poverty. The point is that if you care mostly about inequality, you have to admit you are indifferent to the plight of the poor.

Or perhaps you want a different system that simultaneously reduces inequality and reduces poverty. The problem is that there is no such "other system." The idea that there is an alternative is an illusion. There are no examples of a socialist system managing a system that is either prosperous or egalitarian. Much less both.

I should be careful. Remember, by socialism, I mean a system that relies on state ownership and control of the means of production, state direction of production decisions, and direct state control of education and employment decisions of individuals. If one does not mean those things, then that would require a little more thinking about what "socialism" means.

1. Ownership solves the problem of the commons. But political incentives are very short-run. Presumably we are talking about "democratic socialism." But then it is not clear that state ownership is better than private ownership. In fact, the environmental record of socialist nations in the Soviet bloc and in China is not very good (Ridgeway, 1990).
2. Using prices gives useful signals about relative scarcity, and incentives for decentralized but highly organized individual action. A socialist system sets prices, rather than allowing prices to adjust to reflect the dynamics of fast-moving events.
3. Without prices, we must either rely on the desires of individual dictators or state control. Without prices in the form of salaries, there's no way to direct people toward job shortages except coercive force.

If we want the form of state control to take the form of democracy—and presumably we do want that—then we have to confront a difficulty. That difficulty is at the core of the "ugly pig contest" I discussed above, and it's deceptively simple.

The difficulty is this: Every flaw in consumers is worse in voters. That's deceptively simple sounding, but it's important. Every flaw in consumers is worse in voters.

Voters and Irrationality

Take the individual consumers, the ones who are too dumb, ill-informed, or easily misled to make choices about what size Coke to buy. It may be, as my Duke colleague Dan Ariely—author of *Predictably Irrational* (2010) and other books on behavioral economics—has argued, that people just don't have all the information they need to be able to carry out the role of a fully "rational" consumer in the standard economics model.

But think about it: if we take a large number of such dim bulbs, and gather them together into a mob, are they suddenly able to solve the problem that no one of them understands? Absolutely not. All the problems that Ariely and behavioral economists list, including an undue focus on free stuff, an inability to consider the future, and choices contingent on the set of alternatives, are even worse in voters.

So, there is a real problem for the democratic socialist who starts with the idea that consumers need help. If you think we can use democracy as a replacement for prices, deciding what the "true" value of wages, commodities, and assets should be, you would have to explain that voters are smarter than consumers. Not only are they the same people, but the institution of democracy provides less information and gives less responsibility to the individual.

After all, if I buy a bad car, I have to drive a bad car and I'm likely to think about it more next time. But my vote for President, or a referendum such as Brexit, has no impact on the outcome, and I am free, as Bryan Caplan (2008) has pointed out, to have no connection to rationality at all.

Of course, many people who advocate for socialism don't really think voters are capable of making such choices, and would entrust power to a secular priesthood of experts and bureaucrats. But such a "solution" would have to pursue its own logic to the conclusion that the power of experts must be placed beyond the control of voters. That is simply a recipe for authoritarianism, an unelected and unaccountable oligarchy that rules for its own purposes and with its own goals.

Unsurprisingly, it has been exactly that outcome that all real experiments in socialism have ended up reaching. If you accept that democracy is no better, and is often much worse, in solving problems of information and incentives than markets, than you recognize that democratic socialism is not desirable. If your solution is to suspend democratic accountability, you are conceding that democratic socialism is not possible.

Either way, that first pig, the capitalist pig, is looking pretty good. A clear-eyed comparison of the alternatives actually available to us reveal why all the world's developed nations use some version of capitalism. The only people who advocate socialism are those who don't know how it actually works.

The Three Core Principles of Capitalism

I have to admit that I'm worried that this problem of "not knowing how capitalism works" is widespread. I teach several different "capstone" courses, courses for students about to graduate and go off into the world. One of the most surprising things about these otherwise well-educated students is that they cannot summarize the basic argument for capitalism.

It's fine that they might not be persuaded by the argument; that's a matter of personal conscience and understanding of how the world works. What I find bizarre is that they cannot even summarize the argument coherently. At best, they might say something about self-interest, or freedom. That's even the ones who like capitalism, mind you. The opponents will say something about greed, and inequality, and maybe exploitation.

I have found it useful to summarize the argument for capitalism briefly, and in some ways superficially. First, wealth is stuff that is useful to us. It can be food, drink, or more convenient ways to obtain food and drink. It can be clothing, housing, transportation, or video games or movies delivered to our homes or to theaters, to be available in the event we decide to avail ourselves of the opportunity.

These things are being provided almost constantly, in the background, without any of us really noticing. Ships, airplanes and trucks are operating on tight schedules to deliver remarkably fresh food products to stores. But we only notice those avocados, or MP3 players, when they are already in the bins, ready to be purchased, or not purchased if we decide we don't want them. In other words, consumers get lots of inexpensive, high quality stuff, but all the risks are borne by the system, not by the consumer. That's wealth.

There are three elements to the argument for capitalism, and while they connect in crucial ways they can be separately defined. Those three elements are (a) Division of Labor; (b) Impersonal Exchange Based on Prices; and (3) Economies of Scale Based on Knowledge.

A. Division of Labor

It is only a slight simplification to claim that all the increases in wealth, all of them, since the beginning of time, have been the result of the division of labor. If four of us all produce everything each of us needs, individually, we don't have much stuff. We will stagger along on the edge of subsistence, and some of us may not survive. If the four of us make a deal, and one produces clothing, one shoes, one food, and one housing and water supplies, each of us will get better at doing the one thing we specialize in.[3] The result is that, instead of subsistence, the population can grow. The group can now support more people. Each person faces a "make or buy" decision, and if you can buy something more cheaply than you can make it, you specialize in what you are good at and buy everything else.

This feeds back on itself: instead of one person specializing in each activity, there are now 24 people and six people work in each activity, dividing the making of shoes into six different stages, with the consequent increases in productivity in each stage now multiplying the amount of wealth available. And new activities become possible, with some of the population now providing artistic accomplishment or entertainment. Before, with the small, unspecialized population, music was provided by one guy beating on a hollow log with sticks. Now, with the larger population and division of labor, we reach a population of 10,000 in our city, and we have a string quartet, or maybe even a chamber orchestra. A few people may be spending their time writing new musical compositions (wealth can be culture, not just shoes!).

---

3 For a review, see Munger (n.d.), *Concise Encyclopedia of Economics*.

B. Impersonal Exchange Based on Prices

At some point, the city walls cannot contain the exuberant wealth creation of capitalism. For centuries, city-states were the limiting factor on the division of labor, because institutions of transportation and finance hindered regional trade and made global trade impractical. Trade and exchange took place within the city-state, and larger city-states were wealthier because they could support more division of labor.

But capitalism wants to be global, because the division of labor is limited by the extent of the market. In a larger "market," more different people are working for you. That means that the diversity and quality of products simply explodes, and prices fall. Of course, just as local division of labor meant individuals had to specialize, now cities and regions begin to specialize. Now, cities and regions face the "make or buy" decision, and they become wealthy precisely to the extent that they can focus on what they do best, and buy everything else.

This pressure to expand the extent of the market has some surprising effects. To consumers, all costs are transaction costs. So entrepreneurs turn their creative energies to devising institutions to reduce transaction costs. Transportation, finance, accounting, futures markets, and insurance all become activities that both create value for consumers all over the world and create good livelihoods for their practitioners. The need for an ability to raise and redirect liquid capital, quickly and across great distances, gives rise to an entire financial sector.

The result is that huge and impossibly complex arrays of information are summarized in simple parameters called "prices." Prices signal the relative scarcity of products, inputs, and commodities, and create systems of dynamic adjustment that are breathtakingly efficient. If there is a shortage of something, for a variety of reasons that may be hard to summarize, prices send out the signal of scarcity by rising. Then, almost miraculously, the problem of the shortage is quickly solved, by the three consequences of price increases: (i) consumers buy less, leaving some of the scarce item for others; (ii) producers make more, providing more of the scarce item; and (iii) entrepreneurs devise substitutes, easing the pressure of the shortage.

Folks who don't understand capitalism always want to manage prices. But freely adjusting prices ensure that shortages will always be quickly mitigated, even if no one knows what the cause of the problem is. Prices are signals for all the decentralized actors, in myriad places and without any communication among them, to cooperate in solving shortages.

The result is that each of us buys things from thousands of other people we don't know, will never meet, and yet can trust completely to work for us and make the things we need.

C. Growth based on economies of scale

When someone discovers a better way to do something, or a new way to serve consumers, the results are communicated rapidly through the system. On millions of dimensions, some large and some small, right now entrepreneurs are beavering away looking for knowledge. An improvement in technology or an expansion in the ways we can use liquid capital to create physical capital immediately improves the welfare of the whole world. Economists call this an "economy of scale," which means that specialization and increased social capital in the form of discoveries quickly spread around the world as force multipliers for labor and entrepreneurs.

Where once we lived in a world where there was a relatively fixed amount of stuff, the division of which meant the only way for me to get more is for you to have less, in a world of global capitalism we can all have more, at the same time. Much of the new "wealth" is digital, and takes the form of music, movies, or other entertainment, or software, code that once written down can be reproduced at no cost and transmitted worldwide essentially for free. Products or computer code devised for one purpose can be redirected and reused for new activities that at this point we can't even imagine.

As I said at the outset, I understand that this discussion, with three separate facets of capitalism, is superficial and inadequate. But if our seniors, attending their thousands of graduation ceremonies at all those different colleges and universities, had even this level of understanding of the argument for capitalism it would be a big step forward.

3. Why You Can't Just "Reject" Capitalism

The *Washington Post* (Ehrenfreund, 2016) blared the headline: "Majority of Millennials Now Reject Capitalism, Poll Shows."[4]

I suspect, perhaps unfairly, that this is a matter of some pleasure for the Post's editorial board.

But if you actually read the article, a different picture emerges. In fact, 42 percent of the millennials polled say they support capitalism. In comparison, only 33 percent say they support socialism. So an equally accurate, and less tendentious, headline would have been: "Millennials Favor Capitalism over Socialism by Wide Margin." At a minimum, by the logic of "rejecting capitalism," we should say that "Two-thirds of Millennials Reject Socialism!"

You Can't Just "Reject" Capitalism Any More Than You Can Reject Gravity

Of course, there are some problems interpreting these answers. For one thing, it's not clear that the millennials in the sample (or folks of any age the Post's editorial board) can actually define capitalism,

4 Ehrenfreund, Max. (2016).. "A majority of millennials now reject capitalism, poll shows." Washington Post. April 26. https://www.washingtonpost.com/news/wonk/wp/2016/04/26/a-majority-of-millennials-now-reject-capitalism-poll-shows/.

or for that matter, socialism.

But more importantly, it's not clear that you can "reject" capitalism, any more than you can reject gravity. Numerous accounts of the (now-failed) socialist nations document the emergence of market exchange and production even in the most difficult circumstances. Markets happen, often with the tacit consent of states that officially decry exchange, because otherwise society cannot function. The "transition" from communism in fin de siècle Eastern Europe was largely accomplished before it became official.[5]

Oddly, support for "capitalism" may be stronger in countries that pretend to be socialist. In China, according to Simmons (2014), more than three-quarters of respondents agree that "people are mostly better off in free market systems." Based on this, it would appear that millennials are out of step not just with the U.S., but with the world, and especially with China. What gives?

I think part of the answer is the fact that I have alluded to above: the set of policies required to suppress private exchange and production are so draconian that they are inconceivable. But it is also important to recognize the importance of another explanation millennials have rarely heard: capitalism fosters cooperation, giving desperate people a chance to find creative ways to serve one another. What's not to like?

---

5 "This movement should create a situation in which authorities will control empty stores, but not the market; the employment of workers, but not their livelihood; the official media, but not the circulation of information; printing plants, but not the publishing movement; the mail and telephones, but not communication; and the school system, but not education." Solidarity's Wiktor Kulerski on Poland's parallel society (written while in hiding). Rehmke (2013).

Capitalism Brought Slushies to a Refugee Camp

A recent example is striking, even poignant, because it is both quotidian and yet easily appreciated by anyone with a sweet tooth: slushies.

I don't mean slushies at your local gas station, or some county fair. I mean slushies in a Syrian refugee camp in Jordan. Zaatari has 110,000 "residents." In terms of population, that's about the same size as Topeka, Kansas, almost as big as Charleston, South Carolina.

A respectable size for a city.

Where one might expect squalid conditions and the kind of cheating and bad dealings that scarcity can create, what one finds instead is…slushies. Australian reporter Steve Pennells (2016) tells the story of how slushies, and a lot of other services, provided in an orderly fashion and motivated by profit. It's a simple yet sophisticated system.[6]

Capitalism, in other words.

What Makes Capitalism Happen?

The notion of profit and loss, explained beautifully by Ludwig von Mises (2008), is what drives capitalism. The usual definition of "private ownership of the means of production," is a diversion. The point is that producers get paid if—but only if—they produce more value for consumers than the production uses up in resources. Everyone gets a benefit:

- Labor, owners of machines, and sellers of other inputs all get paid.

6 Pennell, Steve. (2016). "Transcript: Syrian Refugee Crisis." Yahoo Australia. https://au.news.yahoo.com/sunday-night/transcripts/a/23697384/transcript-syrian-refugee-crisis/

- Consumers only buy if the price is less than what they as individuals value the product (Subjective value, anyone?).[7]

Only if there is something left over does the producer get paid. It's a pretty terrific system, and it happens without anyone telling anyone else what to do. In fact, it always happens, even in countries where the government tries to prohibit it.

It's worth watching the whole video, but the part about slushies and other groceries ("We…have….everything!" at 7:30) is particularly fascinating. It covers the story of a budding capitalist who manages to liberate a slushie machine, finds a way to get electric power and supplies, and now sells slushies to…well, to pretty much anyone who wants one.

Refugee camps start out, of necessity, as command economies to a degree that would make any Commissar envious: everybody gets a debit card with $40 a month for the groceries, and a tent for housing, and some bedclothes. But given a chance, people will turn, as they always do, to capitalism.

Maybe millennials will, too.

---

7 For an overview, see Murphy (2011).

4. Anti-Market Atavism Explained

When I lived in Germany in 2009, I often encountered situations that tested my knowledge of culture. After all, my culture was the southern United States; I was immersed in the culture of southern Germany, without in any way understanding it.

I was in Munich, a very large city, and was late for an appointment. I came up to a busy intersection, with a red light, looked both ways, saw no cars were coming, and started to cross the street. I should add that to get to the intersection, I had to push my way through several dozen schoolchildren who were waiting for the light to turn green.

Having taken only a couple of steps, I heard some shrill shouting in German—"Kindermörder! Kindermörder!"—and then felt a pain in my elbow. A little old lady was hitting me, pretty hard, with her umbrella, and accusing me of being a "child murderer." Loudly.

Why would a little old lady physically attack an adult male in a public street? It wasn't because her reason told her to do it. She was angry because I was crossing a street in a dangerous way, directly in front of children who might later do the same thing and be killed. Her body was suffused with a cocktail of powerful "fight or flight" chemicals on seeing a violation of the public norms of safety, and she acted without thinking.

Now, I'm 6'1" and 240 pounds. Even spotting her an umbrella as a club, I probably could have taken her. But I too have an evolved set of responses to violations of norms, even when I'm the violator.

My face turned bright red; I hunched over and tried to make myself physically smaller and less threatening. I crept back to the curb where the children were watching, and tried to tell them I was wrong and that they shouldn't cross against the light.

Good and Bad Rules

That all sounds like the "emotions as norm enforcers" function is actually useful, or what biologists call adaptive. Providing the public good of enforcement, or feeling bad about violating the rules, makes the rules work better and at lower cost. But that may not always be the case, if the rules themselves are bad. Worse, the rules may be the product of the moral intuitions that were evolved for an earlier time period. That's when we may have to deal with such intuitions as atavisms.

For example, suppose you get cut off in traffic. Many of us, especially those of us afflicted with maleness, will act like damn fools, trying to "teach a lesson" to that "*%&^$" who disrespected us. That impulse to correct rudeness may have been adaptive 10,000 years ago, before the Neolithic revolution, when small clans needed cooperation to survive. If you saw someone act badly, you needed to confront them to make sure that the scarce food and other resources of the clan were not wasted on a non-cooperator.

But today, getting upset and perhaps even starting a fistfight or "road rage" incident with gunfire is dumb. It's a holdover, an atavism, from a time when such behavior was adaptive. Most of the time, it doesn't matter and we don't notice it. But sometimes it does matter.

I have long wondered why so many people have such visceral, negative reactions to exchange activities that, to economists, seem either benign or positively beneficial. I've come to conclude that the answer is deceptively simple: whale hips.

The Evolution of Whales

Whales have hips. They don't have legs, at least not anymore. But they still have identifiable hip structures at the point where the legs of the now long-lost legs would have connected. Back when the prehistoric mammals from which whales evolved were romping in the shallows, they had legs, because they had started out on land.

But when these whale ancestors took to the open ocean and dove deep, legs were a hindrance. Natural selection "directed" a smoother shape, with no rear legs to slow the whale-creature down. But the genetic code for legs still hitchhiked along on the modern whale alleles, turned off but latent. There was no particular advantage to selecting for the absence of hips, and a number of muscles were tethered there. So whales have hips.

Biologists call this an "atavism," or (in some cases) a "reversion." Reversions can be bizarre: Some snakes are born with deformed but recognizable legs. The genetic code for legs still hitchhikes in modern snake DNA, but it is normally turned off. Stress in the environment, or other causes that are poorly understood, can result in these genes being "expressed," or turned on, in a given phenotype. It's not adaptive; the snake with legs dies or is eaten by predators, but it happens.

Charles Darwin was interested in reversions. In chapter 13 of his 1868 book Variation of Animals and Plants Under Domestication, Darwin noted that animals that appeared to have been bred into a clear type retained the genetic information of their progenitors. Even two purebred creatures of the new species might produce offspring that had the atavistic form or features. As Darwin put it, "The tendency to reversion is often induced by a change of conditions."

Anger as Argument

Well, whales have hips, and humans have moral intuitions about the value of certain actions in a variety of social settings. Of course, moral intuitions are nothing physical like bones, but they can in some ways be measured. Most human beings have a deep, visceral reaction to seeing a violation of the rules.

The particular rules they care about differ across societies, depending on culture. And things that would upset some individuals are a matter of indifference to others. Still, one is reminded of David Hume's famous observation that "reason is, and should be, a slave to the passions."

The evolutionary function of "the passions" is to provide the public good of norm enforcement. Note that since reason is "the slave" of the passions, this is not a rational or reasoned response. That neatly solves the problem that "rational" human beings — that is, homo economicus — would underprovide the enforcement of norms. But actual human beings are led by a chemical hand to do something they don't intend: enforce norms if they are violated by someone else, or feel ashamed if the norm violation is done by the person herself.

Tribal Norms

What I mean is that moral norms that served small bands of humans well 10,000 years ago — share, cooperate, punish anyone who violates the rules — are no longer very good at helping people navigate commercial society. Ask someone about price-gouging laws, or kidney sales, or generally talk about the role of price as an indispensable signal of scarcity. Most people will get upset.

It may seem that they get upset because they don't have a very good counter argument: "I don't know why that's wrong, but it just is!" The truth is the reverse: the "getting upset" part is actually their counterargument! It's a deep feeling they have, and they will work hard to make up reasons that seem to justify their Stone Age conception of clan life. It's not a choice at all, it's just the way the human mind works.

Ten thousand years is just a blink of an eye in evolutionary terms, given the long human reproductive cycle.

The Hayekian Answer

F.A. Hayek recognized this problem, and thought pretty hard about it. In fact, I had forgotten (until a listener at a talk last year reminded me) that Hayek had even used the biological concept — atavism — when he talked about it.

> It should be realized, however, that the ideals of socialism (or of 'social justice') which … prove so attractive, do not really offer a new moral but merely appeal to instincts inherited from an earlier type of society. They are an atavism, a vain attempt to impose upon the Open Society the morals of the tribal society which, if it prevails, must not only destroy the Great Society but would also greatly threaten the survival of the large numbers to which some three hundred years of a market order have enabled mankind to grow. (Hayek, 1998; p. 304).

And later, in the same book:

> At present … an ever increasing part of the population of the Western World grow up as members of large organizations

> and thus as strangers to those rules of the market which have made the great open society possible. To them the market economy is largely incomprehensible; they have never practised the rules on which it rests, and its results seem to them irrational and immoral.
>
> They often see in it merely an arbitrary structure maintained by some sinister power. In consequence, the long-submerged innate instincts have again surged to the top. Their demand for a just distribution in which organized power is to be used to allocate to each what he deserves, is thus strictly an atavism, based on primordial emotions. And it is these widely prevalent feelings to which prophets, moral philosophers and constructivists appeal by their plan for the deliberate creation of a new type of society. (Hayek, 1998; p. 497).

Interestingly, this notion of the different relative rates of change of economic institutions and social institutions also has some strong reflections in Karl Marx. The idea is that economic relations and institutions of commercial society evolve based on their own logic, which is transaction costs and the calculus of profit and loss. There is no reason to expect that human understanding of these changes, or of the function of even the most important institutions, would be able to keep up.

Now, Hayek thought (in my mind, rightly) that commercial society and market institutions were good, where Marx disagreed, but both agreed that humans found that "the market economy is largely incomprehensible."

So, the next time you find yourself disagreeing with someone about the use of market processes as a means of achieving a decentralized but highly effective order for society, feel free to just shake your head and say, "Whale hips!" At a minimum, the next five minutes will be more interesting.

II

THE ORIGINS OF RULES AND THE PROBLEM OF KNOWLEDGE

One of my dissertation advisers, Douglass North, won the Nobel Prize in Economics in 1993. After one wins the Nobel Prize, or so I am told, there is a period of year or so when your opinions and advice are much sought after. Doug was invited to foreign capitals and feted widely, and then always asked the same breathless question: "Prof. North: You have won the Nobel; what advice do you have about how we can achieve economic and political development?"

North's answer was completely true, but largely unhelpful: "The first thing you'll need is a different history."

What he meant, of course, was that the idea that rules were simply words on a piece of paper, with no underlying cultural significance and no situation in the community norms and customs, was misleading. It is not terribly helpful to tell people what rules they should have, because the set of rules that cause development have been well known for decades, perhaps for centuries. What is necessary is the rule of law to define and protect property rights, sound currency, a reliable and stable financial sector with institutions to attract and direct liquid capital, a professional and noncorrupt police system, a democratic legislature, and an independent judiciary. Every nation that has had those things has prospered rapidly. There are no exceptions.

Some nations, such as China, have managed to have great increases in prosperity even while lacking some of those institutions. Others, such as Argentina, Egypt, Venezuela, and Nigeria, have failed to prosper in spite of possessing large populations and substantial resources. The frustrating thing is the core insight of my subfield of political economy, which is called "Public Choice." That central insight is this: Rules matter more than they should.

The rules may be customs, background culture that people who live in the society may simply take for granted, because they operate in the background. Or the rules may be formal, written constitutions or statutes. Economists have long taken rules for granted, simply assuming that property rights, financial dealings, and the terms of exchange were details of the process and could be assumed away. But that is far from true. The importance of rules, their origins, and the difficulty of assessing a set of rules at a point in time, are the subject of this section.

1. The Secret History of Tamales Offers a Lesson in Humility

I really like tamales, the cakes made from ground corn, stuffed with a savory or sweet filling, and steamed in corn husks or banana leaves. For one thing, they taste good. But tamales are also a powerful historical lesson about humility: most of the time, we don't understand why rules are good, and we certainly should doubt our ability to choose reforms that will be better.

The corn flour from which tamales are made is masa harina, a nixtamalized hominy that is dried and ground up. Corn is an entirely GMO product, the result of thousands of years of Mesoamerican selective breeding. The result is a remarkably hardy and nutritious product that has — after it was "discovered" by Europeans — taken over much of the world; corn (or maize) is by far the largest crop of any grain,[8] with corn output nearly matching wheat and rice output combined.

But Europeans screwed it up, because they were so arrogant about their "science" that they ignored the knowledge dispersed in the traditions of those who had actually invented corn. The Mesoamericans, for the most part Nahuatl (a language and ethnic group that includes the Aztecs), didn't just eat the corn unprocessed, or at

---

8 "Worldwide production of grain in 2018/19, by type (in million metric tons)." Statista. February 15, 2019. https://www.statista.com/statistics/263977/world-grain-production-by-type/.

least not all of it. They nixtamalized it.[9] This concept derives from the Nahuatl word for hominy, whose name in turn comes from nextli ("ashes, lime") plus tamalli ("something wrapped").

Why did the Nahuatl soak the corn in lime (water mixed with wood ashes, which creates a strong basic solution with lots of potassium hydroxide)? Potassium hydroxide is an extremely powerful and potentially dangerous chemical, but the effect on corn is to soften the husk so it can be removed and to cause the kernels inside to swell into the hominy we think of as being almost a different product.

Nixtamalization

It also does something else, something that the Mesoamericans could not explain and that the Europeans did not understand. Nixtamalization liberates vitamin B3, or niacin, in large quantities in the resulting flour. If you grind dried corn, no niacin. If you nixtamalize corn, rinse the "lime" solution away, let the resulting swollen kernels dry, and then grind them, lots of niacin. Nixtamalization also made other nutrients, including protein, more readily digestible, increasing the effective metabolic yield of eating corn.

It's easy to understand why the arrogant, supercilious Europeans decided to skip all those silly, superstitious steps of taking ash from old fires and mixing it into the corn, and then drying the result. It's

---

9 Nixtamalization is a process for the preparation of maize (corn), or other grain, in which the corn is soaked and cooked in an alkaline solution, usually limewater, washed, and then hulled. "Nixtamalization." In Wikipedia, the free encyclopedia. n.d. Accessed June 17, 2019. https://en.wikipedia.org/wiki/Nixtamalization.

inefficient, and clearly just some old superstition, right? The Aztecs, when asked, would say that nixtamalization had been revealed to them by the god of corn, Centeotl, as a secret that benefited them at the expense of their enemies.

Corn seemed like the perfect food for poor people because it grew fast, had huge yields, and provided carbohydrates, protein, and fat all in one package. Plus, it was versatile and could be consumed off the cob, cooked, or dried and ground into flour.

But by the middle of the 17th century, there was a large outbreak of what they called "Asturian leprosy"; in Italy the disease had become very widespread, and was called pelle agra (pelle = skin; agra = sour), which is where we get the modern name for niacin deficiency: pellagra. (For a history of the problem, and current situation, see "Pellagra and its prevention and control in major emergencies," Prinzo, 2009) Symptoms included light sensitivity, aggressive behavior, lesions, weakness, confusion, and sometimes even dementia or paralysis. Many people died.

Unintended Results

The problem was intractable: in South Carolina, 1,306 people died during the first 10 months of 1915; 100,000 Southerners were affected with pellagra in 1916. Unsurprisingly, scientists were stumped, believing that some pathogen or unknown toxin in local corn caused pellagra. That is, people thought pellagra was caused by eating corn, because the people who developed pellagra were poor and ate mostly corn mush and cooked corn, with just a few other food items.

But corn wasn't the problem. The problem was ignoring the concentrated and useful information that had been available all the time. Pellagra was essentially unknown in Mesoamerica, even though the diets of many people were based almost entirely on corn and products made from it. The difference was the "superstition" that those savages were clinging to. They didn't perform the cumbersome nixtamalization process because they knew about niacin, of course; they did it because their religion demanded it.

But the success of tradition is not random, and it is not devoid of information, if you know where to look. It is not hard to imagine the process by which nixtamalization became the dominant process, after all. When corn was first genetically engineered, over the course of centuries of selective breeding, there were likely a variety of practices for preparing and cooking the resulting kernels. Some people may have mixed the dried corn with wood ash, others with chopped cactus or agave, and still others prayed and made incantations. Actually, they probably all prayed and made incantations, and developed a pantheon of gods and a complex set of rituals revolving around the planting, harvesting, and consuming of the sacred maize.

Evolution

Over the decades, in a relatively short span of years by evolutionary standards, it turned out that some practices were favored by the gods. After all, those who engaged in nixtamalization were healthy and strong, and their children were far more likely to survive into adulthood. Those who used any other practice were sick, unlikely to have healthy children, and very likely to die of malnutrition or be killed in combat. It is likely that the evolutionary process homed in on a precise set of optimal practices, in fact, because the societies that were competing were relatively isolated from the outside world but always struggling against each other for supremacy.

Further, humans can mimic and adapt simply by changing behavior. Biological evolution takes time — a giraffe can't make its neck longer just by thinking about it — but institutional evolution can take place through conversion. When outsiders converted to the worship of the suite of Nahuatl gods, Centeotl and nixtamalization came along with the package. It may be true that no one understood why the rules were good, but it was enough that the rules were good and that the society flourished.

My little example has been intended as a small piece of evidence in support of a much larger point. As F.A. Hayek put it in *The Fatal Conceit*,

> To understand our civilisation, one must appreciate that the extended order resulted not from human design or intention but spontaneously: it arose from unintentionally conforming to certain traditional and largely moral practices, many of which men tend to dislike, whose significance they usually fail to understand, whose validity they cannot prove, and which have nonetheless fairly rapidly spread by means of an evolutionary selection — the comparative increase of population and wealth — of those groups that happened to follow them. The unwitting, reluctant, even painful adoption of these practices kept these groups together, increased their access to valuable information of all sorts, and enabled them to be 'fruitful, and multiply, and replenish the earth, and subdue it' (Genesis 1:28). This process is perhaps the least appreciated facet of human evolution. (Hayek, 1991; p. 6).

Does this mean science should be scorned? Of course not. Today, pellagra is once again very rare, at least in developed nations.

Vitamin supplements and other sources of niacin are very effective in preventing the disease.

What's interesting about this "cure" is that it took science more than three full centuries, from 1650 to 1960, to reach the stage of knowledge that had been achieved by Mesoamerican traditions a thousand years earlier.

We may not grasp how essential systems work, but that means that we should always be skeptical of proposals to change those systems based on the "science" that reformers imagine they understand.

2. Pave the Muddy Paths

We often think of "law" and "legislation" as synonyms, but F.A. Hayek famously argued that there are important differences. If we start with individual habits, or patterns of behavior that have become so commonplace that we act almost without thinking, we can understand much of the daily lives of individuals.

Habits that are shared might be called "customs," informal rules that might be written down nowhere. These are agreements, in the sense that we all agree that is the way we do things, even though we never actually sat down and signed anything.

In class I often use the example of the "Pittsburgh left turn" to illustrate the importance of custom and expectations. The example is discussed more in a later chapter; for now, let's just note that the custom in Pittsburgh is to let people turning left have the right-of-way, even if there is no left turn arrow. That's not the law; it's a custom. But it is important that the habit of waiting for someone to turn left in front of you be "agreed" on, in the sense that the expectation is widely shared — and met — because otherwise it wouldn't be effective in making traffic move faster. These customs can come to govern behavior, however, precisely because they shape expectations, and violating expectations may be expensive or dangerous.

Those customs, if they consistently lead to useful outcomes, are "laws." They are discoverable by experience and emerge in the form of traditions. But it is useful to write them down so that they can be enforced more effectively and can be easily learned by new generations. Laws that are written down are rules, commands, and prohibitions we call "legislation."

The problem is that legislation need not arise from law at all. Legislation is any procedures that a set of political actors use to command citizens or restrict their actions. The idea of a speed limit (although see Germany's autobahns!) is probably both a law and legislation. A rule that protects a company from the scolding winds of competition just because government actors own stock in that company is legislation, but it violates the obvious law against artificial privileges in capitalism.

The "rule of law," for Hayek at least, is a situation where all legislation simply codifies and illuminates the law. There may be many laws that are not legislation (some are just "manners," and needn't be legislated), but in an ideal rule-of-law system there is no legislation that is not also a law.

The reason this is important is that Hayek was rightly concerned about the conceit common in "experts" and legislators that they know what is best for everyone else.

The Sidewalk

I often illustrate this with what I call the Hayek University Problem. Imagine that a new university will be built, one dedicated to the principles of F.A. Hayek and Austrian Economics.[10] You are on the "planning committee" charged with laying out the sidewalks. What would you do?

You might walk around, look at aerial maps of the campus, and draw lines to try to guess where people will want to walk. Or you might want to have a purely aesthetic conception of the problem,

---

10 It's not that far-fetched a notion. Universidad Francisco Marroquin, in Guatemala, comes pretty close to having this purpose realized.

and put the sidewalks in places or in patterns that are pleasing to the eye as you look out the windows of the administration building.

But all of that is legislation. No individual, or small committee of individuals, could possibly have enough information or foresight to be able to know in advance where people are going to want to walk. After all, universities are peopled by broadly diverse groups, with heterogeneous plans and purposes. People are often willing to walk on the sidewalks, if that serves their purpose at that point. But you probably don't want to build a sidewalk from every doorway to every other doorway on the campus.

What would a law look like, in this setting? No one person, after all, has any effect walking on the grass, and all the different plans and purposes, taken one at a time, contain no information that you can use. But there is a physical manifestation of the aggregation of all these plans and purposes working themselves out over time. I don't intend to make a path, and neither do you. But if enough of us, over time, find it useful to walk in the same place to accomplish our own idiosyncratic purposes, a visible record of the shared pattern emerges: a muddy path.

So, the law for the Hayek Sidewalk Plan committee will be discoverable if we adjourn for six months or so and then have a drone take some overhead photographs. It is clear now where people, acting as individuals but observable together in the shared result called a muddy path, want the sidewalks to be placed. And the task of the committee is simply to "legislate" by paving the muddy paths.

If we think of the process of discovering law as "looking for the muddy paths," and the legislation we write down as "paving the muddy paths," we have a simple but quite powerful way of thinking about the rule of law.

3. More or Better Rules Will Not Save Us

In life, we go through a cycle in our attitudes toward rules. Most of us, when we are young, are impatient with "This is how we do it," and have impatient and idealistic conceptions of what can be done. In middle age, most of us are more accepting of the rules. And the elderly often cling to the rules, defending them as traditions, the very foundation of "our" culture.

There was a popular song by Bruce Hornsby, from 1986, called "That's Just the Way It Is." The chorus and second verse go like this:

> That's just the way it is; Some things'll never change
> That's just the way it is; Ha, but don't you believe them
> Said, "Hey little boy you can't go, Where the others go
> Cause you don't look like they do."
> Said, "Hey, old man how can you stand, To think that way
> Did you really think about it, Before you made the rules?"

I'm old now (40 with 20 years of experience, you might say), but I never "made the rules." The rules were things that had a separate and superior existence; "that's just the way it is." One notion of conservatism is simply a commitment to the rules that have come down to us from the past. Part of this is a reverence for tradition, and part of it is a skepticism that progressive reason — what Hayek called "the counterrevolution of science" in a book of that name — understands enough of the complexity of social systems to make things better. William F. Buckley Jr., in fact, defined conservatism as "standing athwart history, shouting, 'Stop!'"

But that's also why Hayek wrote "Why I Am Not a Conservative" (Hayek, 2011, p. 397) and why I'm not a conservative, either. Sometimes the rules really are bad. Hornsby's example is hard to argue with: Racial segregation in my hometown of Gotha, Florida, was a full-fledged apartheid system in the 1950s and 1960s. It had no rational basis, and it was actively evil, a perpetuation of slavery in the form of Jim Crow "rules." Even if people did "think about it before [they] made" those rules, they were wrong. Those were bad rules, and they needed to be changed.

There are important elements of truth, then, to both kinds of skeptical claims. It is right to be skeptical that groups of zealous reformers are going to make things better. And it is right to question the traditions that come to us from a flawed historical past. What to do?

I wonder if there is not a fundamental change afoot, one that results from a conception of rules and morals that looks a lot like video games. If you play a video game, there will be a set of rules. Those rules may be arbitrary and contingent, in the sense that they are specific to the game, but they are also clear and can be written down, in list form. The rules of physics, not just of social interaction and reward, are not just something we can make up. You may be able to fly (as in "Second Life"), there may be magic or spells that can transcend "normal" physics (as in "Runescape" or "WOW"), and there may be no social consequences for bad behavior (as in "Grand Theft Auto").

Some games actually allow gamers to rewrite some, or all, of the rules for their own versions of the game. The website OpenSource.

com defines "open gaming" this way:[11]

> Games and software are similar because they are both collections of rules. Just as software is really a set of rules that determines what is and is not possible for users to do with a computer program, a game is a set of rules that defines what players can and can't do in pursuit of a goal.
>
> Open source software is software anyone can modify and enhance because its source code is publicly available (and because its creators have given everyone permission to alter it). Open source games are likewise games that players can adapt to fit their preferences. The open nature of these games allows players to build on designers' ideas.
>
> Taking an open source approach to games means recognizing that the rules governing what people can and can't do are arbitrary — they are not permanent, and people should feel free to tweak and tinker with them. Like writing laws, creating games is the practice of crafting the rules by which people can act. (OpenSource.com, 2019). That's fine for games. It's really fun to be able to change the rules, remaking the norms and physics of the world we live in. In the movie series The Matrix, the heart of the plot turns on the recognition by humans that the rules are arbitrary and can be rewritten.

11 OpenSource.com. "What is open gaming?" Accessed June 17, 2019. https://opensource.com/resources/what-open-gaming

In fact, the rules get rewritten often, to fix glitches or change the rules in a way that benefits the "agents" that control that virtual universe. In the original (1999) movie, Neo sees a black cat. Twice.

> Neo: Whoa. Déjà vu. [Everyone freezes right in their tracks]
> Trinity: What did you just say?
> Neo: Nothing. Just had a little déjà vu.
> Trinity: What did you see?
> Cypher: What happened?
> Neo: A black cat went past us, and then another that looked just like it.
> Trinity: How much like it? Was it the same cat?
> Neo: It might have been. I'm not sure.
> Morpheus: Switch! Apoc!
> Neo: What is it?
> Trinity: A déjà vu is usually a glitch in the Matrix. It happens when they change something.

The gamer view can transcend the game context, of course. In fact, the gamer view of rules is precisely what Hayek saw as scientism in *The Fatal Conceit*:

> Morals, including especially, our institutions of property, freedom and justice, are not a creation of man's reason but a distinct second endowment conferred on him by cultural evolution — runs counter to the main intellectual outlook of the twentieth century. The influence of rationalism has indeed been so profound and pervasive that, in general, the more intelligent an educated person is, the more likely he or she

> now is not only to be a rationalist, but also to hold socialist views (regardless of whether he or she is sufficiently doctrinal to attach to his or her views any label, including 'socialist')....
>
> Intelligent people will tend to overvalue intelligence, and to suppose that we must owe all the advantages and opportunities that our civilisation offers to deliberate design rather than to following traditional rules, and likewise to suppose that we can, by exercising our reason, eliminate any remaining undesired features by still more intelligent reflection, and still more appropriate design and 'rational coordination' of our undertakings.... And since they have been taught that constructivism and scientism are what science and the use of reason are all about, they find it hard to believe that there can exist any useful knowledge that did not originate in deliberate experimentation, or to accept the validity of any tradition apart from their own tradition of reason. Thus [they say]: 'Tradition is almost by definition reprehensible, something to be mocked and deplored'. (Hayek, 1991; p. 53).

This conception of rules, and the implicit idea that the origin of rules is intentional human design, means that the rules can always be improved. Only a cretin or evil troll would oppose this project of improvement. It is difficult to accept that rules in the social world around us are not clear, don't exist in any clear list, and cannot be arbitrarily changed by simply rewriting the "code" of interaction.

I'm not blaming video games, mind you. But the idea that there was any "we" who made the rules, or that those rules can be changed, seems to be an important part of the modern constructivist mindset.

Hayek's worry that "we" do a bad job of explaining the problem is even more pressing today than when he wrote The Fatal Conceit. Society is much closer to a complex biological organism than to a matrix of engineering principles with explicit, contingent rules.

4. The Best Rules Are Those You Can't Write Down

The origin, maintenance, and evolution of rule systems is at the core of our understanding of what makes societies work or fail. My own bias is to think in terms outlined by one of my dissertation advisors, Douglass C. North.

The static version of North's view has two parts. First, institutions are the humanly devised "rules of the game" that shape and direct human behavior. Second, it is important to separate institutions, which are the rules that create incentives and structure payoffs, and organizations, which are humanly devised optimizing responses to institutions.

Institutions, because of path dependence, collective-action problems in voting (along the lines often argued by Bryan Caplan[12]), and failures in our mental capacity to process feedback accurately, are rarely in any sense optimal.

Organizations, on the other hand, are always contingently optimal, given the (possibly pathological) incentives created by institutions.

The dynamic aspects of North's theory are frustratingly vague. To be fair, though, that was in some ways intentional, along the lines of R.H. Coase's famous but frustrating refusal ever to give a clear definition of "transaction costs" (Coase, 1988). North often said (I heard him say it), "The problem for theory is to explain why

12 See, for example, Caplan, Bryan. "Mises and Bastiat on How Democracy Goes Wrong, Part I" and "Mises and Bastiat on How Democracy Goes Wrong, Part II"

institutions almost never change, until they do." Competition among organizations fosters innovation, and innovation can overwhelm institutions that remain relatively static because of "transitional-gains traps," (a la Gordon Tullock).

But by and large, it's hard to say just what the specific rules of the game are, in most social settings. Knowledge of manners, norms, and social expectations usually requires being immersed in the particular culture in which you are trying to live.

Gamer Rules

I would contrast this fuzzy, murky process of rule perception with the "gamer" view I talked about earlier. The gamer view is that the rules, including even the very physics of the social world, are something that can be written down and therefore can be changed. The interactions among rules may be complex, and may affect the state of "play" in complex ways, but, overall, rules can be understood and modified by smart folks.

The alternative view, the view partly articulated by North but more fully developed by F.A. Hayek, is what I would call the "world traveler" view. If you visit another country, it is foreign, partly because you aren't sure what the rules are. The etymology of the word "foreign" is to be on the other side of a door or boundary, to be out of your home territory. What this suggests is that the rules may be different.

Some of the rules you can look up or read about. But often the rules are just assumed because everyone knows them. In many cases, people may be so used to the rules they know that they don't even recognize the possibility that it could be otherwise, unless they are world travelers. I have often told the story of how I tried to take a shopping cart from an old woman in Erlangen, Germany, because I didn't know about the practice of collecting a deposit on shopping carts. No one told me about this, and I thought I recognized the context of "grocery store" as familiar, one where I knew the rules. But I didn't.

Bicycles and Pedestrians

I had another experience in Germany, one that made me think of the importance of what Hayek called "the particular circumstances of time and place." Erlangen, where I taught at Friedrich Alexander University, is a city of bicycles. There are roads, but most are narrow and there are so many bikes that it can be frustrating to drive.

The bike riders, as is true in many American cities, paid little attention to the traffic lights. Often, there were so many bikes that it was not possible to cross the street without getting in the way. But I noticed that people did cross, just walking right out into the street.

I tried this, several times, in my first time in Erlangen. But being from the southern United States, I'm polite and deferential. So, I would start across the street, but then look up the street, and if a bike was close and coming fast I'd stop.

And get hit by a large, sturdy German on a large, sturdy German bicycle. And then I got yelled at, in German. What had I done wrong? Eventually, I figured it out: there had evolved a convention for crossing the street and for riding bicycles. The pedestrian simply walked at a constant speed, without even looking. The bicyclist would ride directly at the pedestrian, actually aiming at the spot where the pedestrian was at that point in time. Since the pedestrian kept moving in a predictable fashion, the cyclist would pass directly and safely behind the pedestrian.

If some idiot from the southern United States, in an effort to impose his own views of "polite" behavior on people whose evolved rules were different, tried to be polite and stop, the system broke down. Though that idiot (me) was stopping to avoid being hit, I was actually being rude by violating the rules. These rules were not written down and could not easily be changed.

In fact, a number of my German colleagues even denied that it was a rule, at first. But then they would say, "Well, right, you can't stop. That would be dumb. So, okay, I guess it is a rule, after all."

More precisely, this rule — like many other important rules you encounter in "foreign" settings — is really a convention. A convention, according to Lewis (1969), is a persistent (though not necessarily permanent) regularity in the resolution of recurring coordination problems, in situations characterized by recurrent interactions where outcomes are (inter)dependent.

Conventions, then, exist when people all agree on a rule of behavior, even if no one ever said the rule out loud or wrote it down. No one actor can choose an outcome, and no actor can challenge the regularity by unilaterally deviating from the conventional behavior. But deviation can result in substantial harm, as when someone tries to drive on the left in a country where "we" drive on the right, or social sanction, as when there is intentional punishment on behalf of other actors if deviation is observed and publicized.

According to David Hume, convention is

> a general sense of common interest; which sense all the members of the society express to one another, and which induces them to regulate their conduct by certain rules. I observe that it will be to my interest [e.g.] to leave another

> in the possession of his goods, provided he will act in the same manner with regard to me. When this common sense of interest is mutually expressed and is known to both, it produces a suitable resolution and behavior. And this may properly enough be called a convention or agreement betwixt us, though without the interposition of a promise; since the actions of each of us have a reference to those of the other, and are performed upon the supposition that something is to be performed on the other part. (Hume, 1978; Book III, part ii, section 2).

Notice how different this is from the "gamer" conception of laws and rules. For the gamer, all the rules can be — in fact, must be — written down and can be examined and rearranged. For the world traveler, the experience of finding out the rules can involve trial and error, and even the natives likely do not fully understand that the rules and norms of their culture are unique.

The Left Turn

One of my favorite examples is actually from the United States, the so-called Pittsburgh Left Turn. In an article in the *Pittsburgh City Paper*, Chris Potter (2006) wrote:

> As longtime residents know, the Pittsburgh Left takes place when two or more cars — one planning to go straight, and the other to turn left — face off at a red light without a "left-turn only" lane or signal. The Pittsburgh Left occurs when the light turns green, and the driver turning left takes the turn without yielding to the oncoming car.

> Pittsburgh is an old city, many of whose streets were designed before automobiles held sway. [That means] that street grids are constricted, with little room for amenities like left-turn-only lanes. The absence of such lanes means drivers have to solve traffic problems on their own. Instead of letting one car at the head of an intersection bottle up traffic behind it, the Pittsburgh Left gives the turning driver a chance to get out of everyone else's way. In exchange for a few seconds of patience, the Pittsburgh Left allows traffic in both directions to move smoothly for the duration of the signal. Of course, the system only works if both drivers know about it. No doubt that's why newcomers find it so vexing.

The Pittsburgh Left is a very efficient convention. On two-lane streets, turning left can block traffic as the turning car waits for an opening. And left-turn arrows are expensive and add time to each traffic light cycle. Far better to let the left turners — if there are any — go first. If there are no left turners, traffic just proceeds normally, not waiting on a left arrow.

Of course, if some idiot from the southern United States (yes, me again) is driving in Pittsburgh, that person expects to go when the light turns green. I blew my horn when two cars turned left in front of me. And people on the sidewalk yelled at me, as did the left-turning drivers. Once again, I didn't know the rules, because I was a foreigner, at least in terms of the rules of the road in Pittsburgh.

Actually, it's worse than that. The Pittsburgh Left is technically illegal, according to the Pennsylvania Driver's Handbook: "Drivers turning left must yield to oncoming vehicles going straight ahead."[13] The written rules, the gamer rules, appear to endorse one pattern of action. But the actual rules, the ones you have to travel around to learn, may be quite different. Real rules are not written down, and the people living in that rule system may not understand either the nature or effects of the rules. It is very difficult to change conventions, because they represent the expectations people have developed in dealing with each other over years or decades.

Hayek understood this clearly, and argued for what I have called the "world traveler" conception over what I have called the "gamer" conception of rules and laws. As Hayek said in 1988, in *The Fatal Conceit*:

> To understand our civilisation, one must appreciate that the extended order resulted not from human design or intention but spontaneously: it arose from unintentionally conforming to certain traditional and largely moral practices, many of which men tend to dislike, whose significance they usually fail to understand, whose validity they cannot prove, and which have nonetheless fairly rapidly spread by means of an evolutionary selection — the comparative increase of population and wealth — of those groups that happened to follow them.... This process is perhaps the least appreciated facet of human evolution. (Hayek, 1988; p. 6)

13 Pennsylvania Department of Transportation. "Pennsylvania's Driver's Manual." 47. https://www.dot.state.pa.us/Public/DVS-PubsForms/BDL/BDL%20Manuals/Manuals/PA%20Drivers%20Manual%20By%20Chapter/English/PUB%2095.pdf

5. What Can and Cannot Be Planned

Emergence is a central idea in economics, but it is also important in other disciplines. The formal definition of emergence appears to have originated with G.H. Lewes in his 1875 book *Problems of Life and Mind*. Emergence, for Lewes, was to be distinguished from "resultant" effects. If an effect is resultant, it arises from the parts or components of which it is composed. Thus, we can add up or otherwise combine the parts and get the effect. Weight, for example, can be obtained by adding up the weights of the components.

Emergent effects are different. Even if you have the components, you may not be able to produce the emergent effect, and even if the effect does emerge it is not understandable in terms of its constituent parts, and it is not reducible to those parts. Emergence is something new, something not present in the parts.

So, fractal geometries are infinitely reducible, or expandable, while preserving an organic unity; they are resultant. Life is an emergent property of chemistry; if I gave you all the chemicals and components of a paramecium, you still couldn't make one. If you took a living paramecium and reduced it to its chemical components, life would no longer be present in those components.

This last point is called "reduction": emergent effects are not reducible; resultant effects are.

Economists have recognized that order in market systems resulting from human action is emergent. One of the first to state this clearly was Bernard Mandeville, who compared society to a bee hive in which no bee cared what the other bees were doing, and the bees were behaving selfishly ("private vices"), yet order ("publick virtues") emerged in the system as a whole. In 1782 Adam Ferguson claimed that social order is "the result of human action, but not the execution of any human design."

The economist most associated with emergence is F.A. Hayek, of course. He advanced a fully articulated set of claims about emergence, focusing in markets on the price mechanism, but also considering social orders in law and culture more broadly. Hayek (1952) argued that:

> many of the greatest things man has achieved are not the result of consciously directed thought, and still less the product of deliberately coordinated effort of many individuals, but of a process in which the individual plays a part which he can never fully understand. They are greater than any individual precisely because they result from the combination of knowledge more extensive than any single mind can master. (pp. 149-150).

The problem, as Hayek saw it, is that no politician can claim credit for doing the socially valuable thing and letting the emergent properties of the price system provide the enormous benefit of directing resources toward higher-valued uses. There are two reasons:

1. In most cases, the best thing for state planners and regulators is not to plan and not to regulate. It's not exactly doing nothing, but doing the "right kind of nothing." Still, having run for governor of North Carolina myself in 2008 I can tell you that a platform of "Vote for me and I won't directly help you!" is not an easy platform to win with.
2. Even if a politician did propose such a platform, it's not clear

that voters would want it. Since the market order is emergent, it is easy to miss its power and value. Hayek (1945) understood this problem all too well:

> The marvel [of the price system] is that in a case like that of a scarcity of one raw material, without an order being issued, without more than perhaps a handful of people knowing the cause, tens of thousands of people whose identity could not be ascertained by months of investigation, are made to use the material or its products more sparingly; i.e., they move in the right direction. This is enough of a marvel even if, in a constantly changing world, not all will hit it off so perfectly that their profit rates will always be maintained at the same constant or "normal" level.
>
> I have deliberately used the word "marvel" to shock the reader out of the complacency with which we often take the working of this mechanism for granted. I am convinced that if it were the result of deliberate human design, and if the people guided by the price changes understood that their decisions have significance far beyond their immediate aim, this mechanism would have been acclaimed as one of the greatest triumphs of the human mind. (p. 527)

As I said above, Hayek is famous in economics for pointing out that a functioning market system is both a discovery process, in which price is the result of uncoordinated human actions seeking to achieve divergent and sometimes contradictory plans and purposes, and also an aggregating institution that reconciles those divergent plans and purposes into a coherent, emergent result. In philosophy and political science, many scholars have asked whether these two functions — discovery process and aggregation mechanism — have analogs.

Public Choice

An entire subfield of political science, one that I myself identify with and that is called "public choice," has examined this proposition. Might voting or other social-choice preference expression play the discovery role of prices? Can parties play the role of firms, competing to offer better platforms? Can the overall political system reconcile harmoniously the contradictory plans and purposes of myriad individuals who don't know each other and cannot easily communicate?

One of the central figures of public choice, James Buchanan, argued that the answer was mostly no. Later work has largely validated this conclusion. There are problems with discovering individual preferences through voting, in part because voters themselves lack the information to make judgments, even about their own welfare.

Political parties face little competition, and so are not disciplined by anything like the "profit test." And overall outcomes can be both socially destructive and stable, since (as Douglass North argued) there is no means by which new entrants can capture the social gains to improved political institutions.

But Buchanan (1979) nonetheless argued that it is important to conceive, and analyze, politics as a form of exchange. It may be true that political action lacks the optimality properties of markets, but it's also true that groups of people can act together to make everyone, and more importantly each one, better off.

The difference, for Buchanan, is that there is no reason to expect "good" rules, by which he meant rules that foster cooperation and the capturing of mutual benefit through collective action, to be emergent. In some cases, and perhaps in many important cases, the rules must be "laid on," or consciously designed by a group of human beings arguing and negotiating. In other words, politics.

To be fair, Buchanan credited the strain of political conservatism that leads through Hume and Burke, the idea that over time good rules will tend to survive and bad rules will be discarded. The problem is that human beings are terrible at telling the difference, and it is not clear that piecewise or additive experimentation tells you much.

Rules systems are dynamic and interactive, like a giant Jenga game. Pull out a stick here, and you create an instability or weakness somewhere else. Still, tradition and institutions such as the common law are valuable, and should receive some deference.

But the most basic rules, the rules about rules, which we call "constitutions"? Buchanan believed that groups must generally constitute themselves, and intentionally, because that is the only way that consent can be obtained. And consent is necessary, for Buchanan, to justify coercion.

If two of us sign a contract, you do the promised work, but I refuse to pay, then it is legitimate to sanction me, even if it is against my will. Likewise, if a group of us agree on some large joint project, but after it is completed I refuse to pay my agreed share, then it is legitimate to sanction me. Actual consent, not tacit consent, plays a key role for Buchanan, but that means an actual choice of rules is required, what Buchanan calls a "constitutional moment."

Buchanan was an admirer of Hayek, but thought that Hayek sometimes came close to mysticism in describing how ignorance becomes knowledge outside of the context of markets. Remember, markets have prices; how does ignorance become knowledge in nonmarket settings?

An Example: Sidewalks Again

As I discussed earlier, an example is useful to illustrate the tension between the Buchanan and Hayek viewpoints: the planning committee for Hayek University! We have already answered one basic question: where should we put the sidewalks?

The answer was, wait and then pave the muddy paths. No one could possibly know enough to be able to lay out the sidewalks optimally, because "path" is an emergent property of the diverse plans and purposes of many individuals, each following his or her own schedule. You've likely seen a lovely set of sidewalks on some college campus, and you've also seen where there is a muddy track going where people actually want to go.

No one created that muddy track; it is the result of individuals going where they want to go. But if enough people walk there, it wears out the grass and makes the ground hard and packed down. The "path" emerges, although no one planned it.

Further, the path's location is informative. Not just a few, but many people find it useful, for their own reasons — we don't know the reasons, and we don't need to know — to walk that path.

The point is that at Hayek University, we don't put down sidewalks for at least two years. We wait until muddy tracks emerge, and that's where we put the sidewalks. Problem solved, with less specific information and with much better results than if we had tried to use a centralized plan based on a map and administrators' best guesses about where people would want to walk.

That's an insight, and I don't want to minimize it. There was no market process at work here, or at least no formal price mechanism. The discovery process was simply the visible consequence of the unplanned, uncoordinated optimizing behavior of many individuals. The result is a path, and paths contain information about where to put the sidewalks.

But, not so fast; let's go back to the Buchanan part of this.. At Hayek University, *where do we put the buildings*? Once the buildings are there, it's true that we can use emergent results to "plan" the sidewalks. The buildings, however, are more likely "laid on," something like a constitution or central plan arrived at by a group of people sitting around a table and making explicit choices.

Buchanan's point in arguing for what he called "constitutional political economy" was much closer to the notion of "Where do we put the buildings?" instead of "Where do we put the sidewalks?" Some architectural layouts are better than others, and the choice requires a central plan, much as the framers of the U.S. Constitution worked things out in Philadelphia in the summer of 1787.

That doesn't mean such central plans are perfect, of course. The point is that we can't rely on emergence. Imagine that we tried to use emergence, and allowed the first year of classes at Hayek University to go forward without buildings.

One might imagine a naturalist, with a Monty Python accent, observing into his microphone in a kind of nature documentary: "Look! Over there! It appears to be… it is! Several sociologists have gathered into a group, in that copse of trees. They seem to be performing one of the primitive rituals called a 'seminar.' This is great, folks. This behavior has never been publicly documented before. Clearly, they are claiming this space for the Sociology

Department, and forevermore that copse of trees will be where Sociology will be located."

Once the various departments had marked their spaces (I don't want to think about how, given the propensity of academic pissing matches these days), then construction can begin.

Said no one, ever. You decide where to put the buildings. Sure, you don't know enough to decide that, but when it comes to rules that's called "the veil of ignorance." John Rawls famously argued that just rules should be devised behind such a veil, to ensure that the rules are fair.

The Sidewalks Rule

So, where does that leave us, in practical terms? I'd say that we should use the "sidewalks rule" where we can, letting knowledge be created by emergent properties of human cooperation. But sometimes we have to have central planning, when it comes to basic rules and the principles that we will use to provide a context for social interactions.

Like Buchanan, I'm a fan of emergence, but we shouldn't just dismiss the importance of choosing good rules. Using good rules that have emerged — deference to unfettered price movements, rule of law, property rights — while trying to design better rules for nonmarket interactions is the challenge that faces public choice scholars. But that challenge, that balancing, is also the reason it's so much darned fun.

6. Car Crashes and Hockey Fights — How Safety Mandates Can Make Life More Dangerous

Suppose you want to reduce deaths in automobile accidents. Should you make cars safer? Seems like a no-brainer, right? But consider: suppose instead of an airbag in your steering column, we put a six-inch dagger. If you hit something hard head-on, you get the dagger through your sternum.

That jerk tailgating you on I-95 would give you more space if his BMW featured an ice pick instead of a soft, comfy airbag.

In fact, economist Sam Peltzman has found that while real mandated safety features in cars reduce the chance that a person in a car will be hurt in an accident, drivers then behave more recklessly, and thus increase the chances of accidents occurring.

This is what we call a "Peltzman Effect." People respond to a safety regulation by increasing their risky behavior.[14] Peltzman Effects happen not only on the road but also on the ice. Hockey, both professional and amateur, has fallen prey to this sort of effect over the last few decades.

---

14 The origin is Peltzman (1978); see for an interesting example Pope and Tollison (2010).

Hockey Helmets

There are three factors that interact to determine player safety in any game, in ways that are hard to predict. The first is the inherent physical riskiness of the sport: zooming around on the ice with 11 other people is just more dangerous than swinging a golf club.

The second is rules and equipment: sometimes equipment evolves, and sometimes new rules dictate substantial changes, as in 1979 when the NHL required players to wear helmets.

The third is behavior, the human element. It's not surprising that this element is the hardest to predict.

We see a pretty clear Peltzman Effect in the behavior of NHL players responding to the 1979 rule requiring them to wear helmets with full face protection. Here's the explanation from Biasca, et al. (2002):

> The increased protection of the face through the compulsory wearing of helmets with full face protection, which was introduced in 1975, appears to have led to a more aggressive playing style perhaps because it is believed that the head, face, and throat are now at less risk. Many believe that, after the mandatory use of helmets with a full facemask, players developed a false sense of security and invincibility leading to excessive risk taking behaviour with a resultant increase in illegal and injurious activity. It is also interesting that increased high stick violation and the use of the full facemask as a weapon were noted … after mandatory use of the full facemask.… Other authors have even speculated that the mandatory use of helmets with full facemasks has increased the risk of neck [and brain injuries].

Hockey Fights — The Code

A similar kind of unintended consequence occurred after a 2003 rule change against fighting.

Players in professional sports are governed, not just by the official rules of the league, but also by what author Ross Bernstein (2006) calls, "the code," the unwritten rules among players. Bernstein argues that for many years, the code of hockey fights actually reduced the level of violent danger in the game as a whole.

Hockey "goons" enforced norms against poking a star such as Wayne Gretzky in the ribs with the butt of your stick. The refs might not catch you, but if you bruised Gretzky you had to face a professional fighter.

Of course, your team would also defend you if you behaved within the code, and send up their own enforcer for the stylized combat. But if you broke the code, you had to fight, and you would likely be both hurt and humiliated.

So Gretzky skated free and had more of the assists and goals that fans paid to see, increasing the salaries even of the players on opposing teams that the Oilers defeated. Hockey thrived because the stylized violence of goons was tolerated, because allowing goons (paradoxically) *reduced* the amount of violence..

Then in 2003, the league cracked down, punishing fighting. This means there are fewer formal fights in the game. But now code-breakers can more easily escape the retribution of the goons. One clear effect of the rule change has been an increase in hard checks on the open ice, and an overall increase in injuries.

Putting these factors together, we can see the unintended consequence of the change in rules and the change in equipment for behavior: more danger. Players can now fly in recklessly, using their (protected) faces to block shots and their shoulders to give hard checks. The shock of the impact is transferred to necks, spines, and joints. And there is no goonery to punish those who injure star players, so we see the paradox: more safety equipment and less fighting imply more injuries.

Peltzman Effects vs The Man of System

The reason for this discussion extends beyond hockey, of course. (Though I like hockey!) The point is that bearing Peltzman Effects in mind helps policymakers and analysts remember that we are talking about people — actual sentient creatures who react and respond, not billiard balls or chemicals in solution, whose reactions are predictable.

There is a tendency among regulators to act like Adam Smith's "Man of System," moving objects around on a chess board.

> The man of system … is often so enamoured with the supposed beauty of his own ideal plan of government, that he cannot suffer the smallest deviation from any part of it.… He seems to imagine that he can arrange the different members of a great society with as much ease as the hand arranges the different pieces upon a chess-board. He does not consider that the pieces upon the chess-board have no other principle of motion besides that which the hand impresses upon them; but that, in the great chess-board of human society, every single piece has a principle of motion of its own, altogether different from that which the legislature might choose to impress upon it. If those two principles … are opposite or different, the game will go on miserably. (Smith, 1759; pp. 233-234)

The "game" may be hockey or public policy; the insight is the same. Unintended consequences may reduce, or even eliminate, the good you expect to result from a policy change. People aren't chess pieces.

III

THE ARGUMENT FOR CAPITALISM

In the first section, I outlined the argument for capitalism in as sparse a fashion as I could manage. The key factors are decentralized management of specialization or division of labor; distributed but efficient impersonal exchange based on prices; and enormous economies of scale based on the rapid sharing of ideas.

An improvement in technology or an expansion in the ways we can use liquid capital to create physical capital immediately improves the welfare of the whole world. Economists call this an economy of scale, which means that specialization and increased social capital in the form of discoveries quickly spread around the world as force multipliers for labor and entrepreneurs.

This last notion may be the most important, and the least understood, because it deals with the way capitalism handles ideas. An improvement in technology or an expansion in the ways we can use liquid capital to create physical capital immediately improves the welfare of the whole world. Economists call this an economy of scale, which means that specialization and increased social capital in the form of discoveries quickly spread around the world as force multipliers for labor and entrepreneurs.

It is by definition difficult to model or predict innovation. This is especially true for technology and ideas, the general category of plans, recipes, knowhow, learning, or, simply, ideas. Once these things exist, because someone gets lucky, or works hard, or just notices something new, ideas spread quickly and are available to anyone with the desire to use them. This ideas-based capital serves as a driving force for expanding the division of labor, benefiting from economies of scale, making us all wiser, creating cascades of improved innovations, and thus spreading prosperity everywhere. (NOTE: This is an idea that Jeffrey Tucker has often discussed, and I should note that his arguments, and in fact his words, are part of the motivation for, and content of, this section introduction.)

This aspect of capitalism is not discussed enough in economic literature. Economics typically deals with the problem of scarcity, and finds answers to this problem in the form of certain institutions like private property, free-floating prices, exchange, and contracts. But ideas and knowledge break the surly bonds of scarcity; knowledge spreads without the need of restraints to allocate and apportion ownership rights.

To take an obvious example, you are reading this book. You can take its ideas. You can carry those in your head for 50 years, or the book might be sent to another country and be discovered in a library or used book store and change the way that reader thinks. The reader can share the ideas with others, or apply the ideas to new problems. Notice, though, that we have broken the problem of scarcity. Your use of my ideas, or Jeffrey Tucker's ideas, takes nothing from us. We still possess the ideas, and can use them with no loss, because scarcity doesn't apply.

And so it goes for billions of others. Everyone can own and use the ideas in this article with no loss of rights to me or anyone else. It's true for all ideas. The problem for society is to find ways to set ideas and information free. "Free" has two Latin meanings: "libre" and "gratis." Clearly, we are all better off if ideas are "libre." But saying that ideas must be "gratis" is a problem, because ideas may require hard work to develop.

What is needed, then, is a system that promotes the radical expansion and sharing of ideas, as fast as possible, but which at the same time allows those who create and apply the ideas to benefit. There are several systems in place to advance this process, including patents, copyrights, and trademarks. Patents, in particular, may be poorly suited to a world where the pace of change is accelerating so rapidly, because patents confer an artificial and extended exclusive right to an idea, giving the "owner" a source of income (solving the "not gratis" problem) but shackling the use of the idea (violating the "set it libre!" imperative).

The alternative system to capitalism is often called "socialism." Like capitalism, it comes in many varieties. But the key feature of socialism is that it inverts the ownership structure that makes capitalism so vibrant and important. Capitalism confers private ownership of physical goods and consumer products, so that private ownership is matched to things that can be scarce. Ideas, on the other hand, can be applied and adapted by anyone, in a system called "permissionless innovation." Socialism collectivizes the private goods that suffer from scarcity, thereby creating "common pool resource" problems. But socialism also privatizes (in the form of ownership by the state) all the ideas and innovations that the system creates. There is no permissionless innovation; only those directions and initiatives approved by the state will qualify for the funding and support that makes the activity possible.

This section explores this problem from the perspective of how the price mechanism, and private ownership, animate the process of decentralized "planning." The system responds quickly to external changes, with no central direction. The value that is created is hard to envision, and almost impossible to measure. But it's very real, and it's no surprise that all prosperous nations are based on capitalist systems of private enterprise. Prices give signals about what is useful, and give rewards (and punishments) to those who attempt to devise new activities using new ideas. Only a price system can ensure that ideas are libre, but not gratis.

1. Everybody Loves Mikey

I pick up the rubber sandals, size 12, bright purple, $1.89 for the pair. I hold them over my head, and start my presentation, loud enough for people two aisles away to hear. This is not what you expect to hear in a beach town drugstore.

"Kevin, why are these sandals here? Do you know why, Brian?"

Pity my poor sons. I often point out things they may have missed about markets. (Now, what teenager wouldn't love that?) Kevin and Brian are hiding behind the film display by now, because they know what's coming. Necks are craning from other aisles, and two employees peek at me from the pharmacy.

"Are these sandals here because someone in China knew that I was going to break a shoe yesterday? Did they want to provide just the right size sandal, in the perfect garish color, for a ridiculously cheap price?" (Pause) "In fact, how could anyone make a profit on a pair of 'flops at $1.89? Why don't they charge more? I'd pay more, because I really need beach shoes. Someone must really love me! There's no other explanation."

Of course, by now my sons do not love me. This next part is what they really hate. The intro differs, depending on the product, but the punchline is always the same. I go on, as if having an inner argument, "Wait... what's love got to do with it? I've never been to China, and besides these were made weeks before I broke my 'flop. It can't be love. It must be..." (pause; at least a dozen strangers' eyes are on me, my sons moaning behind the cooler) "... it must be that those people shipped these sandals here because they can make profits. And, the best part is this: They would love to charge higher prices, and there is no government regulation saying they can't charge a higher price. Nonetheless, the shoemaker and the drugstore have decided that best price for them (not for me, but for them!) is $1.89."

The boys come out from behind the cooler, because they know our work here is now done. I pay for the sandals, and notice another employee is on the phone, probably calling Child Services. We head for the car, and as we drive back to the beach house my older son says, "Good one, dad," shaking his head.

Can't Buy Me Love

Do people do things for us because those people are good, because they love us? Sometimes they do. Your family loves you, and your friends would sacrifice things for you. But for most of us, family and friends is a pretty small group. We can't rely on just those few people for all the things we need in the world. Something other than love, and altruism, has to organize all the thousands of activities and choices we all depend on every day.

We can go to restaurants and get excellent service, and delicious meals. Your mechanic says you need brake work; you pay him $1,200 for the repairs, without physically checking in any way to see if the repairs were actually done. And when you go to Buy Mart to get a VCR, you don't check the contents of the box before you pay the cashier, using a credit card number you trust that cashier not to steal.

All of these actions and choices depend on the cooperation of others, people we don't know, people who might dislike us if they did know us. What keeps them from doing bad things to us? Why don't stores charge us exorbitant prices? Why don't our employers always withhold our health insurance, or cut our salaries in half, or cancel our vacations? Why do we get pay raises, instead of pay cuts? Is it because everyone loves us?

So many people I encounter, smart people, seem to believe that what makes people do good, or prevents them from cheating or acting badly, is personal integrity, good character, and regard for others. I'm not a psychologist, but I wonder if the reason is that they just have trouble with the idea of an intricately interconnected world where all of us are dependent on unknown others. How can we be dependent on others, and not be in their power?

The answer—markets create interdependencies without forcing subjugation, or even allowing abuse—was one of the key insights of Adam Smith's (1776) *Wealth of Nations*. He said: "Observe the accommodation of the most common artificer or day-labourer in a civilized and thriving country, and you will perceive that the number of people of whose industry a part, though but a small part, has been employed in procuring him this accommodation, exceeds all computation." In advanced market economies, we are all dependent on others in ways we may not even have thought of.

Of course, I would prefer the "Everyone loves Mikey!" explanation. If I am treated well, it should be because I am special. The fact that markets create dependencies without subjugation means that I am served well for the benefit of the server; other market participants are prevented from treating me badly not by their good character but by their desire for profits.

This becomes most obvious when incentives fail to discipline sloth or iniquity. What I mean is, that markets don't always prevent all misbehavior, ex ante. Sometimes, things go wrong. But even then, the incentives of the market still come into play. Some background:

I don't change my own oil. I go to the Happy Lube, or whatever they call themselves. Lube and oil change, $24, and it's quick. I could change my own oil, but it would take longer, and I can spend the 20 minutes at the Happy Lube answering phone calls or using my laptop.

Last time I went, an employee came out to my car, eating spaghetti from a dirty bowl. He said, "What do you need?"

I told him I wanted an oil change. He curtly nodded, and pointed at Bay #2. No other words. This was rather odd, as this was not the way I usually get treated at Happy Lube. Courtesy is what I expect, shining happy employees. To be honest, this guy was kind of cool. Like a Jack Black character in a movie about a downtrodden mechanic. Cocky, crusty, but with a heart of gold. Or not, as it turned out.

The oil change finished, I go up to pay. The same food-smeared Jack Black guy starts to ring up the charges. I hand him my $10 coupon. He says, "just put it down there; I'll get to it." I did.

But he didn't. Get to it, that is. He rang up the charge without the coupon. I didn't notice, and gave him my credit card. After I signed, I saw that there was no credit for the coupon. When I pointed this out, he said, "Well, there's really nothing I can do about it now. I already rang up the order. You should have said something."

So, I turned and made a brief speech (I wish my sons could have heard it) to the other customers: "What you have just seen would be a tragedy in any other country. But in the U.S., it is okay. Satisfactory alternatives, Puffy Lubes and Hinky Lubes, are located not too far from here and eagerly await our arrival, though they have no idea who we are. From now on we should all go somewhere else. Because this shop is peopled by thieves, and what you have witnessed here is theft."

All the other customers tried to pretend they were watching Oprah. Which was hard, because the TV was tuned to local news.

Jack became angry about my theft remark. He said loudly that anyone could make mistakes, that I wasn't perfect either… and so on. This was in front of other customers. By this time they weren't pretending to watch anything, except the worst employee in the history of the world. He was shouting at my back as I went out the door.

I sent a letter to the manager. He called two days later, laughing. "This is a great story. Did he actually say, 'What do you need?'" Turns out he had fired Jack as soon as he got the letter, since this was the third or fourth major complaint he had gotten in that one day. This, mind you, had been the manager's first day at the new job: TO DO LIST: Day one—Fire Sketchy Jack Black guy.

And, when the manager stopped laughing on the phone, he offered me a free oil change in compensation. I found this utterly charming, because it proved the manager loved me. Sure, we've never met, but I could feel the love over the phone. As for myself, I love Happy Lube. And God bless America.

2. Capitalism, Not Morality, Ended Baseball's Color Line

In the early days of baseball, in the 19th century (for a deeper history, see Hogan and Tygiel, 2006), the sport was colorblind and open to players of all backgrounds. True, the bigotry of individual players (and fans!) was a problem. Still, as late as 1884 Moses Fleetwood Walker and his brother Weldy played professional baseball for the Toledo Blue Stockings. But protests by bigots, including one of baseball's most famous players, Cap Anson, first baseman and manager for the Chicago White Stockings, led to concerns that players would strike, or fans would become violent, and games would be disrupted.

The problem was that the best black players were much better than the worst white players, and were in many cases better than the best white players in some clubs. The desire to win, and the fact that black players were willing to accept salaries that white players would reject, meant that competition forced the bigots to pay too high a cost, either in lost pay for forfeited games or lost bonuses because when all-white teams did play they would lose to more talented mixed teams.

The solution, as is always the case, was institutionalized racism, or the use of force to oblige even non-bigots to act as if they were bigots. A "gentleman's agreement" was struck, beginning with the end of the 1884 season.[15] It was not written down, but it was clear: no team in

---

15 For a more general history of the "Gentlemen's Agreement" and the history of racism in baseball, again see Hogan and Tygiel (2006). For the particular history of Robinson's own experiences, see Robinson and Duckett (2003).

the National or American League could sign a black player. On July 14, 1887, the issue was settled by two events. Anson managed to force George Stovey, a black pitcher, to be benched in a game between the White Stockings and the Newark Little Giants. And the owners of the International League, the "high minors" of baseball, the feeders for major league talent, voted six to four to ban any new, and to invalidate existing, contracts with black players.

Notice the collective element: the owners could have remained bigots, simply exercising their own racial prejudices and not signing black players. Instead, bigots managed to impose the general policy; it was not enough that I won't sign black players, because the policy will only work if no one is allowed to sign black players. Racism forces everyone to act as if they were prejudiced.

This policy, implicit but binding, stayed firmly in place for 60 years, ending in 1946 with the signing of Jackie Robinson to a minor league contract. Robinson moved up to the major league club, the Brooklyn Dodgers, at the start of the 1947 season.

The hero of this story, in many accounts, was the Dodger general manager, Branch Rickey. But serious scholars have expressed skepticism about this kind of "magic white man-savior" story, and I think they are right. Rickey was a notorious miser, skinflint, and squeezer of contracts, as well as a near-genius judge of talent. Rickey had at least four reasons to break the color line: black players (1) were athletically talented, (2) were underpriced, and (3) were likely to attract thousands of new fans to the Brooklyn ballpark, which was quite close to several heavily African-American neighborhoods.

It is also true that (4) Rickey had long resented the bigotry of fellow owners and the racism of the gentleman's agreement. This sense of the injustice of racism dated (at least) from his time in college at Ohio Wesleyan University, when he had witnessed the systematic racial bigotry of hotels and other teams against black players. I don't want to deny Rickey credit for (4), but the market forces — (1), (2), and (3) — are the real story: Rickey was too greedy to leave easy profits on the table.

Remember, until 1946 the gentleman's agreement had enforced a universal "color line," even in the minor leagues. But baseball requires many skills that have to be developed over years of practice; there had to be some source of black players completely outside the system, or even greed wouldn't have been enough. There was just such a pool of talent, however, because of the development, particularly beginning around 1930, of highly profitable — for some teams at least, including the Birmingham Black Barons, the Pittsburgh Crawfords, and Kansas City Monarchs — parallel Negro leagues. These players had enough talent that they played a highly organized schedule of games before often-crowded stadiums. The salaries of some black stars reached as high as $8,000 per year, with additional bonuses and expenses paid under the table, by 1946. That amounts to more than $100,000 in 2018 dollars, far less than modern ballplayer salaries but still a sizeable sum, enough to attract the talent and effort of young athletes.

Rickey's Dodgers were perennial also-rans, both in New York (where they trailed the Yankees and Giants in attendance) and in the National League (where they always trailed the St. Louis Cardinals in performance). Ironically, perhaps, the strength of the Cardinals was due in part to its innovative "farm system," with organized scouting in tiny communities all over the Midwest. Rickey himself had developed this power system when he worked for the Cardinals (1919-42), and he now had to try to compete against it.

Rickey was frustrated by his inability to sign quality players — at least at the price he was willing to pay — and by his inability to win pennants. Further, he was convinced that the flagging attendance at Brooklyn's Ebbets Field could rebound if he could sell tickets to African-American fans. Further, the skills of the black players, using almost any measure of offense or defense, were consistently higher than those of white players for the same level of salary. Remember, all that is really necessary is that the best black players be better than the worst white players, given the difference in salary. If competition were to be allowed, and if black athletes were allowed a level playing field, racism would have to yield to the cold facts of wins and losses.

All these factors — low attendance, losing seasons, small budgets, and the availability of a huge pool of cheap, high-quality ballplayers in the Negro leagues — led Rickey to sign Jackie Robinson. Rickey is often portrayed as a king or saint, a magic white man who did Jackie Robinson a favor and sacrificed his own reputation for the benefit of African-Americans. But this was a flinty-eyed, green-eyeshade decision and nothing more: Jackie Robinson was signed for a paltry $600 per month even though his skills, defensive prowess, and offensive production quickly established him as one of the premier players in baseball. By 1955, Robinson was the highest-paid Dodger, making more than $35,000 per year, but even that was the result of his market power and not any charity on the part of Brooklyn's management.

Other owners (the "gentlemen" in the misnamed gentlemen's agreement) were infuriated, of course. But that can only be explained by their recognition that the competitive advantage of opening the league to all players based solely on talent would prevent them from indulging their bigoted preferences. The most bigoted teams, or rather their owners and management, by this measure were from New York, Washington, Philadelphia, and (notoriously) Boston. Boston's ownership actually held out until 1959, and gave up only when it became clear that without organized artificial racism the price of bigotry was just too high.

To be fair, the end of the formal color line did not end systematic racism in major league baseball. There is strong evidence that black players either were underpaid or were not hired at all for at least 10 years following Jackie Robinson's emergence on the field. Consider the difference between average players, by race, for the period, comparing the means of batting averages for white and black players and showing the difference in those means.

Table: Comparison of Black and White Player Batting Performance, 1953-1959

Year	Mean Black Player Batting Average	Mean White Player Batting Average	Difference
1953	.288	.257	.031
1954	.262	.244	.018
1955	.271	.251	.020
1956	.270	.248	.022
1957	.264	.252	.012
1958	.274	.249	.025
1959	.265	.246	.019

Source: Rosenblatt (1967, pp. 51-53.)

This table must be interpreted as a measure of the disequilibrium, in standard microeconomic terms, caused by residual bigotry. If there were no racism, meaning that profit-seeking market forces were free to operate to eliminate the performance differences between races, there should be no difference in mean performance. At the margin, owners and managers will hire players based on productivity, as long as the *best* black player they can hire is better than the *worst* white player currently on the roster.

Replacing the worst white players with the best remaining unemployed black players ought, at the margin, to raise the average of white players, as the worst are fired, and lower the average of black players, as marginally less talented players are added. But the process was only partly carried out, meaning that some managerial or owner taste for discrimination (or perhaps a fan taste for discrimination, not wanting "too many" blacks on a team, or player opposition, refusing to play with "too many" black teammates) was still preventing full equilibrium, which would imply that there was no difference at the margin.

One could object that the results shown in the table are the result of selection, but that's the point: at the margin, hiring the best black players not on the roster was far more productive, in terms of cost per unit output, than retaining the least productive whites already on the roster. Note that I am not claiming that black athletes, on average, are in any way naturally superior at running, leaping, or any of the other attributes in bigoted stereotypes. The point is that if the two pools are identical overall, one should expect teams facing competition and caring only about winning to continue adding better black players and firing inferior white players, at the margin, until the mean difference disappears.

I shouldn't be too optimistic or claim too much. Capitalism and market competition are partial solutions, at best, to problems of racism because all markets can do is make bigotry more expensive. The Boston Red Sox had averaged a winning percentage of nearly 61.0 percent during the late 1940s, a remarkable performance, with only white players. In the period when baseball desegregation became general, 1951-59, the Red Sox played at a level just over 51.5 percent, a nearly average performance.

Even in the period following management's surrender to competitive necessity, their reluctance to fully integrate the team held them back, with performances of 45.0 percent or less for much of the 1960s. Only in 1967, with seven black players on the roster, did the Red Sox return to prominence. The "Impossible Dream" team started three black players (Foy, Scott, and Smith) out of eight position players.

Perhaps I shouldn't make too much of the analogy to sports, but there is an obvious parallel with markets in the sense that there is a clear metric to judge performance. Baseball teams are judged on wins and losses, and firms in the marketplace are "judged" by profits and losses. Since performance is objective, there is far more pressure on participants to put aside their prejudices and personal preferences.

This leveling of privilege, in which everyone is judged by their merits, is often lauded as being an advantage of sporting competition. We don't always recognize that markets have the same leveling function, the same corrosion of artificial privilege. The evangelical Christian author Nancy Pearcey noted that this principle is actually general, regardless of whether we are considering religious movements, sports, or markets.

As Ms. Pearcey is said to have put it: "Competition is always a good thing. It forces us to do our best. A monopoly renders people complacent and satisfied with mediocrity." That mediocrity and that complacency was broken by the ending of the "Gentlemen's Agreement," which involved neither gentlemen nor actual agreement. Since Branch Rickey had been part of the baseball apartheid system, the most we can do is acknowledge that he did try to make up for his sins by ending the color line. But the real credit should go to greed and the profit motive, because at some point it became too expensive to maintain the pretense that black players couldn't play at the major league level.

3. Three Undeniable Problems with Anti-Gouging Laws

Price "gouging" is charging a high price for something consumers really need, in an emergency situation. Some folks consider the prices of beer at NFL games (at Oakland's Alameda Coliseum, $10.75 for 12 ounces), or popcorn at the movies (often $10, or more, for a large), to be "gouging," but those are just local monopoly prices for non-essential items.

Real price gouging is often illegal. Anti-price-gouging (APG) laws have three parts: the trigger, the domain, and the limit. Here is the money part of the statute from my beloved home state, North Carolina:

> § 75-38.: Upon a triggering event, it is prohibited… for any person to sell or rent or offer to sell or rent any goods or services which are consumed or used as a direct result of an emergency or which are consumed or used to preserve, protect, or sustain life, health, safety, or economic well-being of persons or their property with the knowledge and intent to charge a price that is unreasonably excessive under the circumstances.

In this case, the "trigger" is the declaration of a state of emergency by the Governor, or an "abnormal market disruption," which according to the statute means "a significant disruption, whether actual or imminent, to the production, distribution, or sale of goods and services in North Carolina, which are consumed or used as a direct result of an emergency or used to preserve, protect, or sustain life, health, safety, or the economic well-being of a person or his or her property."

This could be caused by "a natural disaster, weather, acts of nature, a strike, power or energy failures or shortages, civil disorder, war, a terrorist attack, a national or local emergency, or other extraordinary adverse circumstances."

The "domain," as you can see in the text of the law, is "stuff you really need." So if you charge a really high price for ice, which people without power need, you'd be doing something covered by the law. If you raised your price for the kind of "ice" my wife likes to wear around her neck, and on her wrists, no problem. (Note: My wife just told me that diamonds are actually more of an essential item; no one ever said that "frozen water is a girl's best friend"!)

That leaves the "limit": if the law is triggered, and for commodities or services in the domain, how much can sellers raise prices in the face of scarcity? The answer is quite clear: sellers can't charge a price that is "unreasonably excessive under the circumstances."

So, the price can be unreasonable. It can even be excessive. But it can't be unreasonably excessive. That's actually not clear at all. Apparently, the concrete interpretation of this phrase is 5%, or perhaps 10%, depending on the "circumstances." If you raise your price more than 10% in the face of an emergency, you are "gouging," it seems.

There are 34 states with APG laws, and few others have statutes that could be used that way by an enterprising attorney general. And the laws are popular; there is no movement to loosen the laws, and it appears that large majorities of voters actively favor the laws as they are.

Three Huge Issues

But there are three problems with APGs.

1. Misallocation. Some people need products or services more than other people need them. But if the price is kept artificially low, there is no reason for the person with mild needs to leave some for those still waiting in line, or who will come looking tomorrow for the product. With APGs, the first few people who go to the store buy everything up. APGs, in other words, encourage hoarding rather than sharing.

There's a joke that my good friend Russ Roberts, of Econtalk fame, put up recently on Twitter. A guy goes into a store, to buy some milk. But the milk is $8 per gallon. So he complains to the owner: "$8! That's too much!"

The owner replies, "So, buy it at the store across the street. That guy is only charging $4."

The buyer shakes his head, "I can't, he's out of milk."

The owner nods, "Right. And as soon as I'm out of milk, I'll be able to charge $4, too!"[16]

The point is obvious: it's better to be able to buy milk at $8 than to be out of milk at $4. The low price for things that aren't available is no price at all.

2. Discourage Stockpiling Beforehand. Say there's a hurricane coming. If you know that people really want milk and bread and

---

16 Roberts, Russ. "A Fair Price." Café Hayek. October 22, 2005. http://cafehayek.typepad.com/hayek/2005/09/a_fair_price.html, and "The Reality of Markets." Econlib, October 2005, https://www.econlib.org/library/Columns/y2005/Robertsmarkets.html

other staples to "stock up," then stores could fill their warehouses with needed supplies. That's expensive, and sometimes the hurricane changes course at the last minute, leaving the sellers with a lot of wasted stock. With APGs, there is no advantage to stockpiling, because you can sell things at the regular price anywhere.

3. Discourage New Supplies Afterward. This is by far the worst problem, and the one that APG supporters seem least to understand. The problem is actually not high prices, but scarcity. There is not enough of the desperately needed products and services, and if—by assumption—there is an emergency where we should be doing everything possible to get as much of those supplies delivered, as fast as possible.

For example, it is common to recognize that many people want portable electric generators after a hurricane, because the power goes out. They don't buy one in advance, because they are pretty expensive and no one is sure the electrical grid will go down until it's too late to bring more generators in, in the face of the oncoming storm. (Stores could stockpile beforehand, of course, but see #2 above.)

The hard thing for most people to understand is that the only way to get plentiful supply at low prices is to allow high prices. High prices are a signal that more is needed, and that people serving that desperate demand can be paid enough to make it worthwhile.

But APG laws block this channel of resupply, as effectively as an enemy army might lay siege to a city. A "siege," after all, is when a military unity surrounds a city and prevents needed supplies from getting through. APG laws actually require state and local officials to lay siege to cities. That would be an act of war if another army did it, but when we do it to ourselves it's just "public policy."

Consider this account by Perry (2017), describing the aftermath of Hurricane Katrina:

> Let's use the actual example of John Shepperson of Kentucky, who in 2005 took time away from his normal job to buy 19 generators, rent a U-Haul truck, and drive it 600 miles to the Katrina-damaged area of Mississippi. John offered to sell his generators at twice the price he paid, to help cover his costs and make a profit. Instead his generators were confiscated, Shepperson was arrested for price gouging, held by police for four days, and the generators kept in police custody. They never made it to consumers with urgent needs who desperately wanted to buy them.[17]

Who would have been harmed by the lifting of the siege, meaning that Shepperson, and thousands of other entrepreneurs, had been allowed to sell generators? Presumably, we are concerned about the consumers who would have paid Shepperson's high price, right? It's as if they went to Shepperson, and said that his price--$1,000—was "too high." Shepperson might have said, "Well, go over to the hardware store across the street. Their price is $500."

The consumer would have said, "Yes, but they don't have any

17 Perry, Mark. 2017. "A challenge for supporters of anti-price-gouging laws: when does a 'fair' legal price become 'illegal gouging." American Enterprise Institute. August 31. Accessed June 17, 2019. http://www.aei.org/publication/a-challenge-for-supporters-of-anti-price-gouging-laws-when-does-a-fair-legal-price-become-unfair-gouging/

generators." Well, right. The alternative for the consumer is not being able to buy a generator at the price prevailing a week ago, before the hurricane. The alternative for the consumer is to go without a generator, when the consumer actually values the generator at more than $1,000, maybe much more.

You might object, "What if the consumer does not value the generator at more than $1,000?" Fair enough. She won't buy one. But she didn't have one anyway; for her, in terms of value, "no generator" is the solution regardless of the public policy in place.

The difference is that if APG laws are repealed, those people who do value the generators at more than $1,000 can actually buy one. Let me be clear about the two possible conditions:

Condition I (APG law in place): There are no generators available, regardless of how much consumers want one. People with low valuation can't buy generators, and people with high valuation can't buy generators. Everyone must evacuate.

Condition II (APG law repealed): There are many generators available, because people are bringing them in from surrounding areas. But the price is high; people with low valuation don't buy generators. People with high valuation do buy generators, however, and are able to stay in their houses instead of evacuating.

The bottom line is that people with low valuation (and that does include people who really want generators but are too poor to be able to afford the high price) don't get generators under either condition. The problem is not high price, but scarcity: there aren't enough generators, given the emergency. Imposing an APG law makes the problem of scarcity worse, and does nothing at all to help poor people because APG laws eliminate all incentive to bring in generators from outside.

Of course, one might object that charities, or the state, might supply the emergency goods and services. And to some extent that's true. How could we tell if there is enough? The answer is "price;" if charities and emergency management officials bring in enough supplies, then the price will be driven down to the point where everyone can afford what they need.

But that means that APG laws are unnecessary, and in fact moot. The joke is not funny if the price-gouger says, "Go across the street to the FEMA truck; they are giving milk away for free." The consumer would say, "Okay, I will!" and leave the store. What that means is that APG laws are unnecessary (if the state is as efficient as you think it is) or harmful and dangerous (if the state is as inefficient as I think it is, suggesting private solutions are helpful). Either way, APG laws are either useless or harmful.[18]

---

18 For a wide-ranging discussion of price-gouging, see Tyler Cowen's series on the subject at Marginal Revolution: "Why don't we see more price gouging?" http://www.marginalrevolution.com/marginalrevolution/2003/09/why_dont_we_see.html; "More on price gouging" http://www.marginalrevolution.com/marginalrevolution/2003/09/more_on_price_g.html; "People hate flexible prices" http://www.marginalrevolution.com/marginalrevolution/2003/11/people_hate_fle.html

4. Your Ticket to Capitalism Is Free

How much would you pay for a ticket to Walmart?

That seems like a silly question. You don't have to pay to get into Walmart. In fact, when you get to the door, you usually get greeted by a nice old person who offers you a cart to use.

But how much would you pay? That's the way to think about the value of capitalism, to consumers: What would it be worth to have access to the markets where you can buy the things you want?

Economists have a concept we use to analyze that kind of problem, and it's called "consumer surplus." Consumer surplus is the amount you would be willing to pay to obtain something you want, minus the actual price you have to pay to get it.

So, if you want water (and who doesn't?), the consumer surplus would be the amount you would be willing to pay if there were no other source, minus the amount you have to pay. Let's look at examples of two products, water and diamonds, to get an idea of how that works.

Checking Walmart's website, I see that I can get water for 2 cents an ounce or less, if I buy quite a bit of it. That's more expensive than tap water, of course, but it's pretty cheap. It would cost more if I wanted fancy French or Italian water, of course; that costs 6 cents an ounce or more, or more than a $1 for a half-liter bottle.

I also noticed that Walmart has a nice 6-carat diamond "tennis bracelet" (would you really wear that to play tennis?) for $11,000.

The point being that diamonds are much more expensive than water, at least at Walmart, in August 2018. That's probably generally true, though: a market system is going to "value" a small quantity of diamonds much more highly than even a pretty large quantity of water.

Isn't that a problem? After all, water is more valuable, in terms of the realities of human life, than diamonds. A number of philosophers considered this problem, and in many cases they considered the "paradox" an indictment of the market system of valuing commodities. What kind of cockeyed system would value diamonds more than water?

Plato, in Euthydemus (304 BCE) said: "For only what is rare is valuable; and water, which, as Pindar says, is the 'best of all things,' is also the cheapest."

Adam Smith, in *Wealth of Nations* (1776), said: "Nothing is more useful than water: but it will purchase scarce anything.... A diamond, on the contrary, has scarce any value in use; but a very great quantity of other goods may frequently be had in exchange for it." (p. 33).

Plato's explanation was rareness; Smith's was the difficulty or expense of obtaining the thing, which fits with his labor theory of value. Other analysts have suggested that "marginal utility" is the justification: if we had no water, it would be very valuable, more valuable than diamonds, especially if we happened already to have quite a few diamonds. But since we have lots of water (most of the time), at the margin water is much less expensive.

The Happiness of Consumers

That all sounds very mechanical to me, and not really focused on the main point, which is the actual welfare and happiness of consumers. That is where the real heart of the argument for capitalism lies: consumer sovereignty. And that brings me back to my original question: what is the value of a ticket to the market system?

Suppose that—as is usually the case—your shopping list has more items than "1. Water 2. Diamonds." You want to buy some clothes, some tools, some toys, some fishing equipment, and quite a lot of food, some of it canned or frozen and some it fresh.

You go to Walmart. (You might go somewhere else, of course, but Walmart happens to have all of those things under one roof, so it simplifies my example. There is nothing important about it being Walmart, though!) But this time, at the door, instead of a nice old gentlemen greeter who helps you get a cart, there is a fancy mind-reading robot. The robot takes your list, and scans your mind to see how much you want of each item.

In particular, the robot assigns a value for the maximum amount you would pay for each thing on your list. It might look something like this:

Water: $100,000

Oatmeal: $1,000

Bread: $1,200

Fishing rod: $25,000

And so on, all the way down your very long list.

Those amounts may look like a lot. But remember, these aren't prices. These are the maximum amounts you would be willing to pay for these items. We never have to think in these terms, because we are always presented with choices at prices far less than the maximum amount we would pay.

Think about it: when you go to a store, sometimes you pick up an item and check the price. Then you say, "No, that's too much!" and put it down. But you aren't thinking, "That's more than I value that item." You're thinking, "I can get that cheaper somewhere else," which is completely different. The mind-reading robot's list is much more basic: how much would you pay if you had none of that item, and had no other way to get it?

After compiling the list of values, the robot would then subtract the actual prices being charged inside the store. That would give you the consumer surplus, which is willingness to pay minus price:

Water: $100,000 - $1 = $99,999

Oatmeal: $1,000 - $1.75 = $998.25

Bread: $1,200 - $3.50 = $1,196.50

Fishing rod: $25,000 - $31.00 = $24,969

Again, and so on (it's a long list).

After performing the calculations (which are correct, at least in the sense of matching your subjective valuations, because the robot can read your mind), the robot presents you with a bill. It's the total value of all the consumer surplus you will derive from being able to enter the store. The amount will be considerable, quite possibly $500,000 or more.

No Mind-Reading Robots

Of course, the amount of that ticket makes you exactly indifferent between entering the store and just going back home. By charging back all the consumer surplus you would have gotten from shopping, all the value of shopping is being transferred to the seller. In my example the seller can do that because there is no other source for all these items.

But that's not the way the world works. There are no mind-reading robots, and there are no variable-price ticket booths to get into grocery stores. That's beside the point, though. The real reason the real world is different from my example is that we have a capitalistic market system based on consumer sovereignty. The reason groceries and other stores can't charge a price anywhere close to the maximum you would pay is that groceries have to compete with each other. Walmart, in particular, is constantly trying to find ways to charge lower prices, not higher prices.

The consumer surplus that we derive from buying water, and other items, is enormous, almost incalculable. The fact that all of these products, services, and useful things are available to us at low prices seems automatic, nothing very interesting or important. In fact, the capitalist system operating in the background is performing miracles of production, logistics, and delivery, all to make sure that prices are low.

That means that capitalism is focusing on making sure consumer surplus is high! Since you don't have to buy a ticket to capitalism, it's easy to miss just how much consumer surplus is being directed your way, without you having to make much effort to obtain it.

As long as there is competition, and limits on protectionism, your ticket to capitalism is free. Come on in.

You want a cart?

5. We Can Never Run Out of Anything

Somewhere along about 2005 I started hearing about "Peak _____," where the blank is some resource such as oil, water, food, and so on. Our peak "Peak" pique was based on the notion that "we" (and I'm not sure what that means) had reached the point of maximum production, and that the future was a bleak choice between bad alternatives. Mankind's profligate use of this nonrenewable resource was supposed to presage an era of shortage and shrinking options.

Now, I was familiar with the famous "bet" between Julian Simon and apocalyptic-professional Paul Ehrlich, from the 1980s, in which Simon let Ehrlich choose five resources, and bet that the prices would fall in real terms. The prices of all five did in fact fall. Since then, some people have quite sensibly objected that if other decades were selected, and other resources were chosen, Ehrlich might have won and Simon might have lost. But that's not what happened. Ehrlich lost.

Of course, Ehrlich was used to being embarrassed by having his predictions turn out badly. Remember, Ehrlich had famously said, in his 1968 book, *The Population Bomb*:

> The battle to feed all of humanity is over. In the 1970s hundreds of millions of people will starve to death in spite of any crash programs embarked upon now. At this late date nothing can prevent a substantial increase in the world death rate...The train of events leading to the dissolution of India as a viable nation is already in motion... If I were a gambler, I would take

> even money that England will not exist in the year 2000. (p. 1)

One would assume that Dr. Ehrlich was much abashed by the failure, the absurd failure in fact, of these predictions. But no; the most dangerous place in the world is still standing between Ehrlich and microphone. More recently, Ehrlich has predicted (in an interview with Prigg, 2014) with the same certainty as before that cannibalism was mankind's only hope for survival:

> Is it perfectly OK to eat the bodies of your dead because we're all so hungry? The human race is moving in that direction with a ridiculous speed.

That was five years ago. The amount of poverty, and the incidence of hunger, has actually fallen sharply in those five years. It was the very absurdity of Ehrlich's view of human society and its capacities to work together that led Simon to take what was actually a sucker's bet, though I can't say that I blame Simon: to see supposedly skeptical media types gulping down Ehrlich's garbage science would have provoked me, too.

The point is that Simon was lucky to win, just as a number of people (including the very careful Paul Sabin, in his 2013 book *The Bet*), have said. The reason is that the direction of prices was not, or should not have been, the core of "the bet." Simon's real claim was that we cannot run out of anything if markets are allowed to work. Specifically, what that means is that property rights are specified clearly and prices are free to adjust. Since the most important mechanism that prevents "us" from running out of anything is price increases, I've never understood Ehrlich's preening and apologetics after the fact.

Prices Keep Us from Running Out of Anything, Ever

Here's something you may not have thought of: Is it moral for me to use something that someone else values more than I do? I think you can make an argument at least that the answer is "no." If I know you need something, and I value it much less, but I use it up and keep you from using it then I am acting badly. I may have a reason to act this way, but as a general abstract matter we would like things to be used by the people who value them most.

Is there any way to make sure it works out this way? Well, in many cases this is exactly what the price system accomplishes, though we rarely hear things described this way. Markets combine the information in prices with the incentives to exchange if the person who has something values it less than the person who needs it.

Think about it: Suppose I have a widget, and I value it at $5. You value that widget at $10. We could say that I should just give it to you, but then that imposes a sacrifice on me. Maybe there is a place for charity here, but the point is that if you pay me $7 for the widget I am better off than before, and I'm happy to give the widget up. But you are better off also. I'm better off, and I'm not using the thing that you value more. So I benefit materially, and act morally. Win-win!

What does any of this have to with Simon and Ehrlich? Remember, Ehrlich was predicting catastrophe, scarcity, and shortages, which would imply that prices would go up. Simon was predicting that we would "never run out of anything," which might also mean that prices would go up. For Simon to predict that prices would actually go down was pretty brave.

But it has nothing to do with the basic bet, which is that if there are property rights and prices are free to move we can never run out of anything. The reason is that if we start to run out of something, prices rise. And when prices rise, three things happen:

1. Consumers use less
2. Producers make more
3. Entrepreneurs figure out ways to make substitutes

That is the core of Simon's prediction: we can't run out of anything precisely because prices will go up, and trigger the three self-correcting mechanisms above. So the debate about whether Simon or Ehrlich was right about the direction of prices is just silly. Simon is right (we can't run out of anything, ever) even if Ehrlich is right (prices rise sharply, and trigger reactions 1, 2, and 3).

The "Peak Oil" hysteria of the late 2000's was idiotic. There was never any reason to believe that we were running out of oil. And, unsurprisingly, as soon as prices rose the result was:

1. Consumers cut back, choosing more fuel efficient cars and shifting away from oil as a power source.
2. Alternatives, such as shale oil, fracking, and new areas of exploration were developed, until the current amount of known reserves is nearly double what we knew of in 1985 (that's double, twice as much, more not less, etc.)
3. Engineers and entrepreneurs were spurred to work harder on the problems of batteries, solar power, wind power, and other alternatives.

Of course, we can run out of stuff. We can run out of pelagic fish like cod or anchovies, taken from "open" fisheries in the "commonly-owned" oceans. We can run out of passenger pigeons, and rhinoceros, and other animals that are not owned by anyone and for whom the price mechanism cannot operate. What is the common feature of stuff we can run out of?

It's managed by the state. Because of "market failures," the state manages common pool resources. And that's where the real danger lies. The environment is not safe, not because we are running out of stuff produced by markets but because we cannot control the resources managed by the state.

And that is what is actually scary. Forget Peak Oil; the problem is the Peak State.

6. They Clapped: Can Price-Gouging Laws Prohibit Scarcity?

I'll start the story with the most interesting thing, which is the ending. They clapped. I can't for the life of me understand why the people would clap. Here is what happened:

Hurricane "Fran" smashed into the North Carolina coastline at Cape Fear at about 8:30 pm, 5 September 1996. It was a category 3, with 120 mph winds, and enormous rain bands. It ran nearly due north, hitting the state capital of Raleigh about 3 am, and moving north and east out of the state by morning. The storm also dropped as much as ten inches of rain. In some counties, nearly every building was damaged; total reconstruction cost and damages were later calculated at $5 billion (2006 $).

In the Triangle (Raleigh, Durham, and Chapel Hill), more than a million people were without power the next morning. Humidity made everything sticky. Hundreds of homes had roofs damaged by falling pines and powerful winds. Few residences had any kind of back-up power. Many roads were blocked by large fallen trees. Within hours, food in refrigerators and freezers started to go bad. Insulin, baby formula, and other necessities immediately became susceptible to spoilage in the 95+ degree heat.

The damage was so widespread, and communication so sketchy, that no one had any firm idea of when power would be restored. More than a million people needed ice. And they needed it now.

Resources on the Move… Not

One might think that thousands of entrepreneurs in the surrounding areas, little touched by the storm, would load trucks and head to the disaster area. After all, they owned, or could obtain, all the things that the residents of central North Carolina needed so desperately. Ice, chain saws, generators, lumber, tarps for covering gaping holes in roofs… we needed it all. I say "we" because my family lived in North Raleigh. No power, and 36 large pine trees smashed down like God's own pick-up-stix. We couldn't get out of our immediate Mungerhood, and my underpowered chainsaw burned out on the first tree I tried to cut.

But no such mass movement of resources to their highest valued use took place. North Carolina had an "anti-gouging law," which made it illegal to sell anything useful at a price that was "unreasonably excessive under the circumstances." This had been widely interpreted to limit price increases to around 5% or less. Each instance of violation of this law could result in a fine of up to $5,000. So, ice that happened in Charlotte, stayed in Charlotte. Why drive three hours to Raleigh when you can only charge the Charlotte price, plus just enough for gas money to break even?

The problem for Raleigh residents was all about price, at that point.[19] The prices of all the necessities that I wanted to use to "preserve, protect, or sustain" my own life shot up to infinity. Within a day after the storm, there were no generators, ice, or chainsaws

---

19 Cordato, Roy. North Carolina's Price Control Laws: Harming Those They Are Meant to Help. Raleigh, NC: John Locke Foundation. 2006. http://www.johnlocke.org/acrobat/policyReports/ncpriceregs-maconno2.pdf

to be had, none. But that means that anyone who brought these commodities into the crippled city, and charged less than infinity, would be doing us a service.

Some service was, in fact, on the way. Four young men in the town of Goldsboro, an hour east of Raleigh and largely untouched by the storm, noticed that the freezers at the Circle P's, the Stop Marts, and the Handee Sluggos were brimming with ice. Convenience stores had stocked up, expecting a more easterly course for the storm. Now, there was an ice surplus in Goldsboro, and a shortage in Raleigh. These young men, washed in the milk of human kindness, rented two small freezer trucks, paid $1.70 each for 500 bags of ice for each truck and set off, filled with a sense of charity and the public good.

Okay, I made that last part up. They were filled with a sense of greed, and there was no washing involved. In fact, these guys may in some ways have been bad human beings, real jerks. But who cares? If there had been a benevolent, omniscient social planner, she would have been yelling: (1) Raleigh is desperate for ice. (2) If you have ice, take it to Raleigh. Of course, there could never be a social planner with that level of information and authority, as Hayek (1945) argued so persuasively. But these yahoos acted as if they heard one anyway, speaking through the price system: cheap ice in Goldsboro was expensive ice in Raleigh, so they could make money.

Our icemen came to the outskirts of Raleigh, and headed for the interior, where the citizens waited, icelessly. The path was blocked by fallen trees, but these were yahoos, not idiots. Yahoos have chainsaws, big ones. They rolled the cut logs off the road so their trucks (and, by the way, other cars and emergency vehicles) could pass.

One truck apparently parked in Five Points, near downtown, and another parked a bit west, near wealthy St. Mary's Street, and opened for business. I have not been able to find a definitive claim about price, but it was more than $8. (All three of my personal "sources" knew someone who saw events, but… I'd love to be able to ask the sellers if they knew of the anti-gouging law, but we'll never know, I guess.)

On reaching the front of the line, some customers were angry that the price was so high, but almost no one refused to pay for the ice. I have also been told that the sellers limited purchases to 4, or 6, bags per customer, but I'm not sure. If it is true, it reflects the altruism of the native North Carolinian, even ones who are just trying to make a buck.

But the police are charged with upholding the law, even the dumb ones (laws, not police). Someone must have made a call, because two Raleigh police cars and an unmarked car pulled up to the Five Points truck after about an hour. The officers talked to the sellers, talked to some buyers, still holding their ice, and confirmed that the price was much higher than the "correct" price of $1.75 (the cost of a bag of ice before the storm). The officers did their duty, and arrested the yahoos.

Apparently the truck was then driven to the police impoundment lot in downtown Raleigh, as evidence. The ice may or may not have melted (accounts vary), but it certainly was not given out to citizens.

And now we are back to where I started: the citizens, the prospective buyers being denied a chance to buy ice… they clapped. Clapped, cheered, and hooted, as the vicious ice sellers were handcuffed and arrested. Some of those buyers had been standing in line for five minutes or more, and had been ready to pay 4 times as much as the maximum price the state would allow. And they clapped as the police, at gunpoint, took that opportunity away from them.

What Were They Thinking

I am completely stumped by the clapping. But then I'm stumped on why people support anti-gouging laws. I strongly suspect the two things are related.

Consider some quotes from the Raleigh paper, the *News and Observer*, in the days following the hurricane. First, on September 10, 1996, less than a week after the storm, in two different page 1 stories, we were told:

"Ice shortages are becoming severe in some places—so much so that local counties are asking the federal government to send as much ice as it can."[20]

And:

"At the cabinet meeting, Richard Moore, Hunt's secretary for crime control and public safety, said... he was... deploying the state's Alcohol Law Enforcement officers to investigate reports of price-gouging of products in short supply.

Hunt said both Florida Gov. Lawton Chiles and South Carolina Gov. David Beasley had agreed to send truckloads of ice and other supplies to North Carolina."[21]

When I read these two articles, I started sputtering like a crazy person to my poor wife. And I am still sputtering about it. These articles told me two things: #1—Police and other government officials were being sent out to arrest anyone selling ice at a profit.

---

20 Eisley, Matthew, "New Problems Amid Progress." News and Observer, September 10, 1996, P. A1.

21 Leavenworth, Stuart, John Wagner, and Craig Whitlock. "Residents finally get a peek at battered barrier islands." News & Observer September 10, 1996 P. A1

#2—There was a terrible ice shortage. We were so desperate for ice that the only option is to beg the federal government, or other state governments, for supplies from their ice hoards, because there was no other way to get it.

I'm pretty sure I have a solution: stop doing #1, and #2 will go away like... well, like ice on a steamy September day in Raleigh. Ice is easy to make; just freeze some water. It's hard to make ice without electricity, but most of east, and all of west, North Carolina had plenty of electricity. And, in fact, they had plenty of ice. The problem is that the only real omniscient social planner we have is the market, and she speaks to people through prices. Do this, stop doing that, build something here, move to this city. When the state made it a crime to sell ice at a profit, the price mechanism was struck dumb. Only a few people could hear it. And we threw them in jail, ensuring that even fewer souls would heed the desperate call in the next crisis of deprivation.[22]

Tale of Two Prices

Consider two prices. First, the price of ice before the storm, which most people know, or have a feel for. Second, the price of ice after the storm, which is unknown and highly variable. People who favor price-gouging laws think that the first price, the price before the storm, is the fair price, and that is the price they want to pay. The market price after the storm reflects both the difficulty of getting ice from stores, because the store has no electricity, and the huge bump in demand for ice as thousands try to buy it.

---

22 Avery, Sarah, and Lynn Bonner, "Fran fuels economic boom—but not growth," News & Observer, October 6, 1996, P. A1

Clearly, the relative scarcity of ice after the storm is much higher. The market price rises rapidly to reflect this increased scarcity. This makes people who would have used ice at the old price economize, and use something else. They can drink their bottled water, or their Carolina Ale, warm if they don't want to pay $12 for a bag of ice. So ice only goes to people who really value it. And the higher price also signals yahoos, wahoos, and all sorts of regular folks that one can make box loads of money by taking truckloads of ice to Raleigh. The price system is automatically doing its job, signaling to buyers that they should cut back, and signaling sellers (even potential sellers, those who have to enter the market from Goldsboro) that they should sell more.

If enough people bring ice to Raleigh, of course, the price won't be $12, or $8, for very long. Ice is easy to make and transport, so without market restrictions the price after the storm will quickly be driven down near the price before the storm, because there is so much more ice available. That's what the clapping people must have wanted. Even the supporters of price-gouging laws want low prices and large supplies. But they can't get those things from a price-gouging law. Precisely the opposite happens, as the supply of ice disappears and the effective price, what people would be willing to pay, goes higher and higher. I admit that it's not intuitive, until you think about it. The only way to ensure low prices, and large supply, to buyers is to allow sellers to charge high prices, the highest they can get.

Well, but what if you seek a political solution, rather than trusting markets? What if you pass an anti-gouging law, to symbolize your opposition to scarcity? Scarcity hurts; it means that I can't have everything I want. Let's abolish scarcity; what then? As I have tried to argue, all a state accomplishes by passing an anti-gouging law is to ensure that there is no ice. I can't get it for $100, or $1,000. And too many citizens say, "Help: the market has failed! Let's call on government to rescue us!"

But they are wrong. Markets didn't fail. All that happened was that the price mechanism was bound and gagged, held hostage in the attic of the legislature.

In a way the most interesting way to think about this problem is to compare two people, let's call them Al and Bob. Al sits in his home in Goldsboro, watching tv and feeling bad about the devastation in Raleigh, where the storm hit. Al reflects on the fact that only luck separates those desperate folks in Raleigh and his own safety in Goldsboro, which the storm by-passed. Al feels real sympathy.... for a moment. Then he switches over to FOX to watch NASCAR.

Bob hears about the devastation in Raleigh, rents a refrigerator truck, buys a lot of ice in Goldsboro, where there is plenty of ice, and transports it to Raleigh. Bob then starts selling the ice at a high price.

Here's the question: should both these people be arrested? Should either one be arrested? Most North Carolinians apparently (according to polls, which support laws against price gouging) think that it is fine for Al to do nothing, but that Bob should be arrested for taking desperately needed supplies to a beleaguered city. You are all so concerned that no one get a small underserved reward that you are willing to punish the needy. It doesn't make any sense.

IV

CORE CONCEPTS

I have discussed some of the building blocks of the capitalist system in previous sections. The first and most important, the real explanation for the origins of wealth and prosperity in the world, is division of labor. Division of labor does two things: statically, it increases the amount of "stuff" each of us has, so long as we can rely on other folks to specialize also. I can make spear points, you can make shoes, and that person over they can catch fish, and so son.

Second, as Adam Smith noted, division of labor is one key origin of innovation. If we divide tasks into smaller steps, then the person who spends all day on one small step is likely to develop increased dexterity in that job through repetition. This leads to knowledge of improved techniques. At least as important, repetition will create a setting where the worker looks to do that one little piece of production more efficiently. To put it more simply, it's hard to design a machine that makes shoes, where you put leather in one end and shoes come out the other. But you might be able to design a machine that sews leather uppers to the soles, automating one small step. Many large innovations are the accumulation and sharing of many small ideas, accumulated over time. That's what division of labor makes possible.

There are two other core concepts discussed in this section: Externalities and opportunity costs. The problem of externality is central to much of the policy discussion of welfare economics. One of the earliest discussions of the problem of externality as a focus of public policy was by A.C. Pigou; since markets were unable to solve the externalities problem, the state would be forced to step in. But it turns out the truth is more complicated.

Finally, the question of opportunity cost is is one of the most important problems in economics. The argument for the market system is that prices are the best parametric representation we have of the opportunity cost of resources--subject, of course, to the problem of externalities. Students of economics have grave difficulties understanding opportunity costs in practice, though in principle we can define opportunity costs as the value given up, or the value of the next best foregone alternative use, involved in any course of action.

None of the three concepts--division of labor, externality, or opportunity cost--are well understood by most people. With this analysis and these examples I hope to address that problem. Plus, it's fun to think about!

1. I'm Thankful for Division of Labor

As I write this, on Thanksgiving Day in the United States, I have had one piece of remarkably delicious pumpkin pie. We also feed pumpkin to our dogs, Murphy and Skippy, as a supplement because it is full of vitamins and fiber, and it's delicious even just as pure pumpkin.

It costs us about $1 per day to feed our dogs the canned pumpkin. How can we do that? The answer is division of labor.

Division of Labor

Adam Smith famously made two assertions in the first three chapters of Wealth of Nations (1776). The first was that both the source and meaning of wealth is access by people to goods and services, and that the source of that is what he called "division of labor." The second claim is important enough to be the title of chapter 3: "That the Division of Labor is Limited by the Extent of the Market."

Smith summarized these two conclusions in his deeply insightful discussion of the "woolen coat":

> Observe the accommodation of the most common artificer or day-labourer in a civilized and thriving country, and you will perceive that the number of people of whose industry a part, though but a small part, has been employed in procuring him this accommodation, exceeds all computation. The woolen coat, for example, which covers the day-labourer, as coarse and rough as it may appear, is the produce of the joint labour

> of a great multitude of workmen. The shepherd, the sorter of the wool, the wool-comber or carder, the dyer, the scribbler, the spinner, the weaver, the fuller, the dresser, with many others, must all join their different arts in order to complete even this homely production. How many merchants and carriers, besides, must have been employed in transporting the materials from some of those workmen to others who often live in a very distant part of the country! How much commerce and navigation in particular, how many ship-builders, sailors, sail-makers, rope-makers, must have been employed in order to bring together the different drugs made use of by the dyer, which often come from the remotest corners of the world! What a variety of labour too is necessary in order to produce the tools of the meanest of those workmen! To say nothing of such complicated machines as the ship of the sailor, the mill of the fuller, or even the loom of the weaver, let us consider only what a variety of labour is requisite in order to form that very simple machine, the shears with which the shepherd clips the wool. The miner, the builder of the furnace for smelting the ore, the feller of the timber, the burner of the charcoal to be made use of in the smelting-house, the brick-maker, the brick-layer, the workmen who attend the furnace, the mill-wright, the forger, the smith, must all of them join their different arts in order to produce them. (p. 16)

The "day-labourer," a poor working man, can take advantage of the fact that many people have participated in a process that none of them fully understand, and of which the day-labourer himself may be totally unaware. The plans and purposes of thousands of people are coordinated, and the results organized, even though the activities are widely separated in space and none of the participants know each other personally.

But there is a third, more subtle but clearly articulated, claim that Smith makes about the division of labor: It's portable, and takes the form economists call a "non-linearity." Others might just call it the "work ethic." It goes like this: the more you work on something, the more you know. The more you know, the better you can apply the accumulated techniques and tools that work in the particular local circumstances in which you find yourself.

The surprising thing about this third claim is that it means the division of labor can be cultivated in a setting with no history of prosperity, and highly productive specialization can be fostered even in people who have no special knowledge or abilities at the outset.

In a surprisingly self-aware — and frankly, egalitarian — observation, Smith compares the "philosopher," the person held in highest esteem by the Enlightenment, and the "street porter," a person among the most "lumpen" (ragged, slow-witted) of what Marx would later call the "lumpenproletariat." Smith noted that, while the philosopher might like to think of him- or herself as being innately superior in some way, much of the apparent difference is simply the result of extended application of study and practice, made possible by division of labor:

> The difference of natural talents in different men, is, in reality, much less than we are aware of; and the very different genius which appears to distinguish men of different professions, when grown up to maturity, is not upon many occasions so much the cause, as the effect of the division of labour. The difference between the most dissimilar characters, between a

philosopher and a common street porter, for example, seems to arise not so much from nature, as from habit, custom, and education. When they came in to the world, and for the first six or eight years of their existence, they were, perhaps, very much alike, and neither their parents nor play-fellows could perceive any remarkable difference. About that age, or soon after, they come to be employed in very different occupations. The difference of talents comes then to be taken notice of, and widens by degrees, till at last the vanity of the philosopher is willing to acknowledge scarce any resemblance. But without the disposition to truck, barter, and exchange, every man must have procured to himself every necessary and conveniency of life which he wanted. All must have had the same duties to perform, and the same work to do, and there could have been no such difference of employment as could alone give occasion to any great difference of talents.

As it is this disposition which forms that difference of talents, so remarkable among men of different professions, so it is this same disposition which renders that difference useful. Many tribes of animals, acknowledged to be all of the same species, derive from nature a much more remarkable distinction of genius, than what, antecedent to custom and education, appears to take place among men. By nature a philosopher is not in genius and disposition half so different from a street porter, as a mastiff is from a grey-hound, or a grey-hound from a spaniel, or this last from a shepherd's dog. Those different tribes of animals, however, though all of the same species are of scarce any use to one another. The strength of the mastiff

> is not in the least supported either by the swiftness of the greyhound, or by the sagacity of the spaniel, or by the docility of the shepherd's dog. The effects of those different geniuses and talents, for want of the power or disposition to barter and exchange, cannot be brought into a common stock, and do not in the least contribute to the better accommodation and conveniency of the species. Each animal is still obliged to support and defend itself, separately and independently, and derives no sort of advantage from that variety of talents with which nature has distinguished its fellows. Among men, on the contrary, the most dissimilar geniuses are of use to one another; the different produces of their respective talents, by the general disposition to truck, barter, and exchange, being brought, as it were, into a common stock, where every man may purchase whatever part of the produce of other men's talents he has occasion for. (p. 19)

In other words, the mastiff's muscle does not depend on the spaniel's sagacity; they are just genetically different, and that's that. But the people who are now the philosopher and street porter were once very similar, and in fact nearly indistinguishable. One developed the talent of "being a philosopher." That development depended on a system where others did all the other things — making food and clothing, providing housing and security, and so on — that made it possible for the philosopher to study for decades.

Of course, there are innate differences in talent, mental or physical agility, and so on. Smith's point is that we tend to overemphasize these, and to attribute differences in status to intrinsic merit when a substantial portion of the eventual differences in mature citizens is due to the accumulated effect of many —perhaps 10,000? — hours spent in developing abilities.

Smith does not conclude that therefore these differences are morally or substantively arbitrary, though. In fact, the very stability and prosperity of the system rests on acting on the promised entitlement to the benefits of success.

Smith's division of labor is a hopeful doctrine because even a person with limited advantages, or a region or nation with no apparent comparative advantage, can with hard work develop an absolute advantage by exploiting the opportunities afforded by division of labor. Other people will work to provide all the things you need to go off and specialize, even if the niche your specialization occupies is very narrow, provided the "extent of the market" is large enough to support that niche.

Pumpkins

Pumpkins are a specialized kind of gourd, or squash. The first "pumpkin pie" was apparently obtained by cutting off the top of a pumpkin, removing the stringy insides and seeds, and then pouring in a mixture of spices, honey, and milk. Put that punkin in the still-hot ashes of a fire, put more ashes around it, and in two or three hours, it's yum time!

You can grow pumpkins almost anywhere. But more than half of the world's pumpkin production comes from one state: Illinois. And most of the production in Illinois is centered in an area extending just a few dozen miles from Peoria. Why? Because Peoria is the "philosopher" of the pumpkin patch world; the rest of us are just street porters.

According to the University of Illinois extension service:

> Eighty percent of all the pumpkins produced commercially in the U.S. are produced within a 90-mile radius of Peoria, Illinois. Most of those pumpkins are grown for processing into canned pumpkins. Ninety-five percent of the pumpkins processed in the United States are grown in Illinois. Morton, Illinois just 10 miles southeast of Peoria calls itself the `Pumpkin Capital of the World.'[23]

Economist Timothy Taylor[24] gives a clear explanation for why this small area has such a dominant position:

> Weather and soil are part of the advantage, but it seems unlikely that the area around Peoria is dramatically distinctive for those reasons alone. This also seems to be a case where an area got a head-start in a certain industry, established economies of scale and expertise, and has thus continued to keep a lead. The Illinois Farm Bureau writes: "Illinois earns the top rank for several reasons. Pumpkins grow well in its climate and in certain soil types. And in the 1920s, a pumpkin processing industry was established in Illinois, Babadoost [a professor

---

23 "Pumpkin Facts." University of Illinois Extension Gardener's Corner. Accessed June 17, 2019. https://extension.illinois.edu/gardenerscorner/issue_02/fall_05_05.cfm

24 Taylor, Timothy. "The Dominance of Peoria in the Processed Pumpkin Market." Conversable Economist. November 22, 2017. http://conversableeconomist.blogspot.com/2017/11/the-dominance-of-peoria-in-processed.html

> at the University of Illinois] says. Decades of experience and dedicated research help Illinois maintain its edge in pumpkin production." According to one report,[25] Libby's Pumpkin is "the supplier of more than 85 percent of the world's canned pumpkin."

So the area around Peoria is well-suited for pumpkin growing. But the experience of making maximal use of the local conditions, and developing infrastructure and specialized techniques for planting, managing, and harvesting, is very powerful. The area around Morton, Illinois (the "pumpkin capital of the world") produces more than 100 million pounds of pumpkins each year.[26]

We are thankful for many things, and that's appropriate. We are not always as thankful as we should be for division of labor, however. This Thanksgiving, I tried to make my pumpkin eating more gratefully aware, a testament to Smith's great principle.

---

25 "Climate and Pumpkins." Climate.gov. October 22, 2015. https://www.climate.gov/news-features/climate-and/climate-pumpkins

26 Morton Chamber of Commerce. http://www.pumpkincapital.com/

2. I'll Stick With These: Some Sharp Observations on the Division of Labor

The young woman looked frightened. All I did was ask some pointed questions.

"Why do you have 35 kinds of energy bars, but only one brand of straight pins? And why are those made in China? Why aren't your pins made in America?"

This Kerr drug store was the final stop of my ten "observations," so I had the rap down pat. The poor clerk said, "You can talk to the manager, if you want." The manager came over, after the clerk whispered to him at the far end of the aisle, prepping him on this crazy pin-guy. "Is there a problem?"

"I'm not sure. Do you think it's a problem that you have 35 brands of energy bars, but only one brand of pins?"

He pondered this. I bet he also pondered calling security. "Did you want a different kind of pin? You might go to a shop that sells sewing supplies. We are a drug store."

I persisted: "Yes, but you do sell pins. Why don't you sell American pins? Why are you selling Chinese pins?"

He saw a way out: "Sir, I really don't know. Our purchasing people handle stock. We could order American pins, if you want; have them within two weeks. Do you want to order them?"

The crowning moment! I pretended to think it over. Then, I got to say it: "No. I'll just stick with these."

The Extent of the Market

The point of my "field research" had been to check prices and types of pins available at stores in Raleigh, North Carolina where I live. I'll tell you why in a minute. First, let me report my results.

- Prices ranged from $3.19 down to $2.49 for a box of 500 pins. That was for what seemed to be the standard size, 1 1/16 inch, ball point steel. The highest price was at Eckerds; the lowest was at Harris Teeter.
- Of the ten stores, 8 carried only "Singer" brand pins. The other two carried "Singer," but also had "Dritz" pins (on which, more anon.)
- The largest standard straight pins I found were 1 1/4 inch Dritz-Collins pins, which sold for $2.35 for 350.
- Of the ten stores, only 3 offered to order American pins, which let me use my "I'll stick with these" joke. (Truthfully, it was Russ Roberts's joke, from our podcast; I just thought it was funny).[27]
- Every pin, at every store, was made in China.

So, in my area at least, the market appears to be dominated by Singer. Singer is, or was at one time, an American company. But if you read the fine print on the back, you'll see that the Singer brand

27 Munger, Michael. Interview by Russ Roberts. "Mike Munger on the Division of Labor." Podcast audio. April 2, 2007. http://www.econtalk.org/mike-munger-on-the-division-of-labor/

name on the front is really just that: a front. The pins are "distributed under license" by Dyno Merchandise, Pompano Beach, FL. The labels ("Warning: Sharp product! Keep away from children") on the pins are printed in three languages, English, Spanish, and French. And as the last of these notes, the pins themselves are "Fabrique en Chine."

The reason I had become interested in pins was a passage from Adam Smith. Not the one about the pin factory, though that one is interesting in its own way. No, my interest was in Smith's (1776) observation about the "extent of the market."

> … As it is the power of exchanging that gives occasion to the division of labour, so the extent of this division must always be limited by the extent of that power, or, in other words, by the extent of the market. When the market is very small, no person can have any encouragement to dedicate himself entirely to one employment, for want of the power to exchange all that surplus part of the produce of his own labour, which is over and above his own consumption, for such parts of the produce of other men's labour as he has occasion for. (p. 21).

The market Smith was talking about was the number of potential (and, in an important sense, actual!) customers for the product in question. As the ability of transport and communications to handle trade increases, the size of the factories increases. Let me say that again, because it is so obvious it's confusing. As the number of potential customers you can reach expands, and the costs of shipping and handling fall, factories become fewer and larger. There is far more capital investment in these factories, but fewer workers. And output increases ten-fold, a hundred-fold, a billion-fold.

Let's return to Smith's original intuition, and think of a village artisan. One person, in a shop, making pins. He picks up the wire, spools out a length of it, and then cuts it into pin-size pieces. He sharpens one end of each pin, and flattens the other end for the head, and so on, until the pins are finished and packaged.

These pins are expensive, and one artisan is easily able to supply all the pins demanded in the small village, at that high price. The situation appears to be stable, but it actually isn't. Imagine that the pin-maker gets one large order, even slightly more than he can handle by himself. So, to handle the excess, he hires a temp, a guy who comes in and takes over the second half of the production process. Now, the owner performs the first few tasks, and the other man finishes the pins and packages them.

And our pin artisan, a thoughtful man, notices something strange. The two men don't produce twice as many pins; instead, they produce three times as many pins. And, after a couple of days, as each grows more proficient at a smaller number of more specialized tasks, the two men might produce five times as many pins.

At this point, though, they have a problem: too many pins! After they have filled that one large order, the two men can produce far more pins than is normally demanded in the small village where they live. A pin-maker in this situation might view this as a disaster—what a waste to have all these extra pins! How can he possibly sell them all, living in such a small village? He dismisses the temp and returns to the old ways of making pins. But a more ambitious pin-maker might respond differently.

First, he cuts the price of pins—even at the lower price, profits can be higher because of the increased productivity of the division of labor. So, he sells more pins even in his own village, because the price is lower.

Second, the pin-maker is led, without even really thinking about it, to try to increase the size of his market. He hires a third worker, and spends part of his own time on the road, collecting orders. He doesn't do this because he enjoys it, necessarily. He does it because he has to, to stay in business and avoid drowning in pins (if that can happen). Given his advantage in price, though, he finds these orders easy to get, and the process continues: more steps in production, more division of labor, lower costs, lower prices, larger markets, more sales. The division of labor is limited by the extent of the market. Expand the market and it becomes increasingly profitable to have workers specialize.

Third, as workers' tasks become more specialized, it becomes profitable to design and use specialized tools to aid in the particular individual tasks of each worker. So it is not only the workers who become more specialized but the tools.

Fifty years before Smith wrote *Wealth of Nations*, pins in England were made in small "manufactories" in Bristol, Gloucester, and London, the centers of demand. By the 1760s, pin-making became a decentralized cottage industry, in part because sewing and other activities using pins had also become more decentralized. And this is the period where Smith formed his impression: he saw pins being made by 3-6 men, in a small shop, each of whom performed several tasks at different points in the production process. Smith's widely quoted conclusion, which was actually just a quick estimate, was that there 18 different steps in the pin-making process.

Smith conceived of the process of increasing production as "division of labor" into more and more steps, with each laborer specializing in a smaller slice of the process. But the real revolution took place in the early 1830s, in the U.S., in the mind of a distracted doctor, John Howe. Howe recognized that dividing the tasks of human laborers into smaller discrete steps was not a process that would work forever. Instead (and this is my metaphor, not his) Howe turned to calculus.

In mathematics, calculus is a technique for analyzing and representing change. And a product changes as it moves through the steps in the production process. At each stage, a workman adds something, or takes something away, or performs some operation that changes the product. Division of labor involves using more steps, each one of them smaller than before. The logic of calculus is that at some point, each discrete step gets small enough that as you take smaller and smaller steps, the process gets closer and closer to being continuous.

What Howe did for pin-making was to make the discrete steps smaller and smaller.[28] In Adam Smith's terms, the division of labor made each worker's set of tasks more and more specialized. And workers could devise more and more specialized capital, such as tools or machines, to increase their productivity in that step of production. At some point, the process itself changed fundamentally. Instead of adding better and better tools for each step, it became profitable to mechanize the entire process using a fundamentally different type of tool, the assembly line. Fewer and fewer workers

28 To see the description of the patent, look at the Smithsonian on-line exhibit, "Howe's Patent Model of a Pin Making Machine - ca 1841" https://americanhistory.si.edu/collections/search/object/nmah_848382

were needed to a point where workers became unnecessary in the fashioning of the pins or the good in question and the continuous process could be run by tools themselves. The machines of the assembly line are the limiting case of dividing labor into more and more steps.

By 1833, Dr. Howe had patented his design and built a fully functional pin-making machine. By 1840, he had improved the design by making the machine have a rotary action, involving even fewer points of human interaction and far greater production. Interestingly, the most complex stage of production was packaging them: taking the finished pins and forcing them through folds in a piece of cardboard. Packaging was still done by hand decades after the manufacture of pins was fully automated.

Today, most pin manufacture has moved to Asia. Your first impulse might be to nod and think, "Sure, cheap labor." But that is not an important part of the story. Pin manufacturing is highly capital intensive. Smith's insight on the division of labor, and Howe's idea of making the process continuous and making labor more productive, have combined to expand the market for Chinese pins to the whole world. The number of workers engaged in pin manufacture in China has fallen, not risen, as pin output has expanded. And wages have increased more than ten-fold, as productivity has exploded.

The interesting thing is Adam Smith didn't foresee, and we don't really understand, the implications of the division of labor, and its interaction with the "extent of the market," as production becomes more capital intensive. It would appear that dividing tasks into smaller, more specialized units would increase employment. That is, instead of 1,000 different pin shops, where artisans work away making just a few pins per day, we now have perhaps 100 factories, each employing 18 people making pins, in different stages. Total employment in the industry has gone from 1,000 to 1,800, with the huge increase in output being absorbed by the expanded market because of the new, lower price.

But as the division of labor proceeds, the net effect on employment in the pin industry turns negative, first slowly and then very sharply. And the degree of specialization itself decreases, in the pattern of a "u-shaped" curve. Recall: at first we had an artisan, making the entire pin. Then we move to 18 different tasks, with a worker having specialized in each step. But then, as the process is automated, specialization once again declines: there are only a few workers, with general knowledge of the production process, overseeing the automated production line. Their main job is to intervene in the process only when something breaks down.

The number of people employed in the "industry" is only a tiny fraction even of the original work force of artisans. This in turn allows employment in new industries to expand, industries that wouldn't exist without the productivity driven by the division of labor.

Final Words

I could make my own pins. Working hard, with some wire and some cutters and a file to sharpen them, I might make 100 or more pins a day. But my time is too valuable to spend that way. Likewise, we could make pins in my home state, North Carolina. But the amount of capital required to be competitive with world prices of 10,000 pins for $1 would be… well, it would be a lot. Too expensive, given all the other profitable investments available for capital in North Carolina. The same is true for the U.S. as a whole: we could make our own pins, but it's cheaper to buy them, and exploit our own comparative advantage in activities where division of labor works for us, rather than against us.

So, the next time you think about some foreign product, or even if you actually buy some Chinese pins, rest assured. It's okay to stick with those.

3. The Lighthouse Myth

We all "know" that markets can't produce public goods. The reason is that a public good is non-rival (my use doesn't reduce the amount available to you) and non-excludable (you can't prevent me from enjoying the public good, even if I don't pay). The canonical (cannon-ical?) public good is national defense: What's defended is an area; the cost doesn't go up with population. And the air force can't say, "Okay, you can bomb that one guy's house because he didn't pay. But that's it; no other bombing, because everyone else paid up."

There are two problems with the basic claim about the necessity of state provision. The first is that sometimes people do contribute to public goods, voluntarily or because institutions manage to arrange incentives in a way that solves the problem. The second is that the state has problems of its own and we can't compare real markets (which are imperfect) with imaginary, perfect government. I have made the argument about government failure at some length elsewhere (Keech and Munger, 2015). In this essay, I'm going to consider the possibility that markets can produce public goods more often than traditional economics may recognize.

The problem is not bad design. Our systems of government are the product of long thought and efforts at improved structure over time. The idea that constant reforms and tweaking of rules is the answer is one of the central mistaken conceits that public choice theory was created to combat.

The Dynamics of Institutional Discovery

Supporters of state action argue that governments learn because government action is the consequence of intentional choices and correct motivations. Markets, to the extent that they are simply emergent processes, are not capable of learning. So the difference does not come down to perfection; pro-intervention welfare economists never believed in perfection (see, for example, Pigou, 1920).

Instead, the difference comes down to the possibilities for improvement. The view that government can learn better than markets, which many would say originated at Cambridge and metastasized across the Atlantic to Harvard, M.I.T., Yale, and other universities on the East Coast, is an argument about progress.

As Backhouse and Medema (2012) put it, the difference in learning capacity is important:

> What emerges, then, is that the difference between the Cambridge welfare economists and their modern counterparts at Chicago and Virginia was not that the former were guilty of committing the 'nirvana fallacy' or that they were naive about political processes. Political processes were as central to the policy conclusions of the Cambridge welfare economists as they are to modern public choice theory and the literature on law and economics — indeed, because they did not see government as a homogenous entity, it was even more important for them to examine such processes than it is for modern economists who work with a simplified conception of government. The main difference is that because they were willing to work within the confines of rational choice theory — because, in a sense, they were willing to be more 'neoclassical' — Chicago

> and Virginia developed techniques for analysing political processes that would probably have been rejected by Sidgwick, Marshall and Pigou, even if they had been available to them.

The rational choice approach, with its assumption of stable preferences, is central here, for it effectively rules out the evolutionary view of human improvement that was central to the Cambridge vision.

To put the question more clearly: what are the source and effect of evolutionary pressures in the public sector and in the private (market) sector? To the extent that market processes must take institutions as (more or less) given while the state can change institutions rapidly, this seems to imply that states are our best hope for solving vexatious public goods problems.

Consider the economists Backhouse and Medema mention. Henry Sidgwick, following J.S. Mill, had simply asserted that markets could not handle the problem of public goods. This was taken as a prima facie case for government action: markets can't adjust, so governments must. But there is an interesting story, told in part by R.H. Coase in his 1974 paper "The Lighthouse in Economics." Coase argued that markets are in fact flexible and innovative, even nimble, when it comes to emergent notions of institutions that can solve collective problems, or what look like prisoners' dilemmas.

The Lighthouse

We all recognize that the use of the concept of externality is much older than Pigou, but the debate over lighthouses in the 19th century brings the problem into sharp focus. John Stuart Mill, in his 1848 *Principles of Political Economy*, notes that "no one would build lighthouses from motives of personal interest," because they could not collect the fees necessary to cover costs. Mill's conclusion was therefore that "it is a proper office of government to build and maintain lighthouses … since it is impossible that the ships at sea which are benefitted … should be made to pay a toll."

Later, Henry Sidgwick generalizes from the lighthouse to the existence of a larger set of problems in the first (1883) edition of his Principles of Political Economy. He notes that "there is a large and varied class of cases" in which voluntary private exchange would underprovide goods that produce positive externalities. In particular, Sidgwick claims that "it may easily happen that the benefits of a well-placed lighthouse must be largely enjoyed by ships on which no toll could be conveniently placed."

One is reminded of Pigou's description of what economists "in their studies can imagine," which I discuss at greater length in Section VII, below. In this case, Mill and Sidgwick, sitting in their studies, could not imagine a solution, and so they simply assumed that markets couldn't solve the problem. As I noted above, an obvious problem is the failure to imagine the problems that a real government will have in coming up with a good solution. But in this case, the failure of imagination is not the inability to foresee problems of government, but rather an incapacity to imagine innovations in market institutions.

If, as Mill and Sidgwick claim, a positive externality persists without being captured by those who would benefit, then that means that a group of people are leaving a lot of money on the table. Why would they fail to organize and find a way to provide the useful service?

They didn't fail. In fact, they succeeded. As Coase (1974) shows, as early as 1820, in England (home of Mill and Sidgwick, who could have gotten out of their studies and gone for a walk), most — more than three-quarters — of all lighthouses had been built, and were being operated, by private individuals.

The costs were paid by user fees levied in nearby ports. The whole system operated in the near-total absence of government activity. It is true that the state enforced the collection of the private fees, but that is true of any fee-for-service arrangement, like a clothing store or chocolate shop. That is, it is true that government officials backed the enforcement of contract, and would use force if payment were not made. But Mill and Sidgwick assumed that since they could not imagine a private solution, government provision of the service itself must be necessary.

And that's not true. Markets are at least as adaptable as government, and in many cases the capacity for innovation, especially regarding local externalities, is far greater. In fact, as Candela and Geloso (2018) point out, the range of creative responses can be remarkable. The solution is not a pure market outcome, of course, because government action and enforcement of property rights are an indispensable part of efficient market processes. The lighthouses of coastal England in 1840 were not pure market entities, but rather a kind of hybrid.

It is quite true that a standard bilateral fee-for-service arrangement would fail to provide enough lighthouses — at first. But that failure would have consequences.

Ships need lighthouses, and entrepreneurs want profits. The "externalities mean markets fail" perspective rests on an assumption that entrepreneurs are passive and not very bright. By the time an economist has identified an externality or public good as a market failure, a group of people who stand to benefit may already have devised a private institution that solved the problem. It just never occurs to the economist to check to see what actually happened, because economists are more interested in theory, and in policy, than in actual markets and how entrepreneurs correct errors in allocations.

Further, if we assume static, inert market actors, we should not assume that government agents are active, perfectly informed, and public-spirited. People are more or less the same, according to what public choice scholars call the behavioral-symmetry assumption. If there is a difference based on sorting, you have to ask yourself which way it goes. Do impatient, innovative people go to work for large bureaucracies or private companies? It's not plausible to think that positive innovations occur exclusively, or even primarily, at the level of the state.

4. Bosses Don't Wear Bunny Slippers: If Markets Are So Great, Why Are There Firms?

When I teach political economy, I start with the neoclassical theory of consumption, and then cover production. And I show students how miraculous it is that the actions of millions of people who have never met can be directed by prices. Resources move toward their highest valued use, and consumption goods are delivered to the consumers who want them.

For example, the United States promoted ethanol as an auto fuel. This sharply increased the price of corn worldwide. As Brazilian reporter Kieran Gartlan put it: "Higher prices are leading Brazilian farmers to plant more second crop corn this year, and the country's modest corn exports are expected to expand [from 42 million tonnes to 48 million tonnes, an increase of 230 million bushels.]"[29]

No one directed the Brazilian farmers to shift to corn production. The article puts it perfectly: "Higher prices are leading farmers…." The leadership comes from the prices themselves! The farmers may have had no idea why the price of corn had increased, to $4.00 per bushel. (After all, Brazil uses sugar, not corn, to produce its ethanol.) But Brazilian corn production increased within a year, by

29 Quoted in the Agriculture Policy Analysis Center, https://www.agpolicy.org/weekcol/344.html. Original was a DTN report, March 2, 2007.

nearly 15%. No one made the farmers switch; they made choices. Other corn producers, in Argentina, Mexico, and several African countries, followed suit. No one talked about it, no one gave any orders; prices led them.

There is nothing wrong with this lesson, nothing I would change in my presentation to students. But there is a problem of emphasis, for someone who wants to understand, fundamentally understand, markets. And the problem is this: Prices are the central force directing resources and shaping consumption in a market economy. But most economic activity seems (at first glance) to take place without any influence from prices at all. Most employment choices, and in dollar terms most production decisions, are not directly guided by any observable price.

Most people work for a firm, a company, or a large organization, and they have a boss. There are people who provide computer services, janitorial services, legal advice, and myriad other day-to-day activities who are paid a salary. They are directed by their boss, not by prices. The boss has to gauge (guess?) whether that worker is carrying her weight and adding to the profitability of the firm.

In such a setting, the boss also must try to figure out if there are enough servers or computers (my hunch? Your IT guy says, "no." Never enough). Now, the manager does buy this equipment on the market, and pays real prices. But he doesn't sell the computer time to the staff. He gives it away. Is it worth it, in terms of somehow increasing profits or raising the company's share values? The boss has to guess. Many different bosses, in many different firms, make different guesses. Some of the firms are profitable, some are not. No one knows what specific choices led to increased profits, or to bankruptcy.

Then one day, in one firm, one manager, perhaps on a whim, outsources the computer services or janitorial services or legal advice. Not to India or Ireland but simply to another company across town or across the country. The boss signs a contract, after taking bids from several companies that provide similar services. These companies are forced by the scolding winds of market competition to provide excellent service at low cost. By looking at the different prices in the bids offered in this competition, the boss learns something. He learns how much the service costs to provide. And he learns how much money he saves by laying off the employees who used to provide the service in-house.

It's hard to fire employees, particularly since most employees are smart enough to work hard enough to get acceptable performance reviews. The boss also has a hard time motivating the in-house staff, because watching each employee is expensive and tiresome. But it's easy to fire contracted employees, because you just sign a new contract with a competitor. Why not let the market system do your motivation work? Let's suppose that our outsourcing boss sees the company's profits rise dramatically, and the stock price goes up 18% in six months. Life is good, for the boss.

So, one day the boss has this crazy thought. He asks himself a question that has never occurred to him before: Why have any employees at all? Why have a building? Why not just sit home, wearing his jammies and bunny slippers, sipping a nice cup of tea, and outsource everything? He can write contracts to buy parts, he can pay workers to assemble the parts, and he can use shipping companies to box and transport the product.

The boss is elated. He never really liked these people anyway.

Always asking questions, constantly looking for direction and expecting him to know the answers. He fires all his employees, effective one month from now, and takes bids on all the design, parts manufacture, assembly, and shipping that those people used to do.

On day 31, after all those wasteful employees are gone and the new contracting efficiency regime is in place, the boss has a nice breakfast, pours his tea, and puts his bunny-slippered feet up on his desk at home. Checking his email, he notices he has 1,239 new messages. He turns on his cell phone, and sees he has missed 485 calls. What the heck?

It turns out that coordinating all those contract employees, and making all those different transactions work together in time and space, is a really hard job. The manager shucks the bunnies, puts on his suit, and hurries over to his primary contract supplier of inputs. "What are you doing? We have a contract!"

The supplier says, "Who are you again?"

The boss gives his name, frantically. Not one of the other contracts can be fulfilled if he can't get these parts.

The supplier checks, "Oh, yeah, I see the order. Sorry, we're running behind. We'll have the stuff to you by the end of the week, maybe the following Monday."

Within three days, the boss is fired, because the company is plunging into bankruptcy. Stock prices fall by 75%, and a desperate effort is made to rehire most of the old employees back to their old jobs.

The Theory of the Firm

If prices and competition do such a terrific job of directing resources (and they do!), then why are there firms? Why are there hierarchical organizations that are internally directed by command and control, rather than the price system? Why not outsource everything? Why don't bosses sit home wearing bunny slippers?

Some firms come close, buying many of their inputs on the market and selling contracting for manufacture and assembly using piecework contracts with temporary workers. But many, and in employment terms most, firms are much more than a shell. What gives?

To appreciate this puzzle, let's go back to Adam Smith's (1776) famous "pin factory" example.

The pin factory showed the power of the market, through division of labor. The factory divides pin-making into a number of smaller, more specialized tasks. Increased dexterity, improved tools, and economies of scale raise productivity so much that just a few workers could make thousands more pins than they could themselves use. So, we conclude, markets organize huge quantities of labor into more and more productive tasks.

Or… do they? What would a pure "market" pin factory look like? Nothing done in-house, only out-house! There would be no direction, no hierarchy, only individuals responding on their own to prices of inputs and outputs. The first man draws the wire, and then take bids. The high bidder pays for the wire, get his change back, and then carries the wire to his own shop, where the cutting machine can be stored safely. Then the cutter sells the little pieces of wire.

One potential buyer might be a pin sharpener. He calls several cutters, and checks out their reputations on Epinbay, a bulletin board that describes buyer reputations. (This is 1776; I mean a literal bulletin board, with wet scraps of paper blowing in the wind, held in place by sharpened pieces of cut wire, since there are no pins yet).

And so on. Each step, each break in the production process from one artisan to another, would require negotiations, a transaction, payment, and transportation of the product to the next step.

Obviously, that's silly: no pin factory could work that way. The cost savings from division of labor would be swamped by the increased cost of negotiating and carrying out transactions, and monitoring quality. That's why the "firm" is not really a market at all. This factory is instead a group of individuals who have contracted to cooperate in a particular way that saves the costs of conducting and monitoring separate transactions. The contract extends across the individual workers, and provides for a scheme of payments that focuses on wages of labor, rather than the prices of commodities. The form of the contract negotiated by each worker is for a much longer term than a one-off purchase or sale transaction.

The task of the economist, then, is to explain two phenomena with just one theory. First, why are firms more efficient than markets at organizing some transactions? Second, if firms are so efficient, why are there any market transactions at all? What determines the margin where the firm stops organizing additional transactions internally, and buys goods or services instead through the market?

The problem was stated in just these terms by one of the pioneers of the transactions costs approach, Ronald H. Coase. His remarkable 1937 paper in *Economica*, "The Nature of the Firm" contained two key insights. First, firms are contractual means of reducing transactions costs. Division of labor requires groups, sometimes large groups of workers. But it would be too expensive and time-consuming to negotiate sales of labor, services, and products at every stage of production. So, an entity called "the firm" is created, which specializes in directing these activities. Firms compete with each other, but within the firm, activities are directed by command and control.

Second, Coase argues that the optimal size of firms responds directly, though in undirected ways, to market forces. This is true both for vertical integration (owning suppliers, and retail outlets) and market share (the number of units sold, total). So the market is at work after all, since the expansion or contraction of the firm is directed by prices and the actions of consumers and suppliers. Firms that guess wrong, and expand (or contract) too much will lose profits, and may even be "selected" for extinction by bankruptcy.

The important thing to remember about the importance of price is that it is an overall guide, not an indication of what anyone other than the marginal buyer or marginal seller thinks. In fact, every transaction we see on the market reflects disagreement, not agreement. It is only possible to agree on a price when the buyer and seller disagree about the value. If buyer and seller agree about the value, then that is a reimbursement, not an exchange. Firms, and managers, make money precisely by finding differences between price and value, and then selling things to consumers or other users who value it more than the price.

Final Thoughts

In this essay, a serious question has been asked, and I want to make sure the reader sees why it is important. Outsourcing, either across town or across a huge ocean, is a form of transforming a transaction from one organized within a firm to one organized through a market. All firms use some combination in-house work and outsourcing (no computer company makes its own furniture, grows the wheat for bread in the employee cafeteria, or makes waste paper baskets). Where is the line? How does the company decide what to buy, and what to produce?

The answer is: profits. The company has to decide which

approach, at every stage, costs less, improves quality, or in some other way increases profits. Price is an important consideration, of course, for managers. But the day-to-day activities of most employees, in most firms, are not directed by prices the way that price directs the choices of farmers. Workers are for the most part paid salaries, or by the hour.

Ah, you might say, but that's where prices come in! Workers work, and change jobs, for wages. Sure, and the Brazilian farmers could change jobs, too. They could go from being farmers to woodcutters, or factory workers. My point is that the farmer looks to prices to say, "What will I plant today?" The worker in a firm doesn't look to price, but rather asks his boss, "What will I do in the plant today?"

Most importantly, bosses can't contract out all the activities of the firm, in most situations. The coordination and monitoring function (Alchian and Demsetz, 1972; Klein, Crawford, and Alchian, 1978) may be the real reason that firms exist. The problems of transactions costs, and management, are complex and hard to solve. If you want to run your own firm, make sure you keep your wingtips, or at least a pair of sensible pumps. You are going to be doing a lot of walking around and giving instructions to people who don't have prices to direct them.

5. Rent-Seek and You Will Find

"I don't know if we should stay in this business." That city official was just being honest, but his framing of the problem surprised me. The "business" he was referring to was writing and winning grants from the Department of Housing and Urban Development (HUD), the federal agency charged with improving home ownership and low-income housing availability. Fifteen years ago, when I had this conversation, I didn't understand what he meant.

As Director of the Master of Public Administration Program for UNC-Chapel Hill in the early 1990s my job was training city and county managers, sending them out to serve the public weal. Public grants were the mother's milk of city management; why would any city official think twice about getting free money to help citizens?

The answer is one of the paradoxes of public choice: free money isn't free. In fact, you have to pay for free money twice: first you have to collect the money, out of tax revenues. And then you have to pay for the money again, because the benefits are dissipated by what economists call "rent-seeking." Let me explain.

The technical definition of rent is any return to investment, or effort, that exceeds the opportunity cost rate of return. So, Alex Rodriguez of the New York Yankees earns a large rent, or premium, because of his scarce talents as a baseball player. He could earn a living as a banker, or a waiter, or something else. But it is unlikely that he could earn anything close to the $25 million per year he once made as a baseball player, or the $20 million he makes now doing commentary for ESPN. Those rents encourage competition. And in most economic situations, that competition for profits produces benefits. But in politics, competition for those rents is often destructive.

The greater the rent, the greater the costs people are willing to incur to win it. When government hands out what appears to be free money, people are going to scramble to get some of it, incurring costs as long as those costs raise the chances of winning the "free" money sufficiently.

Robert Tollison (1982), one of America's premier students of public choice and government, defines rent-seeking this way: "Rent seeking is the expenditure of scarce resources to capture an artificially created transfer." Competition for government goodies—rent-seeking—is a wild goose chase, no matter how well-intentioned the goose or the chasers.

The city official told me that his office employed 15 people whose sole jobs were to identify and win federal grants. Their total salaries, and the staff and utilities required to support them, exceeded one quarter of the federal funds they had secured in grants the previous year. It seems like a pretty good deal to spend only 25 cents to win a dollar. But if you think about all the other cities doing the same thing, you realize that this system of distributing grants has some pretty perverse costs.

And the costs were climbing. Other cities around the nation, in the mid-1990s, had begun to get better at the HUD-grant game. At first, Charlotte had been able to win grants with a relatively short proposal, and some supporting documents. But as time passed, the amount of effort and resources required to win was increasing. Not only was Charlotte spending more and more city tax dollars just to win grants funded by federal tax dollars, but Charlotte was winning less and less often. It did sound like a dysfunctional system.

But I was stumped: this just seemed like competition. Isn't competition supposed to be good? How could the outcome seem so bad? It turns out that rent-seeking "competition" is a contest for a fixed price, a zero-sum problem that works like a transfer, at best. Competition in markets has no fixed price, and is robustly positive-sum. In politics you try to move money around and take credit for it. In markets you try to create value and make profits.

Competition in Other Places

My understanding of competition, after all, was that of the economist who studies markets. Lots of choices, lots of choosers, prices driven down toward the cost of production. New goods and services come constantly to the market, because producers' self-interest forces them to think of new and better ways to serve customer needs.

Can public policy work the same way? To put it in other terms, is competition always good? Is an increase in competition always the first solution we should think of, to any problem?

In political markets, there is good competition and bad competition. The fundamental human problem is to foster the good and block the bad. If the design of the institution fails to render the clash of self-interests beneficial to the community, then competition can make bad things happen to even the best people.

Not all political competition is bad. Madison, in Federalist #51,[30] famously argued that a government characterized by separation of

30 Madison, James. Federalist No. 51. 1788. Bill of Rights Institute. https://billofrightsinstitute.org/founding-documents/primary-source-documents/the-federalist-papers/federalist-papers-no-51/

powers among its branches would be more stable and more reliable than other forms. The reason? Competition! "Ambition must be made to counteract ambition...." But, as we will see, not all political competition works this way.

Tullock Lottery

In my classes, I ask students to imagine an experiment that I call a Tullock lottery, after one of the inventors of the concept of rent-seeking, Gordon Tullock (1980).

The lottery works as follows: I offer to auction off $100 to the student who bids the most. The catch is that each bidder must put the bid money in an envelope, and I keep all of the bid money no matter who wins.

So if you put $30 in an envelope and somebody else bids $31, you lose both the prize and the bid. When I run that game with students I can sometimes make $50 or more, even after paying off the prize. In politics, the secret to making money is to announce you are going to give money away.

Take a walk along K Street in Washington, DC. It is lined with tall buildings, full of fine offices and peopled by men and women with excellent educations and a real sense of ambition, a desire to make lots of money and achieve great things. What are those buildings, those people? They are nothing more than bids in the political version of a Tullock lottery. The cost of maintaining a D.C. office with a staff and lights and lobbying professionals is the offer to politicians. If someone else bids more and the firm doesn't get that tax provision or defense bid or road system contract, it doesn't get its bid back. The money is gone. It is thrown into the maw of bad political competition.

Who benefits from that system? Is it the contractors, all those companies and organizations with offices on K Street? Not really. Playing a rent-seeking game like that means those firms spend just about all they expect to win. It is true that some firms get large contracts and big checks, but all the players would be better off overall if they could avoid playing the game to begin with.

My students ask why anyone would play this sort of game. The answer is that the rules of our political system have created that destructive kind of political competition. When so much government money is available to the highest bidder, playing that lottery begins to look very enticing. The current Congress has, to say the least, failed to stem the rising tide of spending on domestic pork-barrel projects. Political competition run amok has increased spending nearly across the board. And sometimes, you have to bid just to keep from having money taken away from you through regulation.

In a well-functioning market system, competition rewards low price and high quality. Such optimal functioning requires either large numbers of producers or relatively low-cost entry and exit. Suppose that Coke and Pepsi not only had all the shelf space for drinks, but asked in addition if they could make their own rules outlawing the sale of any other drink. As Adam Smith (1776; p. 278) pointed out, "To widen the market and to narrow the competition is always the interest of the dealers…"

In the market system, we have safeguards set up, however imperfect they are. If nothing else, the Federal Trade Commission would not look favorably on the request, or the industry.

But in our political system, we have an industry dominated by two firms, Republicans and Democrats. Together they have a 99 percent market share. They have undertaken actions at the state and national levels to make it practically impossible for any other party to enter. This system forecloses good competition, the kind that raises new ideas or asks embarrassing questions. We have been fooled into thinking the system is competitive, because we constantly see vigorous rent-seeking competition for access to the public purse. This bad competition is an expensive gladiatorial combat, where Congress keeps a lot of the ticket receipts. Some of the rest of the spending is simply wasted building those expensive office suites on K Street and using the time of those lobbyists who could be doing something more productive.

Rent-Seeking: Politically, You Can't Lose

When they set up a rent-seeking contest, politicians are gambling with house money. To simulate the real world of rent-seeking more closely, I would need to amend my classroom exercise. First, collect $10 from each student. Next, run the auction, giving the students a chance to buy their money back. I'm not sure what would happen, but this procedure would give you the "pay for it twice" aspect that real political rent-seeking games exhibit. And I wouldn't be surprised if some students just stayed home sick that day, as a way to avoid playing the game at all.

What did Charlotte decide? Did they drop out of the game? Of course not. True, spending city money to win pretty much the same amount of federal money makes little sense economically. But it makes a lot of sense politically. As long as politicians are able to claim credit for bringing new federal spending to their state, district, or city, it doesn't matter that each dollar "won" actually cost 30 cents, or even $1.20. On August 1, 2005, a story was published in the Charlotte Observer:[31]

> WASHINGTON, DC—Senator Richard Burr today announced $8,329,494 in United States Department of Housing and Urban Development (HUD) grants for the City of Charlotte. The funds will expand affordable housing and emergency shelter to the homeless and sick and extend homeownership opportunities to low-income and minority households.

Homeless, sick, low-income, and minority households? Who could object to that? Besides, it's free money! Isn't it?

31 https://www.burr.senate.gov/press/releases/burr-announces-83-million-in-grants-for-charlotte

6. A Fable of the OC

There's this concert. Green Way is coming to town. To hear those great songs from American Dolt performed live you are going to stand in line, camping out for tickets. You get to the box office about midnight, but don't sleep much because it's noisy. Finally, sleep does come. It only seems like a few minutes later when the clank of the ticket window opening wakes you at 8:00 am. In the sunlight, you notice that there are way more people in line than you thought. Thousands, in fact. You may not get tickets, even after camping out.

Three hours later, the line has snaked along nearly to the window. You can see the guy behind the glass, taking money and handing back tickets. But you are getting more and more anxious. And with good reason: the ticket window clanks loudly again, this time on its way down. Sold out? SOLD OUT! Oh, no. Your main squeeze was counting on those tickets. She just loves Green Way.

Now you walk alone towards home, head down, disconsolate. But then you hear a hubbub across the street. It seems that some people who were first in line were not Green Way fans at all! They bought up tickets just to resell them. And reselling them they are, busily and noisily. Excellent—you may still get lucky.

You scurry across the street, and join the crowd surrounding the (to put it nicely) "resellers." When you hear what they want for a ticket, though, you are incredulous: "Three hundred bucks, dude. Cash only."

What's even harder to believe is the fact that people are paying $300 per ticket. You have to stop and review the pros and cons. It happens that in your state, "scalping" entertainment tickets is legal.

Further, you yourself have no moral compunction about scalping. You have enough cash saved up to pay $600 for two tickets. And all tickets are general admission, so there are no reserved seats.

When economists refer to the "opportunity cost" of a resource, they mean the value of the next-highest-valued alternative use of that resource.[32] If, for example, you spend time and money going to a movie, you cannot spend that time at home reading a book, and you can't spend the money on something else. If your next-best alternative to seeing the movie is reading the book, then the opportunity cost of seeing the movie is the money spent plus the pleasure you forgo by not reading the book.

But you start thinking about opportunity cost, the big OC. You recall from economics class that the OC is about foregone alternatives. In other words, the cost of doing one thing is all the other things you don't get to do as a result.

And $600 is a big cost. You don't so much mind the money, but if you were going to spend $600 you could buy every Green Way CD ever made, plus a first-class MP3 player to play them on. And you'd have enough left over to take your boy/girlfriend to dance clubs and dance to Green Way songs every Friday night for a month. (It's a safe bet the clubs will play Green Way, since that is all they play right now, especially that ecological anthem, "Nader of Suburbia").

The point is that money itself is not the whole cost of any activity. The true cost is what you give up: spending the money on X means you don't have that money to spend on Y. So the real cost of X is...

---

32 Henderson, David R. "Opportunity Cost." In *Concise Encyclopedia of Economics*. The Library of Economics and Liberty. https://www.econlib.org/library/Enc/OpportunityCost.html

Y. Some economists have claimed that money is simply a "veil," masking the fact that money prices are measures of relative scarcities of commodities.

If you go to the concert, you would be giving up 10 CD's, at $20 each, an X-pod MP3 player for $250, and $150 worth of cocktails down at the dance club. All for just one 2 hour concert. You think about it some more, and then shake your head. It's not worth it.

Having decided, you set off toward home, your chin drooping toward your chest. After going twenty blocks or so, you notice a scuffed up envelope, out in the road a little way from the sidewalk. The outside of the envelope is blank.

You pick it up with a strange feeling, a quickening heart. You tear the envelope open…and in it are two Green Way concert tickets! Oh, baby!

But then… guilt. These tickets aren't really yours. On the other hand, if the envelope blew out a car window, the people who lost them could be miles away by now. They may not even know they lost the tickets.

Still, you wait for nearly an hour. Every time a car goes by, your shallow heart's the only thing that's beating. But no cars slow down, and nobody comes by on foot looking for an envelope. You can hardly just hold up the tickets and say, "Anyone lose these?" And since the concert is festival seating there is no way to identify the true owner anyway. The tickets are yours, fair and square.

So, you call your consort on the cell phone, and you tell him/her the great news.

End of Story.

Now, a question: What's the news? Do you go to the concert, and if so, why? Assume you are "rational," in the conventional economic sense.

I used this fable (sort of—it was Bruce Springsteen then) as a test question in my intermediate Microeconomics class at Dartmouth College in spring term, 1986. I assumed that the question would be easy. The kids at Dartmouth are smart, and they clearly knew the definition of opportunity cost. In fact, they had the OC down cold.

But more than half of them missed the question; some of them missed it completely. Let's consider some things you might tell your boy/girlfriend on the phone, as well as the grades I would assign to each answer.

1. "I have free tickets! We can go to the Green Way concert!"
Grade: F
You fail; back to school. The tickets are not free. Remember, you don't mind scalping, scalping is legal in your state, and you saw scalped tickets actually transacting at a price of $300 each. And you established, after careful thought, that the concert is not worth the $300 opportunity cost for each ticket. The opportunity cost of attending the concert is still $300, even if you found the tickets on the ground.

2. "We can go buy some CDs, and an MP3 player, and go out tonight. I found $600!"
Grade B+
Too simplistic on the other side of the question. Remember, you do have to walk twenty blocks back to the area where tickets are being sold, and then hawk the tickets. So, if you are going to sell the tickets, you have to say why. It is actually not obvious that you sell them, any more than it is obvious that you keep them.

3. "Babe, we are going to the Green Way concert! I found two tickets, which is like finding $600 minus the $50 transactions costs I estimate for converting the tickets into cash (walking twenty blocks back to place where you can sell the tickets, hawking them, etc.) So using the tickets only really "costs" us $550. Combine this with the implicit income or wealth effect of finding the tickets, and you are going to the concert.
Grade A+
Perfect.

Now we could debate my grading scale. It might be that a student would mention income effects, and transactions costs, and still decide not to go, and that would also be an A+ answer. But the point is that "I have free tickets! We're going to the concert!" is always wrong, completely wrong, brutally misguided.

Yet more than half of my students put "They are free! We are going!" as their answer. What a bad economics teacher I was.

Opportunity Cost is Not the Way People Think

I whined about this outcome to my professor colleagues. The economists I talked to weren't really surprised. "People don't understand opportunity cost. For that matter, they don't understand lots of other apparently simple economics concepts. That's why we should study economics more." I'm not sure this is right. It reminds me of Bill Niskanen's (1971) observation about Ludwig von Mises. Niskanen argued that many people, including von Mises, were too optimistic, resting their conclusions on "the hope, almost pathetic in retrospect, that a broader education in economics will reduce the popular support for large government and the consequent pervasive bureaucracy."

Niskanen was not persuaded that economics is quite so self-evident, at least not to the large mass of the public.

Instead, it would appear that the answer is simpler: people just don't think this way, even if you try to teach them economics as a way of thinking. My evidence for the claim is that most people don't find my explanation persuasive. And my colleagues from other disciplines consider the apparently obvious economics argument to be empirically false from the outset, at least as a description of human behavior. "Of course people go to the concert; if you found tickets for free, and didn't take your partner to the concert, that relationship would be over, for sure! Don't be so analytical!"

Anthony de Jasay wrote an interesting article at Econlib[33] describing the importance of analysis. Jasay repeated Frédéric Bastiat's admonition to focus on what comes down to opportunity cost:

> When a man is impressed by the effect that is seen and has not yet learned to discern the effects that are not seen, he indulges in deplorable habits, not only through natural inclination, but deliberately.[34]

To be fair, there is some support in the psychology and behavioral

---

33 Jasay, A. D. "The Seen and the Unseen. Part II. The Costly Mistake of Ignoring Opportunity Cost." The Library of Economics and Liberty. January 10, 2005. https://www.econlib.org/library/Columns/y2005/JasayunseenB.html.

34 Bastiat, Frederic. "Selected Essays on Political Economy." The Library of Economics and Liberty. https://www.econlib.org/library/Bastiat/basEss.html?chapter_num=4#book-reader

economics literature that people often do not seem to take opportunity cost into account in the way more traditional economics would predict. It appears that we value gains differently from losses; once we have the tickets, we would be giving them up, which is different from deciding whether to spend money to acquire the tickets. The fact that the value ($600, in this case) happens to be the same for the gain or the loss is largely irrelevant. This perspective is related to the "heuristics and biases project" in cognitive psychology (as developed by Kahnemann, Tversky, 1974, and others). This particular bias, known as the "endowment effect," rests on the empirical claim that people value things they already have more than they value something they haven't yet purchased or acquired, even if it is the same thing at the same price.

But I'm not convinced. People may just get it wrong. (To be fair, Kahnemann and Tversky also think the choice is "wrong," from a rational choice perspective, so I am not disagreeing with them in any important way). Expecting them to get it right rests on the hope, "almost pathetic in retrospect," that citizens are educated in basic economics.

I put my little OC question to people on airplanes, or ask it of people I meet at conferences. And they are decidedly split, even after I explain the "correct" answer. More or less the same problem comes up all the time regarding basketball games at Duke University, where I teach. The face value of a basketball ticket to Cameron Indoor Stadium is $40. But for most games one could get a lot more than that. For some games, in fact, like Duke vs. UNC, the value of a scalped ticket is well over $1,000. In 2006, the value was more like $2,500. So, when faculty ask me (as department chair) for a raise at the end of the year, I will remind them that they don't need more money, because they are already rich.

"What do you mean?" they ask.

I reply, "Well, you can afford to spend $2,500 to go to a basketball game. You must be wealthy."

They show me the ticket. "$40! It's a $40 ticket!"

My response? "Tell you what. I have $50. Will you sell me the ticket for that price? After all, you claim it's a $40 ticket."

So far, I haven't been able to buy any tickets that way, even from people who tell me that opportunity cost is a stupid concept.

7. Orange Blossom Special: Externalities and the Coase Theorem

I grew up on a Valencia farm, in orange country south of Orlando. Twice a year, in December and June, the air was perfumed with orange blossoms, advertising their sweet nectar. Bees filled the air, harvesting that nectar. But the bees looked as if they were wearing thick yellow gaucho pants, carrying pollen from flower to flower.

An old guy with skin like leather, whom we knew as "Bee Man," would bring his hives in, and arrange them in a row. I found that if I looked sad he'd give me a piece of comb, dripping honey (and bee droppings, to bc honest) to gnaw on. The bees produced enough honey that Bee Man could pay us in honey and still make money.

Thinking back on it, I was in the middle of one of the most interesting and complex economic situations around. But the sun-warmed, honey-soaked wax comb tasted so good that I missed what some economists call "externalities," bees fertilizing fruit and flowers giving bees nectar for honey.

Externalities

If I do something that affects you, positively or negatively, without your consent or without my own ability to withhold a benefit unless you pay, then that is an externality.

Economist A.C. Pigou (1920) expressed the problem as a divergence between supply price (what a buyer pays) and the "marginal supply price" (the total amount something costs). The price paid might be less than true cost (a negative externality) or more than true cost (a positive externality). A commonly alleged example is a lighthouse, a positive externality. As Henry Sidgwick put it, nearly 150 years ago, "It may easily happen that the benefits of a well-placed lighthouse must be largely enjoyed by ships on which no toll could be conveniently placed."

This conclusion seems perverse, and it is. Folks who would benefit from increased production of a positive externality will try to come up with a solution. As another economist, Ronald Coase, pointed out, Pigou was ignoring an important fact: in real markets, externality problems are often solved privately, which means that the externality disappears. In fact, as I discussed earlier, Coase did a little digging, and found something interesting: in 1820, in England (home of Sidgwick!), more than three quarters of all lighthouses were built and operated privately.

Coase gives a general analysis of externalities in his landmark 1960 paper, "The Problem of Social Cost." He makes three fundamental points. First, externalities are reciprocal. Second, externalities persist only if transactions costs are high. Finally, if transaction costs are low, market processes will lead to the same efficient outcomes, irrespective of the assignment of property rights.

Let's see what a Coasian analysis would tell us about the externality I was interested in. Let's think about bees.

A Coasian Analysis: Cheung's "Fable of the Bees"

In 1952, an economist named J.E. Meade published a paper in the Economic Journal. Meade thought that he had discovered a truly new phenomenon, an externality relation so intricate that markets could not handle it. As you can see in the sidebar, Meade thought the result would always be inefficiency, because the orchard grower cannot capture all the benefits created by bee-keeping. Consequently, he argued, some kind of subsidy or government provision is required.

But Meade was wrong. The first reason is that, unlike oranges, apple blossoms don't produce enough nectar to make "apple blossom honey" viable. Yes, you can buy something called apple blossom honey. It is made mostly from wildflowers that grow in the orchards. But "apple blossom honey" sounds way better than "weed flower honey."

Further, all externalities are reciprocal. Economically, the bee and the flower are as interconnected as the chicken and the egg. And the gains to solving the problem are significant. Meade's claim about the "failure" of markets to capture the externality would have been news to apple growers, as later work by economist Steven Cheung (1973) demonstrates.

Remember, the general problem is supposed to be that positive externalities cause underproduction. And Meade argues that the specific problem of beekeeping is a perfect positive externality. Bees kept in one orchard, unless it is very large, will cross boundaries into the neighboring orchard. So pollination is "external" to the decision of any one landowner. And that means that there will be too few bees. Bring in the Federal Bee-reau of Apiation! We need subsidies, and we need them now.

Cheung ignored the economists, and looked at the economics. He found that apple growers had solved the problem. Bees fly far in their search for nectar, sometimes a mile, maybe three miles. Apple orchards can be big (the average size is a little over 50 acres), but bees might easily cross the property line and pollinate trees in the next orchard. So, suppose I have a moderate-sized orchard in the middle of several other orchards. Suppose further that I expect the growers around me to invest in bees. I can free ride, after all! Much, perhaps most, of my orchard will be pollinated by roving bees from the surrounding growers.

But if some economist with a blackboard can figure this out then surely the apple growers can, too. There are real gains to solving this problem, which is local and involves only small numbers of orchardists. Stephen Cheung describes a powerful implicit contract, the "custom of the orchard," that gets farmers out of Meade's predicament.

"The custom of the orchard" is an understanding that a certain number of hives are required to pollinate some fixed area, on average. It is true that some bees from farm A will end up on neighboring farm B, and vice versa, in what look like random search patterns. But if both farmers purchase the correct average number of hives, and the bees randomly search for pollen and nectar, then the externality is entirely internalized. My bees pollinate some of your trees, and yours some of mine, but the average and marginal allocations of resources are fully optimal! If there is money to be made, and transaction costs are not too high, people will figure out something on their own.

Orange Blossom Special

Still, what is the market price of bee services? How can markets solve that problem? Cheung (1973) proposed a simple answer: since the possible externality is reciprocal, pollination might be worth more, or honey production might be worth more. So, the exchange will be some combination of money and honey, and it is not clear to an outsider who will pay whom. But the actual parties to the exchange can solve the problem among themselves.

Remember that in Washington, apple blossoms produce relatively little nectar. The result is that the beekeepers in Washington are producing more value in pollination than they are taking out in honey. So, apple orchardists pay beekeepers, over and above whatever honey the beekeepers produce, and keep. But the apple orchardists pay less for bee services than if no honey were produced at all.

Orange blossoms, by contrast, are an enormous source of valuable honey. And, the direction of payment is reversed: In Florida, until recently, beekeepers pay the grove owner. (The "until recently" caveat is necessary because bee populations have shrunk in the last few years, in many parts of the country, including Florida, so that now grove owners pay beekeepers.)

Thus, at its simplest level, we can see that a remarkably complex theoretical problem is solved in a simple and straightforward way by the price mechanism. Beekeepers will make offers, and so will farmers. Both parties to such transactions benefit. Who pays whom, and how? An outsider might have trouble guessing. The prices will signal the relative scarcities of the inputs (including the bees!), and the demand for the farm products. In apple orchards, the farmers pay the beekeepers. In orange orchards, the beekeepers pay the farmers.

And no one had to tell them what to do to make honey. Sweet.

V

IN DEFENCE OF PROFITS

One of the most common tropes of dogma is that profits are theft. Some people believe that profit is the return to capital, and capital is "barren," so whatever share is taken for capital is being stolen from the working class. Another view is that entrepreneurs are just middlemen, and in a system with poorly functioning matching of buyers and sellers profits may be a necessary evil. But in a properly designed technocracy the entrepreneurial function can be dispensed with, because experts will make the decision of how much to make and who gets what.

Earlier, in chapter III, I discussed Adam Smith's "man of system," the autocrat or technocrat who designs a social system for others. Such people are always surprised when things don't work out.

Frederic Bastiat, in *Economic Sophisms*, famously took on one of the most famous (and persistent, even unto this day) "systems," the system of mercantilism. Bastiat imagines a dialogue:

> you say:
>
> "It is better to make things oneself, even if it would be less expensive to buy them from another."
>
> Now, gentlemen, setting aside theory, demonstration, and reasoning, all of which seem to fill you protectionists with disgust, which of these two assertions enjoys the sanction of universal practice?
>
> Visit fields, workshops, mills, and stores; look around you everywhere; examine what is done in your own household; observe your own actions at every moment; and then say which principle it is that guides these farmers, workers, industrialists, and merchants, not to mention your own personal practice.
>
> Does the farmer make his own clothes? Does the tailor raise the wheat that he consumes? Does your housekeeper continue to bake bread at home when she finds she can buy it more cheaply at the bakery? Do you propose to give up the pen for the shoebrush in order to avoid paying tribute to the bootblack? Does not the whole economy of society depend on the division of labor, i.e., on exchange? And what is exchange but the calculation that induces us, so far as possible, to discontinue direct production whenever indirect acquisition enables us to effect a saving in time and effort?

We could have some complex multilateral contract, obliging the farmer to farm, the tailor to sew, and the baker to make bread. But in large groups this contract would be cumbersome and hard to enforce. It seems like this system would be efficient, of course, because if everyone works hard for everyone else we'll all be better off.

The profit system simplifies the contracting and enforcement problem, dramatically. And note well that contracting, monitoring, and enforcement by some superior party are all costs, even if we could trust that party to work hard and to care for the public interest. In a way, it's an empirical question: is it cheaper and more productive to assign specialized tasks to everyone, from each according to their abilities, and then to watch over all those workers and punish them when they shirk? Is it better if all of us work for each other?

Or is it better if each of us works for ourselves? That is, we work for profits, or we work for companies that can make profits even after paying our wages. There is nothing stopping anyone from trying the first approach, and of course many nations have tried. The Soviet Union tried it, until it died a death of economic self-strangulation. China tried it, until Chinese leaders decided that it would be better to switch to markets and get rich. North Korea, Cuba, and more recently Venezuela have tried it, and found that profit is not all that costly after all.

Profit is the reward to entrepreneurs for directing economic traffic, and for designing and making new products cheaply and practically. If you think of profit only as a cost, you are missing the fact that profit is a signal, a big flashing sign saying, "Do more of this!" Rather than having to make everything ourselves, or to watch everyone else to be certain they are keeping up their part of some mythical social contract, we can rely on others to make the things we need and provide the services we want simply because it is in their self-interest to do so.

This section, then, seeks to define, and to defend, and sometimes to celebrate, profit.

1. It's Profit, Not Greed, that Is Good

In the movie *Wall Street*, Gordon Gekko delivers an iconic speech:

> Greed, for lack of a better word, is good. Greed is right. Greed works. Greed clarifies, cuts through, and captures, the essence of the evolutionary spirit. Greed, in all of its forms; greed for life, for money, for love, knowledge, has marked the upward surge of mankind.[35]

But few defenders of free markets, not even the oft-maligned Ayn Rand, can be read as defending greed. In fact, if greed or selfishness is understood as exploiting others, then greed is impossible in a system of voluntary exchange.

It is more accurate to say that some form of self-interest is always lurking in the background, contingent on the rules and norms of a society. Human institutions can usefully be arranged to make the clash of self-interest a benefit, rather than a harm, to a society. And that is just what market exchange can do, under a limited set of circumstances: markets can make human interaction mutually beneficial even if those same humans could be greedy in an authoritarian system.

What, then, of profits and the income disparities associated with market processes? Is not profit the animating spirit of capitalism? No. Capitalism is consumer sovereignty. Full stop. Profits, and

35 *Wall Street*. Directed by Oliver Stone. 1987.

income inequality, are signals, byproducts of the attempts by entrepreneurs to serve consumers. As in any other context, the idea that the world would be better if the level of byproducts were reduced to zero is quite mistaken. Pollution, for example, is a sign that something is being produced. Profits, in fact, are a sign that we need even more of the things being produced.

Throughout this book, I have argued that the price system creates enormous value for the consumer because many products are available for much less than the consumer would be willing to pay. That benefit of markets is widely recognized, and even some of those who are worried about inequality would admit that the front end, the price-and-production side of markets, is indispensable.

But what about the back end, the distribution side? John Stuart Mill certainly thought otherwise. As he famously put it in *Principles of Political Economy* (1848), there is a crystal-clear distinction between production decisions and distribution decisions:

> The laws and conditions of the Production of wealth partake of the character of physical truths. There is nothing optional or arbitrary in them. Whatever mankind produce, must be produced in the modes, and under the conditions, imposed by the constitution of external things, and by the inherent properties of their own bodily and mental structure....
>
> It is not so with the Distribution of wealth. That is a matter of human institution solely. The things once there, mankind, individually or collectively, can do with them as they like. They can place them at the disposal of whomsoever they please, and on whatever terms. Further, in the social state,

> in every state except total solitude, any disposal whatever of them can only take place by the consent of society, or rather of those who dispose of its active force. Even what a person has produced by his individual toil, unaided by any one, he cannot keep, unless by the permission of society. Not only can society take it from him, but individuals could and would take it from him, if society only remained passive; if it did not either interfere en masse, or employ and pay people for the purpose of preventing him from being disturbed in the possession.

In other words, the so-called free market distribution is just as arbitrary as any other distribution the state might select. The state not only can but must choose the best distribution from the perspective of the society as a whole.

The problem with this formulation is the idea that we can assume production and distribution are separable. "The things once there"? Seriously? And economists get mocked for their facile assumptions? There is no reason to assume that "the things" will be there, unless prices and profits can perform their directive functions. In fact, as Venezuela has recently learned to its great harm, without the lure and signal, the *things* are not there to distributed.

In a larger sense, the things won't even be "things." Innovations are just ideas that no one ever thought about until some entrepreneur came up with them. Potential profits are a signal to entrepreneurs. And entrepreneurs serve consumers. Greed won't help, because the task of the entrepreneur is to imagine what the consumer wants even though the consumer doesn't know it yet.

The idea of entrepreneurship appears to derive from the French verb entreprendre, meaning "to undertake." One of the first clear statements using the modern meaning comes from J.B. Say:

> An entrepreneur is an economic agent who unites all means of production — land of one, the labour of another and the capital of yet another and thus produces a product. By selling the product in the market he pays rent of land, wages to labour, interest on capital and what remains is his profit. He shifts economic resources out of an area of lower and into an area of higher productivity and greater yield. (1834;

But entrepreneurship is more than just buying low and selling high. Israel Kirzner gives what I think is the best description of the relation between profit, value, and entrepreneurship:

> Let us consider the theorem which Jevons correctly called "a general law of the utmost importance in economics," which asserts that "in the same open market, at any one moment, there cannot be two prices for the same kind of article." … Now the existence of such a tendency [toward a single price] requires some explanation. If the imperfection of knowledge (responsible for the initial multiplicity of prices) reflected the lack of some "resource" (as where means of communication are absent between different parts of a market), then it is difficult, without additional justification, to see how we can postulate universally a process of spontaneous discovery.…
>
> We understand, that is, that the initial imperfection in knowledge is to be attributed, not to lack of some needed resource,

> but to fail to notice opportunities ready at hand. The multiplicity of prices represented opportunities for pure entrepreneurial profit; that such multiplicity existed, means that many market participants (those who sold at the lower prices and those who bought at the higher prices) simply overlooked these opportunities. Since these opportunities were left unexploited, not because of unavailable needed resources, but because they were simply not noticed, we understand that, as time passes, the lure of available pure profits can be counted upon to alert at least some market participants to the existence of these opportunities. (p. 89).

Kirzner defined entrepreneurship as awareness, the constant searching for profit opportunities. But Kirzner conceived of errors much more broadly than the above passage would suggest. Rather than simply correcting errors in the price system and causing the convergence of prices of a single existing commodity, entrepreneurs imagine alternative futures, possible ways of organizing production, and new products that consumers may well not even be aware that they could have, much less want.

Steve Jobs, of Apple, famously observed in 1989 that entrepreneurs could not rely on static conceptions of demand: "You can't just ask customers what they want and then try to give that to them. By the time you get it built, they'll want something new."[36]

A decade later, Jobs went further: "But in the end, for something this complicated, it's really hard to design products by focus groups.

36 "Interview with Steve Jobs." (1989). Interview with *Inc. Magazine* for its "The Entrepreneur of the Decade Award" (1 April 1989).

A lot of times, people don't know what they want until you show it to them." This view, if it is correct, suggests how entrepreneurship may be destructive, at least from the perspective of those other firms and enterprises still trying to make what people used to want. If an entrepreneur shows folks what they really want but don't know they want … boom![37]

The Sony Walkman was an extremely popular (and profitable) device that allowed people to move around or even exercise while listening to the radio or to cassette tapes. At one point, the Walkman captured more than 50 percent of the mobile-music market. But then MP3 players were invented. MP3 is short for MPEG-3, an abbreviation for Motion Picture Expert Group codings. Codings are means of reducing the amount of information (bits of stored digital information) to encode a song without losing quality.

The first patents for MP3 encodings were issued in the United States in the late 1980s and the early 1990s. The first commercially viable MP3 players went on sale in the late 1990s, and by 1999 they were relatively common in stores. The first iPods from Apple were released in January 2001; by the end of 2002, 600,000 had been sold at prices exceeding $400 (in 2002 dollars).

So even though people didn't know that MP3 was how they wanted to buy, store, and carry their music, it turned out to be so. The most successful MP3 player, for more than a decade, has been the iPod, made by Apple. Steve Jobs and the Apple engineers imagined a different arrangement of productive resources.

None of the resources needed to be invented, and none of the digital processes for storing the music were especially difficult or

---

37 *Business Week*, (1998). "Interview with Steve Jobs." (25 May 1998).

innovative. But the package, the iPod, was something new. It was a thing that wasn't there, and then it was there, and people wanted it. Perhaps Steve Jobs did it for glory, but his company did it for profits, and profits made it possible.

2. Distribution in Markets Is Always Just

Many modern political controversies are often not about production as such but the distribution of what is produced. To whom does the value of what has yet to exist belong? What's more, how are we to enforce that judgment once it is made, without letting the enforcer change the agreement on its own?

Let's consider the topic carefully.

Arnold is building a new house; he needs a roof. Brenda is a competent contractor, installing roofs at competitive prices. Arnold values the new roof at $10,000 and Brenda estimates she can pay her roofing roustabouts all the costs of wages, nails, shingles, and other material, for $5,000.

Brenda doesn't work for free, so she also takes $500 from the final price for hiring the workers and organizing the job. Brenda's roofing can do the job for any price over $5,500. Clearly some mutually beneficial arrangement is possible.

Part of the problem, for both Arnold and Brenda, is the need for policing fulfillment of the agreement. The workers want their pay, the building supply company wants its bill paid for shingles and nails, and Brenda needs her profit. Further, and not least, Arnold wants some assurance that the work is done.

The risks are costs, something that economists call "transaction costs." Much of the profit earned by entrepreneurs arises precisely from finding ways to reduce transaction costs—for both workers and customers—to manageable levels. The entrepreneur also accepts the risk if the expected revenue does not fully materialize.

Both parties would pay for assurance against such risk, contracting with a third party to extract some painful or expensive bond. Notice that this means that Arnold and Brenda are, in effect, paying to be coerced, because assurance is cheaper than risk. This point was famously made by Milgrom, North, and Weingast (1990) and elaborated by Leeson (2007) and Stringham (2015).

Commit to Comply

In economist Oliver Williamson's terms, the problem is the "Fundamental Transformation": before we sign the contract, both of us recognize that breach is a problem and we try to commit to compliance. But after we sign, everyone tries to find a hole in the arrangement and exploit it. My present self is willing to bind my future self to comply, because that lowers the price I have to pay.

Arnold and Brenda hit on a clever solution: they need a big strong dog to bite cheaters. Since this is a valuable service, required by anyone who wants a cheaply enforced contract, some entrepreneur likely specializes in renting out just this sort of dog; the dog is named Uht. Uht's job is simple: bite the legs of anyone who breaches an otherwise valid contract.

The whole point of renting Uht—large, loyal, sharp-toothed, and not very bright—is to ensure that the costs of complying are cheaper than breaching. In equilibrium, the enforcement services can be rented out to enforce many contracts at the same time, because Uht has no one to bite. And many new contracts are negotiated because enforcement is cheap and sure.

So, our story has a happy ending. Arnold can buy, and Brenda can sell, a new roof at a price benefitting both. The new roof is worth much more than Arnold is obliged to pay, and Brenda would be willing to accept a price far less than what she actually gets from Arnold. Both are better. And transaction costs are low enough that the cooperative contract is not precluded by risk of breach.

Maybe Not

But maybe that's not the ending. Maybe it's not even happy. After a heavy snowstorm, Brenda knocks on Arnold's door. She points out (correctly) that the value to Arnold of the roof is far greater than what Arnold paid her. In fact, without the roof, the house would be uninhabitable, and the warm family scene Brenda can see through the window would be impossible. Arnold owes Brenda more money, in this view, because the value of having a secure roof is so great.

We could just say, "A deal's a deal!" If Brenda tries to renegotiate after the fact, Uht the Contract Dog should just bite her, right? Not so fast. Brenda actually is raising a philosophically interesting point.

Suppose that Arnold is rich, and that the roofing business is very competitive. It's true that Brenda was unable to negotiate a very good deal, and it's true that her workers won't get paid very much. But is that fair? Shouldn't society do something to ensure that Brenda actually makes more profit, or that she pays her workers more? They are the ones creating the value, after all. The benefits of the new roof are considerable; how should those be benefits be distributed, from a moral perspective?

That question harks back to John Stuart Mill's famous distinction between production on the one hand, and then—"the things once there"—distribution of the benefits the production creates.

> The laws and conditions of the Production of wealth partake of the character of physical truths. There is nothing optional or arbitrary in them. Whatever mankind produce, must be produced in the modes, and under the conditions, imposed by the constitution of external things, and by the inherent properties of their own bodily and mental structure. Whether they like it or not, their productions will be limited by the amount of their previous accumulation, and, that being given, it will be proportional to their energy, their skill, the perfection of their machinery, and their judicious use of the advantages of combined labour. . . .
>
> It is not so with the Distribution of wealth. That is a matter of human institution solely. The things once there, mankind, individually or collectively, can do with them as they like. They can place them at the disposal of whomsoever they please, and on whatever terms. . . . Even what a person has produced by his individual toil, unaided by any one, he cannot keep, unless by the permission of society.

So, yes, production is economic. But distribution is ethical and the province of philosophers and devotees of social justice.

There are two problems with this reasoning, as has been pointed out by a number of people but perhaps most directly by Anthony de Jasay. The first problem is that it is simply false to think that production and distribution can be separated, much less that they should be. Second, if an authority capable of registering and ruling on such ex post claims is created, the compliance enforcement function is compromised beyond recognition.

No One Produces Without a Distribution Plan

In a market economy, there are no actual examples of production-then-distribution sequence. Inputs negotiate, and then are paid, the value of their marginal products. Each input will be able to negotiate in a competitive setting to obtain its increment to physical output, multiplied by the price that output commands in the downstream market. This process cannot be stopped or even manipulated in a pure market setting, and the resulting payment according to the "value of marginal product" is actually the very essence of justice.

The reason this is important, according to de Jasay, is that Mill—and many of the more recent adherents of this view—want to bake the cake first, and then decide how it will be sliced. But that's not how cakes get baked, in market systems: no one bakes a cake until after it has already been divided, prospectively.

Brenda went around to workers, and to suppliers, and made offers. If these offers were accepted, those are the "slices" of the value cake Brenda is contemplating. When the roof is installed, each of the workers and suppliers are paid in full (otherwise, Uht would have bitten Brenda). It makes no sense to start over "the roof once there," and then decide how to divide up the value slices. That's already agreed on by all the participants; all the slices of the cake are spoken for, before the "fundamental transformation" of signing the contract.

Output and Distribution

Similarly, the contractor herself cannot renegotiate and demand more of the cake after it is baked. The reason that the cake was baked (in this case, the contract was signed and the roof was put on) is that an agreement on distribution of the surplus created by the job was agreed on between the homeowner and the roofing contractor. It's perfectly true that the house would be worth much less, and in fact be uninhabitable in winter, without the roof. But that does not give the roofer legal or moral cause to renegotiate the agreement ex post.

As Anthony de Jasay puts it:

> it as wages in exchange for the effort; owners of capital get some of it as interest and rent in exchange for past saving. Entrepreneurs get the residual as profit in exchange organization and risk bearing. By the time the cake is "baked," it is also sliced and those who played a part in baking it have all got their slices. No distributive decision is missing, left over for 'society' to take.[38]

What about Uht the Contract Dog? This is what is most clever about Jasay's argument. Most people think that there is something different about the dog and the services it provides.

Jasay thinks so, too, but for different reasons. To see Jasay's second problem, remember that Uht's job is to enforce contracts. But who will enforce that contract, the one that says citizens will pay and Uht will enforce contracts between citizens? In other words, if people can't trust each other, why can they trust Uht without some third party enforcement mechanism? It seems naïve to think that Uht will bite himself.

---

38 Jasay, Anthony de. "Parrot Talk: The Repetition of Common Fallacies." Cato Journal 28, No. 1 (Winter 2008): 148. https://object.cato.org/sites/cato.org/files/serials/files/cato-journal/2008/1/cj28n1-10.pdf

Imagine that one day Arnold comes home. Brenda has stopped bothering Arnold, with Uht's help, so Arnold expects a quiet night. But on opening the door, Arnold encounters a surprising sight. Uht the Contract Dog has taken out Arnold's guns, and is cleaning Arnold's AK-47. The dog is also drinking some of Arnold's best scotch whisky, and watching Bundesliga soccer on the big screen. This is particularly amazing because Arnold never signed up for the expanded cable package; Uht must have called the cable company and charged the new channels to Arnold.

Arnold is upset. "Look here, Uht! You don't have my permission to come into my house, take out my guns, drink my scotch, and watch soccer! BAD dog! Bad!"

Uht coolly replies: "Yeah. About your 'permission.' I was thinking. You wouldn't have this house if it weren't for me. You couldn't have had contracts to build the bathrooms, or put on the roof, or to provide security now. I think it's time I got my fair share of the value my services create. This is MY house; you didn't build it, I did. This is MY scotch, and my gun, and my television."

Arnold is furious. "Stay! You are trying to change the rules in the middle! We had an agreement! Stay! STAY, Uht!"

Uht has now reassembles the gun, and loads it, looking at Arnold without blinking. Arnold shouts, quickly: "Stay, Uht! Stay-Uht! Stayht! STATE!"

Uht the dog has become a state. The power to provide coercive enforcement services seems different, because somehow the "social" contract is supposed to enforce itself. If the plumber comes back and says, "You wouldn't enjoy this house without the toilet, pay me!" it seems silly; we already paid. If the roofer wants more money, we reject the request. But for security services the state keeps coming back, over and over again.

That makes no more sense than saying your dog owns your house, as Jasay pointed out.[39] The difference is that once a state is established, there is no way for citizens to prevent ex post recontracting in violation of the original contract, because the state gets to decide what the contract is and whether to enforce it.

Jasay does not dispute the value of credible commitments for contracts. His quarrel comes when constitutional contractarians, ranging from Rousseau to Buchanan, use this mythical argument to justify actual states. He reserves special scorn for those who argue that contracts would be unenforceable without a state, and then simply (as he puts it) "jump over their own shadows" to say that a larger, "social" contract is the answer. Who, pray, could be expected to enforce that contract, the one from which all other contract enforcement is derived? On the other hand, is it possible to have private providers of coercion services that remain private, or is coercion inevitable, because states are inevitable?

The real force of this argument is that it turns the usual claims for "social justice" on their head. The unrefined, unfiddled-with, results of market processes are always just, because that cake is baked with the slices already allocated. The problems for social justice arise when coercion is misused, precisely because our "contract" with the state is unenforceable.

---

39 Jasay, Anthony de. "Your Dog Owns Your House." *The Library of Economics and Liberty*. April 22, 2002. http://www.econlib.org/library/Columns/Jasaydog.html

3. Market Makers or Parasites?

A "middleman" buys cheap, sells dear, and does nothing to improve the product in the meantime. Middlemen are everywhere and probably have been since the very first exchanges started to improve the lives of primitive humans. Marco Polo and his family were middlemen. So is Ebay. Between them, in time and complexity, lie millions of highly specialized, highly profitable actions and transactions. But are middlemen good for market systems? Or are they just parasites?

My Own Good Name

It's all there, in my name. "Munger" comes from "monger," a dealer or trader, often in illicit or smuggled goods. The name has very old roots: in the Saxon writings of the 11th century, we find it as "mancgere." According to the Etymology Dictionary, the Latin noun was "mangonis," a trader or merchant (often, sadly, in slaves). And mangonis, in turn, has its roots in a Greek word manganon, a war machine or contrivance for deceiving an enemy. The Trojan Horse was a manganon. Given that origin, it is not surprising that traders were seen as deceivers, thieves, and parasites. So, there is little to place on the positive side of the etymological ledger, at least until 1000 A.D. or so.

By that time, the river of meaning had forked: There were war machines (such as the medieval "mangonel," or catapult), and traders in the market (the mancgere). Sharon Turner's remarkable three-volume History of the Anglo-Saxons (1836), quoting an old source from the 11th century, states:

> In the Saxon dialogues, the merchant (mancgere) is introduced: "I say that I am useful to the king, and to ealdormen, and to the rich, and to all people. I ascend my ship with my merchandise, and sail over the sea-like places, and sell my things, and buy dear things which are not produced in this land, and I bring them to you here with great danger over the sea; and sometimes I suffer shipwreck, with the loss of all my things, scarcely escaping myself."
>
> "What things do you bring to us?"
>
> "Skins, silks, costly gems, and gold; various garments, pigment, wine, oil, ivory, and orichalcus*, copper, and tin, silver, glass, and suchlike."
>
> "Will you sell your things here as you brought them here?"
>
> "I will not, because what would my labour benefit me? I will sell them dearer here than I bought them there, that I may get some profit, to feed me, my wife, and children."
>
> (pp. 115-6; original in MS. Tib. A 3; * brass)

Quite a drama: risk, greed, profit. But the "mancgere" of 1050 AD was no parasite, at least not in his own eyes. In fact, he claims he is "useful." Can that be right? The mancgere freely admits he does nothing to change or improve the product. All he does is transport it and then sell it at the highest price he can get for it. We'd be better off without him, wouldn't we? Isn't the trader simply preying on people's needs for goods and providing nothing of real value himself?

No. Not even close. Without middlemen, we couldn't have modern markets. And the story about why that's true is one of the most important, and most misunderstood, in all of economics. I am going to consider two classic accounts of middlemen, from R.A. Radford (1945) and F. Bastiat, to illustrate how markets work through middlemen.

Middlemen in Action I: WWII Prison Camp

During World War II, British economist R.A. Radford was captured and placed in a German P.O.W. camp. Radford noticed the universality of exchange in the various camps in which he was imprisoned. Being an economist, he knew that exchange, in the presence of full information and in the absence of coercion or fraud, always makes both partics to thc cxchangc bctter off. The interesting thing about the prison camp setting is that each prisoner had precisely the same endowment or total wealth. Each prisoner received (a) daily rations from what Radford delicately calls "the detaining power;" and (b) sporadically, the contents of a Red Cross packet: tinned milk, jam, butter, biscuits, tinned beef, tinned carrots, chocolate, sugar, treacle (molasses), and cigarettes.

What I mean by "makes both parties better off" is this: If I like two carrots more than, say, one milk, and you like one milk more than two carrots, we can trade. This is actually quite important: There is no increase in the total amount of food in the area, but the total welfare of the group is improved. It seems like magic, because it has such a big impact, but we never give it a second thought. Whenever you have different preferences, but similar endowments of resources, then voluntary exchange can make everyone better off. In this case, because the main source of trade goods was the Red Cross packages, endowments were identical. So, barter and exchange made everybody happier.

And people don't have to be told this. They recognize it quickly. As Radford puts it, "Very soon after capture people realized that it was both undesirable and unnecessary, in view of the limited size and the equality of supplies, to give away or to accept gifts.... 'Goodwill' developed into trading as a more equitable means of maximizing individual satisfaction." There's the first point I want to make: Trade is more equitable than relying on gifts or charity because voluntary trades always leave both parties better off.

So, let's accept that trade and exchange are good. But what about middlemen? Aren't they a problem? The prisoners in the camp thought so. Radford mentions a (possibly apocryphal) story of a priest with a sharp eye for exchanges. "Stories circulated of a padre who started off round the camp with a tin of cheese and five cigarettes and returned to his bed with a complete (Red Cross) parcel in addition to his original cheese and cigarettes."

There is the second, more important point, a truly fundamental paradox: *middlemen profit by making other people better off*. The padre never made a fraudulent claim or misrepresented what he was offering to trade. The commodities were standardized and interchangeable (one tin of cheese is just like any other; cigarettes are machine-made, and indistinguishable; a tin of jam is always the same). At each and every step, in every transaction, the exchange with the padre made the other party better off. And yet, the padre accumulated "profit" of a full Red Cross parcel, a small fortune in the setting of the camp.

It might seem that the wandering padre only took value, buying cheap, selling dear, and changing or improving none of the products he exchanged. But just like the Saxon "mancgere" in 1050, the padre created value at every step in the process. He did this by finding A, who would pay six (or fewer) cigarettes for a tin of beef, and then finding another man B, who would sell a tin of beef for three (or more) cigarettes. Of course, if these two traders had happened to meet each other, they would have exchanged directly. But finding just the right person to trade with is time-consuming and may take a little luck. The mancgere/padre, by searching across trades, arbitraged the difference: He could sell the beef to A for five cigarettes after buying it from B for four cigarettes. Thus, both A and B are better off by at least one cigarette and the padre "profits" one cigarette by finding the exchange opportunity.

Although I don't want to overstate the importance of one example, the positive role of the middleman is universal. And the parable of the itinerant padre is the starkest form of the argument that I have ever found. Remember, the question is this: If every exchange makes both parties better, how can the padre have produced any profit? Shouldn't profit always be a sign of exploitation, especially in a setting in which nothing new is produced, as here?

Middlemen in Action II: Bastiat and the Stomach that is Hungry

To resolve the paradox, let us turn to the other example, from the work of Frédéric Bastiat, first published in 1850. The entire essay, "What Is Seen and What Is Not Seen," is full of insight, but I want to focus on just Section 6, "The Middlemen."

While this quote is rather lengthy, the gist of Bastiat's argument is easy to state: There are three ways of getting food from farm to market. First, every consumer goes off on his own, with a cart. This is inefficient and too slow to answer the needs of the hungry (as David R. Henderson illustrates in his discussion of price controls in the aftermath of World War II, German Economic Miracle[40]). Second, middlemen can buy, transport, and resell the products. Third, the state can buy, transport, and resell the products, or give the products away for free.

Bastiat notes that many claim that the state can always perform the function of middlemen more efficiently because the officers of the state are motivated by public service, not by profit. But this is disastrously wrong. First, agents of the state are not, in fact, motivated by the public interest. They are no better than anyone else and act to benefit themselves. Second, without the signals of price and profit provided by middlemen, no one knows what products should be shipped where, or when. In short, without middlemen, the state would act more slowly, less accurately, and at the wrong times.

Once again, the point seems paradoxical. It is because of profit that middlemen create value. And the seeking of profit by middlemen, buying cheap and selling dear, ensures that, as Bastiat put it, the "wheat will reach the stomach" faster, more cheaply, and more reliably than any service the state could possibly create. The system of middlemen performs what seems like, to Bastiat and to me, a miracle: "Directed by the comparison of prices, it distributes food over the whole surface of the country, beginning always at

---

40 Henderson, David R. "German Economic Miracle."Concise Encyclopedia of Economics, Library of Economics and Liberty, Liberty Fund, Inc. http://www.econlib.org/library/Enc/GermanEconomicMiracle.html

the highest price, that is, where the demand is the greatest. It is impossible to imagine an organization more completely calculated to meet the needs of those who are in want…"

Final Thoughts

The merchant, the middleman, the mancgere. Many people tend to think of him as a necessary evil, raising prices and exploiting nearly everyone. But this is quite wrong, and is wrong in a way so fundamental that it makes one wonder why most people seem to have no conception of how real economics works.

The fact is that middlemen are the means by which markets become "perfect" or, at least, approach perfection, where perfection means a single price and reliable quality. Arbitrage is the discipline that reduces differences in price, providing accurate signals on relative scarcity and engendering enormous flows of resources and labor towards their highest-valued use.

In fact, now that I think of it, I'm proud to be a Mancgere!

4. The Origin and Meaning of Profits

The definition of profit is the excess of revenue over costs. The underlying activity that produces the revenue, and incurs the cost, can be almost anything. As Robert Nozick pointed out in his 1974 article, "Why Intellectuals Oppose Capitalism,"[41] intellectuals find this amorphous aspecificity of the goals and reward structure of capitalism frustrating. After all, intellectuals have spent their lives going to the best schools, getting the best grades, and congratulating each other on being the most important members of society.

By comparison, entrepreneurs and business people are often uneducated, even coarse. Socially, we tend to think of Al Czervik from the movie "Caddyshack": If you make or do something, and a bunch of people happen to like it, enough so that you can charge more than it costs to make that thing....what kind of achievement is that?

For example, do you remember the "Pet Rock" of the mid-1970s? If not, ask your (grand)parents. In 1974, a guy named Gary Dahl was in a bar, listening to some friends complain about how much work it was to keep pets. He decided that a pet rock would be a lot less work. He bought nearly a ton of ordinary gray stones at a building supply warehouse. He marketed them in cardboard boxes with air holes cut so the rock could "breathe."

The real idea was a 32 page "owner's manual," with instruction on

41 Nozick, Robert. "Why Do Intellectuals Oppose Capitalism?" Libertarianism.org. 1998. https://www.libertarianism.org/publications/essays/why-do-intellectuals-oppose-capitalism

training the pet—"sit" and "stay" were basic commands, graduating to "roll over" and ultimately "attack" if the rock were thrown. The fad lasted about six months, with a burst of sales around Christmas of December 1975. More than 1.5 million Pet Rocks were sold, and Dahl was moderately wealthy.

It appears that in 2012 an updated version of the Pet Rock was offered, with a USB cable for "added functionality." It is no longer available, as far as I can tell, but I am pretty sure that the USB port and cable didn't actually add any functionality at all. Nonetheless, quite a few people bought them.

Did Gary Dahl produce any value for society? Does a "Pet Rock" that earns profits mean that someone should get rich? An intellectual would say, "I got straight A's, and you didn't even finish college, you filthy entrepreneur. We need redistribution based on social merit! Some idiot who sells rocks doesn't deserve to be wealthy!"

The Origins of Profit

This kind of question simply reverses the cause-and-effect relationship between merit and desert. (That's "des-ERT," or deserving a reward, not the really dry hot place). The problem with the standard view of desert is that wealth is, or should be, a reward for merit. But "social" merit is very hard to define; as Thomas Hobbes noted, in Leviathan: "A man may be Worthy of Riches, Office, and Employment, that nevertheless, can plead no right to have it before another; and therefore cannot be said to merit or deserve it."

Right. But profit is not wealth awarded to people who have intrinsic social merit. Profit is the end consequence of a discovery process, a search for value that is distributed among all the many nooks and crannies of a modern economy.

Somerset Maugham wrote a famous short story, "The Verger."[42] Mr. Foreman has been working hard as a verger—a lay assistant to the Vicar in the Anglican Church—for more than 15 years, since he was a teenager. A new vicar is appointed, and is shocked to learn that the verger cannot read or write. The vicar demands that Mr. Foreman become literate, or leave the church's employ.

Mr. Foreman doubts he can learn to read. He is sacked. He wanders, looking for a cigarette. But there is no tobacconist anywhere on all the long street of shops. Mr. Foreman has an idea, hardly a profound idea but an idea nonetheless, that he might open a shop. He makes substantial profits. Before long, he opens another, and then several more, in every case using the simple, in fact obvious, strategy of finding an area of the city with many shops but no tobacconist.

He amasses a fortune. Worrying about having to mind all that cash, Mr. Foreman visits a bank, where he is told by an executive that he should invest the money. Mr. Foreman declines to invest in complex financial instruments, confiding in the banker that he cannot read or write. The banker is thunderstruck, finding it remarkable that an illiterate man could acquire substantial wealth.

The banker wonders out loud, given what a success Mr. Foreman without literacy, how things might be if he could read. As Maugham puts it, "'I can tell you that sir,' said Mr. Foreman, a little smile on his still aristocratic features. 'I'd be verger of St. Peter's, Neville Square.'"

Did Mr. Foreman deserve to become wealthy? He didn't have any merit, at least as intellectuals measure such things. All he did

---

42 Quoted in Klein, Daniel B. "Discovery and Economic Freedom." *Independent Institute.* September 1, 1997. http://www.independent.org/publications/article.asp?id=309

was to make it possible for people to buy a product they wanted, at a lower price (counting travel) than had been possible before. What's so hard, or so admirable, about that?

Mises himself is honest about this feature of the profit and loss system.

> The entrepreneurs are neither perfect nor good in any metaphysical sense. They owe their position exclusively to the fact that they are better fit for the performance of the functions incumbent upon them than other people are. They earn profit not because they are clever in performing their tasks, but because they are more clever or less clumsy than other people are. … If the grumbler knew better, why did he not himself fill the gap and seize the opportunity to earn profits? It is easy indeed to display foresight after the event. In retrospect all fools become wise.

Kirzner (1978) defined entrepreneurship as "awareness," the constant searching for profit opportunities. But Kirzner conceived of errors much more broadly than the above passage would suggest. Rather than simply "correcting" errors in the price system, and causing the convergence of prices of a single existing commodity, entrepreneurs imagine alternative futures, new products, and possible ways of organizing production.

It is difficult to overstate the importance of this distinction. An entrepreneur does not (just) take advantage of errors (i.e., differences) in prices. An entrepreneur cultivates a character of alertness, looking to anticipate what consumers want. But that means that the system is ultimately driven (though perhaps passively) by consumers, not entrepreneurs. Entrepreneurs are the active agents in the system, but consumers decide what firms produce and which productive activities will be rewarded and which punished.

The verger, Mr. Foreman, corrected an error in the system. There should have been a tobacconist there, in that spot. No one else recognized that, but the absence of a tobacconist was a mistake. Consumers wanted a store there (though even consumers may not have recognized this fact!).

That's what I mean about being confused about the direction of causation: one doesn't have merit, and then receive rewards. The entrepreneur seeking profits creates something new, correcting a mistake. If the costs of correcting the mistake are less than the benefits in terms of the consumer surplus created, the result is profits.

There is no particular reason to expect that education or intellectual interests are an advantage in cultivating a habit of awareness of the sort Kirzner highlights. But there are very good reasons to argue that profits, deserved or not, are something that entrepreneurs should be legally entitled to seek.

VI

GENERAL PROBLEMS OF STATE ACTION

A mistake often made by market "enthusiasts" (as I have been called, and not as a compliment) is to attempt to defend the perfection of markets. This is a mistake, on two grounds. First, the notion that universal ignorance results in perfect information borders on mysticism, and it's not a persuasive argument. Second, the argument for markets is not perfection of the price mechanism; it's the universal imperfection and entropic tendencies of human life.

It is common for policy analysts to advocate for the "market failure" paradigm, where the failings of markets are defined with reference to an unobservable--and, in fact, imaginary--benchmark of competitive equilibrium. Since in the blackboard model market outcomes are not perfect, it must be possible for the state to sweep in and perfect what markets have fouled up.

Notice the intellectual sleight of hand: markets as they are, are found wanting. So we substitute the state as we can imagine it. We imagine that the state has information required to solve the problem that markets botched, and we imagine that the human beings who make up the state want to achieve the idealized equilibrium rather than act in their own self-interest.

Both claims are just as nonsensical as thinking markets are perfect, and in fact for the same reason. The government also faces a knowledge problem, and the government also has a problem of incentives and monitoring. Taken together, these claims are known as the "public choice" objection to the market failure justification for state action. Remember, the problem is that prices are assumed, in a market failure setting, not to convey accurate information about opportunity costs. But then where is the accurate information to be obtained? As FA Hayek and others have argued, this simply reprises the "socialist calculation debate," because price is the only mechanism for conveying accurate information about opportunity costs. Prices are not an input to the process, as assumed by "market failure" enthusiasts; rather, prices are the result of the discovery process, and there is no other means of generating that kind of information.

In the case of public goods, or citizen demands for state provision of private goods, it is true that the state will do something. But there is no more reason to believe that the result will be a Pareto optimum than market provision. Both are deeply flawed, and problematic. The difference is that markets do generate some price information, and markets likewise foster innovation and new institutions that encourage cooperation. States are mostly concerned with power, and protecting the privileges of those who have power.

1. It's Not Only about Markets vs. the State

Many of us operate using a false dichotomy: everything that is not a for-profit market process is "the state." That's logically wrong, and concedes far too much to the state. It leaves us defending the "perfection" of the market, which is a fool's errand.

The best argument for markets is not the perfection of the price mechanism; it's the imperfection of the world. Everything is in the wrong place, and information about how to make things better is dispersed and hard to obtain. Decentralized, voluntary mechanisms for organizing humans socially are the key to solving those problems.

The "state" depends on centralized, coercive means of organizing people socially. That's almost always a mistake. But it may also be a mistake to insist that market processes, using explicit prices, are the answer. As I argued in my book (with son Kevin) *Choosing in Groups*, the answer is often found in the suggestions of James Buchanan, one of the founders of Public Choice, who saw politics as a kind of exchange using non-market institutions.

Tocqueville

There is a substantial scholarly foundation for this kind of approach. One of the most famous is Alexis de Tocqueville, who wrote in 1831 in Democracy in America that the particular genius of the United States was precisely the ability of Americans to use decentralized voluntary associations that were neither state nor market.

> Americans of all ages, all conditions, and all dispositions constantly form associations…religious, moral, serious, futile, general or restricted, enormous or diminutive. The Americans make associations to give entertainments, to found seminaries, to build inns, to construct churches, to diffuse books, to send missionaries to the antipodes; in this manner they found hospitals, prisons, and schools. If it is proposed to inculcate some truth or to foster some feeling by the encouragement of a great example, they form a society. Wherever at the head of some new undertaking you see the government in France, or an aristocrat in England, in the United States you will be sure to find an association.

Tocqueville was worried that state action, and democracy in particular, was displacing voluntary private action in France. He thought that private groups were actually the primary cause of the American capacity for self-governance. Notice the difference: governance, not government. This distinction has recently become important again, in part because of Edward Stringham's deeply insightful book Private Governance has refocused our attention on the fact that if the government doesn't interfere citizens can find ways to govern themselves.

Tocqueville claimed that Europeans had lost "the habit of acting in common," a marked difference compared to standard "Progressive" dogma, which holds that citizens are only capable of acting in concert through the intercession of the state. According to Tocqueville:

> Amongst democratic nations…all the citizens are independent and feeble; they can do hardly anything by themselves, and

> none of them can oblige his fellow-men to lend him their assistance. They all, therefore, fall into a state of incapacity, if they do not learn voluntarily to help each other….
> [Some claim that] the more enfeebled and incompetent the citizens become, the more able and active the government ought to be rendered, in order that society at large may execute what individuals can no longer accomplish. [But it] is easy to foresee that the time is drawing near when man will be less and less able to produce, of himself alone, the commonest necessaries of life. The task of the governing power will therefore perpetually increase, and its very efforts will extend it every day. The more it stands in the place of associations, the more will individuals, losing the notion of combining together, require its assistance… (Book 2, Section 2, Chapter 5; emphasis added)

Cornuelle

This insight was taken up by Richard Cornuelle in his book 1999 *Reclaiming the American Dream*, where he describes "Progressivism" as perceiving " a mounting agenda of problems so large and complex that only government, the largest single force in sight, seems big enough to handle them." (Chapter 4).

The Great Depression and its aftermath made things even worse:

> Our habit of sending difficult problems to Washington quickly became almost a reflex. A one-way flow of responsibility to the federal government, begun by Depression remedies, has continued and gained speed. In less than thirty years the government has nearly cornered the market for new public responsibility. (Chapter 4).

Cornuelle's diagnosis is that, far from mitigating or solving these problems, Progressivism had made them much worse. The voluntary private sector had shriveled, just as Tocqueville had predicted in 1831. But the fault was not just the mistakes of Progressivism, according to Cornuelle. Private market advocates had themselves given away the store by ignoring the importance of what Cornuelle called "the independent sector." The economist who had led the push for private action had simply failed to recognize the significance of other kinds of voluntary collective action:

> We know that the Progressive movement had two distinct branches—one statist and one voluntarist—of comparable intellectual vigor. We know that before America's Great Depression, there appears to have been a formidable alternative to government action for almost every aspect of the public business, from disease control to economic stabilization. And we know that by 1958, in The Affluent Society, John K. Galbraith could write about American society as if it had only two sectors—one public, by which he meant governmental, and the other private, by which he meant commercial—and that no one noticed the omission for years.
>
> How could we lose a sector of this size and scope is something of a mystery. Perhaps the decline of this dimension of our pluralism began when Woodrow Wilson set out to use his extraordinary wartime powers to jail all our most gallant, original, and entertaining misfits and rationalize American society. By 1946, the American tradition of independent, nongovernment action on the public business had been buried alive…

Cornuelle called for a recognition of the importance of the independent sector, in effect saying that the motto of anti-statism should be "anything voluntary," not just "markets are great!" Voluntary charitable and other private associations seem unimportant to market advocates, but they are a crucial part of a strategy of effective decentralization and liberation. The problem is that, like markets, such institutions have "... a natural competitor." Cornuelle explains:

> Both sectors operate in the same industry: public service and welfare. Sometimes, over the years, leaders on each side have sensed their competitive positions and built a fascinating record of both creative competition and deliberate collusion. The quality of life in the U.S. now depends largely on the revival of a lively competition between these two natural contenders for public responsibility. The struggle would enhance the effectiveness of both.
>
> The government doesn't ignore public opinion because the people who run it are naturally perverse. It isn't wasteful because it is manned by wasteful people. [The problem is that] without competition, the bureaucracy can't make government efficient.... Innovation painfully disrupts [bureaucracy's] way of life. Reform comes only through competitive outsiders who force steady, efficient adjustment to changing situations.
>
> The independent sector will grow strong again when its leaders realize that its unique indispensable natural role in America is to compete with government. It must be as eager as government to take on new public problems. It must be

> imaginative, vigorous, persistent. Independent groups must line up in Washington, not begging for help but looking for bigger jobs to do.

Tocqueville and Cornuelle should be libertarian heroes. "Voluntary collective action" should be our motto. This obviously includes markets, to be sure. But there is no reason to cede the vitality, attractiveness, and exuberance of the non-profit independent sector to ownership by the state. Voluntary private organizations belong to everyone.

2. Government Is Not What Makes a Country Great

Can you distrust the government and yet still be loyal to your country? I say yes.

I spend quite a bit of time in Europe. Friends "across the pond" are always incredulous about some dumb thing the U.S. government has done. They expect me to be defensive; in fact I'm usually able to supply some detail or additional outrage they hadn't heard yet.

Someone will take me aside later, and ask if I am thinking of moving to another country. After all, if I am that scornful of the U.S. government, how can I stick around?

Wait. I can be a patriotic American, but also think that U.S. politicians are ninnies. Both can be true: our country is great, and our government is terrible. To be fair, European political officials are a pack of clowns and thugs, too.

Become a Great Country

Countries are great when they can overcome bad politicians, because the core rules and the values of the citizens are bulletproof. Citizens must somehow have both the ability and the courage to face down governments when that government becomes too oppressive or too arbitrarily focused on the personal power of temporary leaders.

That, I think, is where my Euro-friends disagree. The reverence for "democracy"—by which Europeans mostly mean "majority rule"—is almost unknown here. Many of our government institutions—the Senate, the Supreme Court, the Electoral College—are explicitly and intentionally anti-majoritarian. It has never been clear to me why this faith in majorities is so strong in countries that love government.

If you start with one person, too dumb to be able to choose what size soft drink to buy or to buy lunch from a food truck without government help, and gather a whole pack of them into a poorly informed and undisciplined mob, then they can make extremely complex decisions about foreign policy that affect the entire world.

H.L. Mencken, in Notes on Democracy, (1982) shared my skepticism. Or, to be fair, I guess I share his:

> [In the electorate,] one hears, lies a deep, illimitable reservoir of righteousness and wisdom, unpolluted by the corruption of privilege. What baffles statesmen is to be solved by the people, instantly and by a sort of seraphic intuition.... The cure for the evils of democracy is more democracy.
>
> This notion, as I hint, originated in the poetic fancy of gentlemen on the upper levels - sentimentalists who, observing to their distress that the ass was over-laden, proposed to reform transport by putting him into the cart. (P. 154).

One might object, of course, that the problem is not the lack of information voters possess, since the very idea of anyone knowing enough to organize or plan a society is ludicrous.

Societies that work organize themselves, using higher level rules that structure their interactions and allow innovation. As Mises and Hayek argued, the notion that planning can be achieved through "calculation," either by experts or by voters, is both eternally appealing and dead wrong.

Mencken said something else about democracy, something that I can't help thinking about in the aftermath of...well, of pretty much every election in my lifetime. There is a fatal internal contradiction in seeing "democracy" as being nothing more than majority rule, rather than a set of restrictions on majority rule:

> Does [democracy] exalt dunderheads, cowards, trimmers, frauds, cads? Then the pain of seeing them go up is balanced and obliterated by the joy of seeing them come down. Is it inordinately wasteful, extravagant, dishonest? Then so is every other form of government: all alike are enemies to laborious and virtuous men. Is rascality at the very heart of it? Well, we have borne that rascality since 1776, and continue to survive.
>
> In the long run, it may turn out that rascality is necessary to human government, and even to civilization itself — that civilization, at bottom, is nothing but a colossal swindle. I do not know: I report only that when the suckers are running well the spectacle is infinitely exhilarating.
>
> But I am, it may be, a somewhat malicious man: my sympathies, when it comes to suckers, tend to be coy. What I can't make out is how any man can believe in democracy who feels for and with them, and is pained when they are debauched and made a show of. How can any man be a democrat who is sincerely a democrat? (P. 168).

Much of the genius of the U.S. has always been that we are not a majoritarian system. A naïve faith in the racist, greedy, homophobic, and immigrant-hating majority is no basis for government.

Trust Not Authority

Sure, elections and majority rule are the best tools we have to curtail tyranny, but we don't have to worship our tools. People didn't vote to end segregated schools; the Supreme Court overruled the will of the majority in Kansas, and President Eisenhower sent elite troops, the U.S. 101st Airborne, to force voters to do that which they didn't want to do: treat all children equally.

But the U.S. is now becoming more like Europe, in the sense that we are trusting more and more of the authority to use force to naïve majority rule. When President Obama said, "Elections have consequences, and I won!" he was elevating elections over rule of law. When he said that he had a pen, and he had a phone, and could use those to govern through executive order rather than depending on the Congress, the rule of law took another hit.

Since November 2016 several Duke University colleagues have come into my office, closed the door, and said, "Okay. You were right. Are you happy now?" Since the U.S. response to 9/11, with the Patriot Act and expansive use of executive power, I had been complaining.

What if a tyrant is elected? What if these huge new powers fall into the hands of someone you disagree with? The problem is that the exceptions to the rule of law persist, but the policies you want will be obliterated.

Well, in the minds of many that "what if" is no longer hypothetical. And much of what made the U.S. distinctive has been heedlessly destroyed. We are conflating loyalty to our elected leaders with patriotism, and it scares me.

3. The Welfare State Is a (Bad) Polygamist

Polygamy is an ancient practice, rooted in patriarchy, that effectively enslaved women in societies where females had no status and little power. Restrained by their circumstances, women were better off "sharing" husbands who had power and resources than living alone or taking as a partner a man who could barely even feed himself.

Fortunately, those days are long behind us. Or are they?

In many countries, including the U.S., the state has become a polygamist, and a jealous one at that. Bound by poverty and dutifully "supported" by welfare, women find themselves trapped in a vice. If they try to get a job or have a relationship with a partner, the state will react in a jealous rage and kick them out.

Of course, that's not how the people who have constructed our rickety welfare state actually think about it. To hear welfare state apologists tell it, the state is protecting women who are otherwise defenseless, or have no way of gaining access to the resources they need to raise their children.

The problem is that these "benefits" are contingent, and the conditions are surprisingly similar to those of the ancient polygamists. It's fine for women to have furtive liaisons, and the state is even willing to pay for the children that issue from these casual affairs! But any kind of serious relationship, and the jealous state cuts women off.

An economist might put it in a more sterile fashion: the highest marginal tax rates in the U.S. fall on the very poor, especially women with small children, considering the fact that they often lose more than they gain by getting married and obtaining a job.

How the State Creates a Cycle of Poverty

The American welfare system was established with a wide range of contingencies and safeguards to ensure that welfare recipients are facing a "real need" and to avoid "fraud" (the "welfare queen" is a powerful political trope).

For this reason, those at the very bottom receive benefits that are, for example, "tied" to an activity in the form of a voucher. Food stamps and section 8 housing vouchers provide the poor with the sustenance and shelter they need to live lives of relative dignity and to ensure that they spend their welfare money on essentials, not luxuries and vices. But this means that they have no other way of obtaining the food or housing those vouchers provide. And as soon as they get a job, they lose their benefits. As soon as they get married, they lose their benefits.

In some cases, the effective marginal tax rates for very poor women with children can approach, and possibly even exceed, 100%. A woman with two children, who lives in Section 8 housing and receives food vouchers, whose kids receive subsidized meals at school, and who depends on "low-income energy assistance" programs to heat their apartments, can lose $20,000 worth of benefits for the first $25,000 she earns in income. As the Center for Hunger-Free Communities points out, this is called the "Cliff Effect":

> "Families that successfully increase their earnings should not find themselves worse off due to the consequent loss of benefits…. While a higher income can be an important step

> in a family's progress towards self-sufficiency, the increased child food insecurity in this group suggests they may be experiencing the 'cliff effect.' This occurs when an increase in income causes an overall reduction in total resources due to a loss of benefits or increased tax liability."[43]

Not Intentional, but Still Evil

People who support this sorry state polygamy don't actually want to be evil; in fact, I'm willing to concede that their motives are good. But the problem is the conceit that "We have to DO something!" to solve every problem.[44] Here is how this logic plays out in practice:

1. It is a huge problem that some people are poor.
2. If you are a good person, you care about the fact that some people are poor.
3. Therefore, we should do something.
4. Housing subsidies, food subsidies, free school lunches for children, and other "poverty programs" are all something.
5. Therefore, we should do those things.
6. If you object that those programs actually don't work, and in many cases are actively harmful, you hate poor people!

---

43 "Earning More, Receiving Less: Loss of Benefits and Child Hunger." Center For Hunger Free Communities. http://www.centerforhungerfreecommunities.org/sites/default/files/pdfs/cliffeffect_brief_sept10-1.pdf

44 Michael Munger, "We Have to DO Something!" https://www.learnliberty.org/blog/we-should-do-something/

What the state polygamists fail to recognize is that sometimes doing something hurts more than it helps. In the case of welfare, this "benefits trap" is clearly unintentional.[45] But it's real. It consigns women to hopeless lives, depending on a state that doesn't really want them, but is too jealous to let them go.

45 Cochrane, John. "Benefits trap art". The Grumpy Economist. December 27, 2012. https://johnhcochrane.blogspot.com/2012/12/benefits-trap-art.html

4. Truthiness and the Origins of "Fake News"

Ten years ago this January I published an article about "truthiness."[46] The word comes from the The Colbert Report on October 17, 2005. Colbert did a segment called "The Wørd," and "Truthiness" was the guest of honor.

We tend to think of public debates, and to some extent even voter choices in elections, as distinguishing between truth and error. But Colbert's act illustrated that this distinction was false, or at least incomplete. He proposed a neologism: "truthiness." It caught on and became the American Dialect Society's 2005 word of the year:

> Truthiness (noun): the quality of stating concepts or facts one wishes or believes to be true, rather than concepts or facts known to be true.[47]

Colbert occasionally put a suit on truthiness when it was time to step out, calling it "Veritasiness." Regardless, my point (as I put it in 2007, and I'm just quoting from that paper, don't blame me for

---

46 Munger, Michael C. "Blogging and political information: truth or truthiness?" Public Choice, 134, Issue 1–2, pp 125–138. https://link.springer.com/article/10.1007/s11127-007-9205-6

47 "Truthiness Voted 2005 Word of the Year by American Dialect Society." American Dialect Society. January 6, 2006. http://www.americandialect.org/Words_of_the_Year_2005.pdf

being prescient) was that "Truthiness trumps truth — intuition based on feelings or values is more important than debate and evidence."

Fact-checkers in pajamas

The blatant disregard for the facts that set off the protests against "fake news" actually preceded Colbert's segment. In the run-up to the 2004 presidential election, there were serious questions raised about George W. Bush's war record.

On September 4, 2004, the television show 60 Minutes broke the explosive story: Bush had failed to report for a physical while supposedly on active duty. The most important document was a direct written order issued May 4, 1972, by Lt. Colonel Jerry Killian.

But shortly thereafter, a variety of bloggers and other voices on the Internet argued that these documents were obviously forgeries. On the night of September 9, the executive vice-president of CBS News, Jonathan Klein, appeared on Fox News to debate Weekly Standard writer and pundit Stephen Hayes, who agreed with the bloggers' claim. Both Hayes and the host demanded that CBS acknowledge they had been duped, and in fact had no evidence for their claims against Bush.

Jonathan Klein responded with a level of smugness that showed he didn't realize that CBS's place as a news source that others would simply defer to was already gone forever.

> You couldn't have a starker contrast between the multiple layers of checks and balances [i.e., fact checkers at 60 Minutes]

> and a guy sitting in his living room in his pajamas writing.[48]

That turned out to be true, though not in the way that Mr. Klein intended. After further scrutiny, it is clear that there were significant irregularities in the documents. CBS had failed to authenticate them before going on air with the evidence. But that meant that the "multiple layers of checks and balances" had gotten it wrong, and the bloggers in pajamas had it right: no reputable news source would have used those documents to support that story.

Why had CBS gone ahead, then? Because they believed the story more than they believed in the need for evidence. That is truthiness.

News anchor Dan Rather, in particular, was convinced that George W. Bush had been AWOL, saying that the "essential truth" (Rather's words) of the claim transcended any nit-picking problems with those particular documents.

Now, even today we can't be certain, by any means, that the contested documents were actually forgeries. The problem is that there is little reason to believe they are real.

The focus of the argument moved to apparently simple features of the primary letter in particular, the one in which the supposed "direct order" was issued. The most obvious problem was with superscripted letters, in a smaller font size, on military unit numbers (like 41st or 53rd). This way of typing would not be conventional on most military typewriters, as it would have required changing the type ball and manually moving the carriage to create superscripts.

---

48 Liberman, Mark. "You Couldn't Have a Starker Contrast." Language Log. September 17, 2004. http://itre.cis.upenn.edu/~myl/languagelog/archives/001459.html

This, it was pointed out on dozens of blogs, is nearly impossible to do consistently. Furthermore, other (legitimate) letters from the files at around the same time from the same office showed a completely different, non-proportional typeface.

None of this is proof, of course, but the questions kept coming as more and more people independently studied the letter. There was no conspiracy among the bloggers, no clandestine coordination. Many people looked at the evidence, and concluded it just didn't hold up. Before long, the supposed "source" for the letter had changed his story about where he had gotten it, and CBS eventually threw in the towel. Dan Rather issued a tepid, narrow apology for the use of the letters, and CBS News fired four people, including the (apparently) overzealous producer Mary Mapes.

Right up until the end, though, Dan Rather defended the story as "essentially" accurate. That is, even though these particular documents might be fake, the story itself was true. On several occasions, as documented in the Thornburgh-Boccardi (2005) report and elsewhere, senior CBS personnel (including Dan Rather) flatly stated that they could prove the essential truth of the story. But they had no real evidence, other than their own certainty about the correctness of their views. The president's guilt was a foregone conclusion; the news producers' only job was to get the word out.

Fake news is bad news

When Stephen Colbert first talked about "truthiness" and the problem of "essential" or "gut" truths that transcend evidence, trust in the media exceeded 50%. That is, more than 50% of Americans consistently answered "a great deal" or "a fair amount" in response to the question "In general, how much trust and confidence do you have in the mass media—such as newspapers, TV, and radio—when it comes to reporting the news fully, accurately, and fairly?" By 2016, this number had fallen to 32%; today it is more like 25%.[49] That is, three-quarters of Americans now answer "not very much" or "almost none."

That's bad news for civility, and civic discourse. Every fact is contested, every disagreeable claim is scornfully dismissed. The social function of news media — the curation of facts, a kind of elite intermediation — is indispensable in a world where the flood of information overwhelms our ability to parse and interpret.

Just last year, on November 5, 2016, just three days before the election, the Huffington Post invoked a truthiness of its own. At the time HuffPo's Ryan Grim, like most journalists, believed that Hillary Clinton would almost certainly win the presidency.[50] But the prediction-and-punditry site FiveThirtyEight, headed by Nate Silver, had pointed out that Trump's polling in many key states was within the margin of error. In other words, Trump could win.

Huff-Po's response to Silver's heretical reporting of actual facts was to accuse him of cheating — "putting his thumb on the scale."

Instead of recognizing that honestly pointing out the problems with conventional wisdom is the key job of the media, HuffPo rejected FiveThirtyEight's facts and doubled down on its own

---

49 For the poll source see https://news.gallup.com/poll/195542/americans-trust-mass-media-sinks-new-low.aspx

50 Grim, Ryan. "Nate Silver Is Unskewing Polls — All Of Them — In Trump's Direction." HuffPost. November 5, 2016. https://www.huffpost.com/entry/nate-silver-election-forecast_n_581e1c33e4b0d9ce6fbc6f7f

beliefs. And three days later the sky fell, because it had only been supported by columns of truthiness.

If I have my news, and you have yours, and both of us rely on truthiness — the uncontestable "essential" truth of our beliefs, regardless of facts — it's impossible to have a conversation. And when people who disagree can't have a conversation they are much more likely to fight. Ten years ago, when I was first writing about "truthiness," it was still a pretty new notion, one that seemed kind of funny and whimsical. It's not that funny now.

5. Why a Canadian City Tore Down the Staircase Its Residents Had Always Wanted to Build

Toronto city officials recently threatened a man with fines for building an unlicensed staircase in a local park. Then they tore down his staircase, which had cost him $550 to build, and replaced it with one that cost $15,000.

Now, there's a lot going on in the world. So you'll be forgiven if you missed these events in Canada. But there's a lesson to be gained here about why government workers do the seemingly strange things they do.

The brief version of the story goes like this. A lovely section of wooded Tom Riley Park, right along Mimico Creek in Toronto, had a steep, rocky, muddy slope. But it was the shortest path from the parking lot down to the community garden lot and soccer fields, saving at least 100 yards of walking. For more than a few elderly guests, or women wearing fashionable shoes, this path was treacherous, and folks fell or slid down the slope. One garden club member recently broke her wrist.

Apparently Toronto had studied the slope as a candidate for a staircase, but determined that it would cost $65,000 (CAN) to build. That's a lot for a staircase, so the plan was shelved.

Don't you dare do it yourself.

But the residents of Toronto are civilized. It's not some redneck hangout like Mississauga, where sliding around in mud is date night. An elderly gentleman, Adi Astl, a retired mechanic, decided to take matters into his own hands. Enlisting the aid of a local homeless man, Mr. Astl built a stairway, with sturdy 4×4 timbers and a handrail.[51] It wasn't a perfect stairway, but it worked and it was much safer than the muddy slope it replaced. The whole thing appears to have been less than six vertical feet, just eight stairs.

And then all heck — it's Canada — broke loose. The city blocked the stairs, and hung yellow CAUTION tape, because "the railing is unsafe, the incline is uneven and there is no foundation." They also threatened Mr. Astl with thousands of dollars in fines for "building without a permit." All this even though the stairs seem to have made the spot less dangerous than before.

Some days later, the city tore up Astl's wooden stairs, and put in some poured, reinforced concrete stairs with metal railings. And they did it for $15,000.[52]

Now, you may think that the city's inspectors or bylaw officers or the parks department in general behaved badly here, because (1) they didn't act until they were embarrassed, (2) they threatened Mr. Astl and destroyed the useful stairs he built, and (3) their replacement stairs cost 27 times more than his did. Why couldn't the city officials just use some common sense, leave Mr. Astl alone, and let park users enjoy his donated staircase?

---

51 "Toronto man builds park stairs for $550, irking city after $65,000 estimate." CTVnews. July 19, 2007. https://www.ctvnews.ca/mobile/canada/toronto-man-builds-park-stairs-for-550-irking-city-after-65-000-estimate-1.3510237

52 Bykova, Alina. "Controversial staircase at Etobicoke park to open Saturday, city says." *The Star*, July 28, 2017. https://www.thestar.com/news/gta/2017/07/28/controversial-staircase-to-open-saturday-city-says.html

Public officials are no worse, but also no better, than the rest of us.

Well, here's the problem. Officers of the government don't have discretion in these matters, and in fact they shouldn't. Some folks probably just think, "That's petty. They should have left the stairs up." But that's wrong: if we give discretion to bureaucrats and the police, they will impose their own biases and sympathies. They're just human, after all. And that is one of the key insights of public choice: the recognition that public officials are no worse, but also no better, than the rest of us because they are us, just human.

The rule of law requires that the law applies to everyone, equally. Discretion allows the representatives of the government to indulge their racism, their sexism, or to give privilege to those they favor. So, we're stuck. We're stuck with rules that seem blunt and clumsy and we have to enforce those rules without discrction or exception. That is the very nature of the state, to restrict the discretion of bureaucrats and law enforcement. They have to enforce the law. And the law is cumbersome and inefficient.

Here's the bad news.

The people who work in Toronto's parks department may actually do a pretty spectacular job, given the restrictions on the ways bids can be taken, plans drawn up, and work executed. But if they don't follow the rules about railings and foundations and the intricacies of the bid-procurement process, they get fired.

The problem, in short, is not that those funny bureaucrats are lazy, or dumb. In fact, pretty much the opposite is true. Many of them are well-educated and actually dedicated to public service. But don't you see? That's the bad news, right there: even good people can't fix a bad system. And centralized state provision of goods like parks and staircases is often a bad system. There are too many rules, and control is too far removed from the citizens who, like Mr. Astl, have exactly the right local knowledge to do what needs to be done.

Edmund Burke had it right, then, when he said, "In vain you tell me that Artificial Government is good, but that I fall out only with the Abuse. The Thing! the Thing itself is the Abuse!"

Blaming people is a mistake. The system is the problem. If you want things provided by the state, you can't complain when that provision is slow, expensive, and hard to manage.

6. Tragedy of the Malecon: Is Cuba "Domestic" Politics?

On September 30th, the University of Miami in Coral Gables, Florida will host the first of the Presidential debates, focusing on domestic policy. What's odd is that "domestic" policy has a little different meaning down there. Lots of Miamians are second or third generation Cubanos, and they have some questions for the candidates. Like, "when do we get our property back?" and "what are you going to do about Castro?" While the moderator will steer talk toward conventional domestic topics, such as the economy, health care, and taxes, the audience will want the debate to look southwest, to Cuba, so close and yet so far.

Coral Gables is just over 220 miles from the Malecon, Havana's breathtaking front porch on the ocean. That's closer than Tallahassee, the Florida capital, and for Miamians that proximity means something real. For the rest of us, it seems strange that the politics of another country should have such an impact on our Presidential election. But there's no question that tens of thousands of Cuban-Americans in Florida, by supporting Bush, changed the outcome of the election in 2000. They may do it again in 2004. Is this domestic policy, or foreign policy, or some unique mix, a spicy guiso that can't be unmade?

I traveled to Cuba in 2001, and got to form my own impressions. I went on an educational exchange program, exempting me from U.S. travel restrictions. With some other American academics, I gave a series of lectures at the Center for the Study of the United States, at the University of Havana. Our hosts were particularly impressed with my color overheads. Being well paid to make the trip, I paid for the overheads myself rather than bill them to Duke—they had cost me about $1.50 per page to produce. Our hosts were professors and were also well paid, earning in some cases more than $20 per month. The idea that someone would pay nearly $30 to make 18 overheads, on his own, amazed them. I later found out that many of the professors also drove taxis on nights and weekends, since they could make a month's salary in tips in a couple of days.

While you needed a visa in 2001 (and now, under President Trump, you need one again…) to get into Cuba, you may as well leave your Mastercard on your dresser at home. Cubans take plastic, but they cannot accept cards issued by U.S. banks (because of the U.S. law). So Americans have to use currency. This is less of a problem than you'd think, because the currency everyone uses is American dollars. In fact, Cuba is one of the most dollarized economies in the world, and has been for more than a decade. If you try to change dollars for pesos, people look at you like you're crazy, or American. About the only thing pesos will buy, from the "state" stores, is dead flies and old soap powder solidified into bricks.

One thing you can do with your dollars is go out touring. We had a semi-private, but government- approved, tour guide who went with us by taxi to several places around Havana. He was friendly, bright, and very energetic. I'll call him "Trino."

At lunch, I asked Trino about himself. It turns out he had an advanced degree, the closest equivalent one could find to an MBA in Cuba. He wanted to start his own business, and had several plans about how to make it happen. We talked in general terms about what would happen when Castro finally passed on, the inevitable chaos of transition and the uncertainties afterward. I slowly realized that Trino was boiling mad, furious at the system he had to live in. More than anyone else I met, this tour guide made me feel the tragedy of "modern" Cuba.

He had big plans, huge ambitions. But he had to go to Morro Castle, or Hemingway's house, or some other attraction, every day and listen to idiot tourists (like me) ask the same questions. Idiot Tourist: "Do they have those six-toed cats here?"

Poor Trino: "No, no, that was Hemingway's other house, the one in Key West." (KILLMEGOD- KILLMEGOD- KILLME!).

Trino's life was ticking by, and he couldn't make any money, in spite of living in the greatest potential tourist/development profit spot in the world. He knew just what to do, and how to do it. But Castro's secular religion of sacrifice and fake altruism kept Trino in chains.

There was prime real estate, in 2001, and it's still there now, right on the Malecon, where the breeze is cool, the ocean vistas are unsurpassed and the buildings are uninhabitable. Some visitors ask if these buildings were damaged in the revolution. No; they have been damaged by the Revolution, a little at a time, for nearly four decades. Whole blocks are crying concrete tears, which lay in the streets, exuding defective rebar. These crumbling monuments to human stupidity crowded right up to the waterfront, just where the grand mansions full of light and joy and employed people should have been.

I asked our hosts back at the University why these properties weren't being renovated, or just torn down for new development. They earnestly explained that investment in real estate was complicated by the facts that (1) one couldn't obtain loans, because capital is barren and interest is theft, and (2) one can't own property anyway, because it is owned by the state.

I tried to argue that there was a big difference between a complicated situation and a set of rules that elevated control over liberty, privileging conformity over achievement. I didn't get very far, though, so I went back to eating camarones and drinking rum, without getting angry, and knowing I would leave soon. Trino, on the other hand, had to ride by these great gold mines every day. No wonder he was angry—it was tragic. Literally no one is served by the existing system, because in the Cuban system self-interest doesn't count. All you would have to do is take ten 26 year-old entrepreneurs like Trino, open up a financial system for direct foreign investment, and endorse private property. Within three years, each Trino would be making $25,000 a month. Hundreds of people would be employed, each of them also making good money, on the projects that Trino would create out of the ragged nothing that is there now. The world would see a net increase in value, because of focused and directed economic activity, if the damned state would just stop trying to focus and direct all economic activity. The Malecon would be beautiful, even if you turn away from the ocean and look across the street.

One other guy I met is worth mentioning. He is not unique to Cuba; his ilk is found in any police state. He was charming, amusing, and completely untrustworthy, so we liked him immediately. "Evaristo" was selling contraband cigars. The cool part is that he was doing it openly, in (I'm not kidding) the government cigar shop. To be fair, he wasn't actually selling cigars there. He was trying to hook people into walking across the street with him and buying the same cigars at less than half price, avoiding all those nasty taxes and laws and things.

I fear tax dodges and black market transactions, since governments have men with guns. So, I paid $80 for ten cigars in the government shop, and got my receipt for U.S. Customs. Then I followed Evaristo and the other profs half a block (good hiding spot!) to the "private" cigar shop.

There was nothing on the first floor, including light or air (I may have been hyperventilating by this time). Being a coward, I hung back while they went upstairs. After two days, or maybe 20 minutes, my colleagues came down beaming. They had gotten twice as many cigars, at less than half the price.

My tour guide Trino was, in his own mind at least, a failure. But Evaristo the cigar man had found a niche, a way to be successful. These archetypes embody Cuba's tragedy and her hope. On the plus side, the population is smart, reasonably well-educated, and hungry for a better life. They respond to incentives, just like economics predicts.

On the negative side, the incentives of the Cuban system are necrotic. Entrepreneurship (making money by creating value) is sharply discouraged. Police, financial restrictions, explicit laws and informal norms of "equality" all combine to suppress investment.

But rent-seeking, working outside the rules to profit from the arbitrage or theft opportunities created by the rules themselves… now, that is Cuba's national occupation. Evaristo wasn't producing anything. He was just moving goods around and reselling them, his profit margins created not by resource scarcities but by tax differentials. He was making money hand over fist, but creating no value whatsoever.

The thing that you have to understand about Cuba, the thing that

I myself can't really grasp and have so much trouble communicating, is that this mess is not an accident. Neither is it the product of Yankee oppression. Cuba is this way because that's how thinkers of the Revolution designed it. To get some hint of what they were trying to achieve, consider this passage from Che Guevara's "Man and Socialism in Cuba" (1965).

> Society as a whole must become a huge school.... We can see the new man who begins to emerge in this period of the building of socialism. His image is as yet unfinished; in fact it will never be finished, since the process advances parallel the development of new economic forms. Discounting those whose lack of education makes them tend toward the solitary road, towards the satisfaction of their ambitions, there are others who, even within this new picture of over-all advances, tend to march in isolation from the accompanying mass. What is more important is that people become more aware every day of the need to incorporate themselves into society and of their own importance as motors of that society.

Honestly, I admire Guevara. He was an impossibly attractive combination of intellect, physical vigor, and sensitivity to suffering, and looked hot in the beret. But he was dead wrong about the good society. For one thing, there are no "new economic forms." There are command economies, where people are told to do things they don't want to do. The alternative is market economies, where people do what they want to do. It is actually people pursuing "the satisfaction of their ambitions" who are the real motors, the only motors, of a healthy society. Forcing citizens to "incorporate themselves into society" creates tragic figures like Trino, bright ambitious people descending into a living grave.

Fidel Castro died in November, 2016. It's not clear he was actually aware that Donald Trump had won the Presidency of Cuba's enormous neighbor to the north. But Trump's roll-back of the (feeble) reforms implemented by Obama have had little effect. The "Revolution" continues.

Cuba is no longer our enemy. Its armed forces are toothless, and its anti-US rhetoric is tired, repeated out of habit rather than conviction. The current sanctions, imposed unilaterally by the U.S. and widely flouted by other nations, should be ended as soon as possible. The economic benefits to the U.S., and a decent concern for ending the suffering of the Cuban population, demands that travel restrictions, trade restrictions, and limits on foreign investment should all be relaxed. But Cuba is still controversial. When Democratic Presidential candidate Bill de Blasio quoted (apparently unwittingly) Che Guevara in the first 2020 Democratic Debate, there was an explosion of criticism. True, the debate was held in Miami, and whoever wrote that line for de Blasio is pretty out of touch with the politics of Cuba in southern Florida, but it's surprising that a small foreign nation is still such a flash point in American politics.

The Miami debate still matters for Cuban expatriates, living in Florida and yearning to return. Their claims are real, their losses enormous. Until I traveled to Cuba, I thought that the problem was insoluble. How could the Cuban exiles be compensated, or have their property restored?

But my visit changed my mind. Economies are not static, and the amount of value in the world is limited only by human ingenuity. I saw that Cuba's flaw is also its virtue. This beautiful nation is so economically depressed that gains from exchange and growth will dwarf any claims that the returning exiles will make on its resources. The free market, if it is allowed to flourish there, will attract all the brains and talent that flowed out in the decades following the Revolution.

7. Planning Order, Causing Chaos: Transantiago

I sat in the office of the Decano, or Dean, of the School of Government. Out the window, the sun sank into the Andes in a Dr. Seuss palette of pastels. I must have been distracted. Because I thought I heard el Decano say that, according to his survey results, the biggest problem facing the citizens of Santiago was… the bus system.

The bus system? Really? How could the capital of privatization-friendly Chile have botched buses?

The answer, though entertaining to an outsider, is a parable about the combustible combination of optimism and ignorance. Add a spark of "two hours late to work," and you have riots hot enough to match the sunset. Let's go over a bit of history.

Santiago's Private Buses

With more than five million residents, and real economic growth averaging six percent over the last decade, Santiago is a boom town, the economic engine of Chile. Nestled in a broad basin of the Andes, Santiago has the density (21,800 people per square mile) and the wealth (banking center and headquarters to more than one hundred international corporations) to make a mass transit system work.

And work it did. The underground, or Metro, was built in the early 1970s and had high ridership, more than 2.5 million per day. Like many municipal subway systems, it received government subsidies to operate, but, compared to Washington D.C.'s fiscal black hole, "Metrorail," Santiago's was a model of efficiency. (If you are keeping score at home, the D.C. Metro gets annual direct subsidies of more than $175 million and average construction subsidies of nearly $1 billion per year; Santiago's Metro gets about one third that much operating funds, and less in construction, in a metro area twice as large as metro D.C.)

But the real jewel in Santiago's transit crown, or so I would have thought, was the bus system. Hundreds of different bus lines, most of them entirely privately owned, operated freely throughout the city. Some of the lines ran on surface streets parallel to the Metro, adding transport redundancy in case the Metro was having mechanical problems or was simply overcrowded. Competition among bus lines kept fares low, and drivers were paid according to the number of passengers they transported. Other bus routes delivered riders to Metro stops, not because anyone had ordered them to do so, but because that is where passengers wanted to go. And there were several classes of service, ranging from posh express buses that charged high prices down to claptrap jalopies that charged pennies and stopped every few blocks.

There were two problems with the Santiagueño bus system, however—as a survey of newspaper articles in El Mercurio and La Segunda in this period illustrate. Both had to do with greed, or the public perception of it.

Problem one: dangerous incentives. Drivers were paid based on the number of passengers, rather than on time or distance driven. But a moment's thought reveals the problem: Take one bus stop with a crowd of passengers, and then add two buses with a lot of empty seats. The result is a 40-mile-per-hour bus race on streets full of cars and pedestrians. The drivers were taking tickets, making change, watching traffic, and reenacting the chariot race scene from the movie Ben Hur all at the same time. Not surprisingly, there were accidents, and more than a few deaths. The number of motor vehicle accidents had risen from about ten per 100,000 population in 1990 to nearly fifteen by 2005. Further, 700 pedestrians per year, nearly half of all traffic fatalities in Santiago, were killed by cars or buses, a number much higher than in many other cities in Latin America over the same period. Worse, both trends (motor vehicle accidents and accidents resulting in deaths) rose over the period 1990-2005, compared with falling rates in nearly all of Chile's neighbors.

Problem number two was a little hard for me to believe when first I heard it. But even a few moments of research proves that it was true: The private bus system was operated without any public subsidies, or losses. That's right: a major municipal mass transit system was operating in the black! And that's a problem… why?

Well, of course, that's not the way that detractors described things. For a privately owned asset to be operating "without losses" means that the owners were either breaking even (some years) or making actual profits (most years).

For more than a few members of La Concertacion, Chile's center-left ruling government coalition, having companies profit by providing a public service smacked of theft. And so a consensus started to build. Citizens were upset about the rude, aggressive bus drivers. And the "planners" who run city agencies objected (first) to having only routes people seemed to want, and (second) to the injustice of different levels of service. They preferred a comprehensive, "rational" transportation plan, one that treated everyone equally badly, like the DMV in the United States.

The result was the new "Transantiago" public bus system, rolled out on February 10, 2007, during the summer vacation period, when

Santiago seems asleep. Nonetheless, almost overnight, the new "planned" system cut mass transit ridership, increased congestion everywhere in the city, and tripled average commute times from forty minutes to two hours.[53] As President Michelle Bachelet later said in a speech, "It is not common for a president to stand before the nation and say, 'Things haven't gone well…. But that is exactly what I want to say in the case of Transantiago…. The inhabitants of Santiago, especially the poorest, deserve an apology."[54]

The roll-out was not a total disaster, however. The new planned system did solve one of the major problems it had targeted: profits were eliminated overnight. Where the old system had made $60 million a year, the new planned system immediately began to lose, and has continued to lose, more than $600 million per year. Mission accomplished.

Transantiago: Publicly Private Chaos

It's always easy to criticize, with hindsight. But optimism about planning and ignorance about the information provided by markets nearly always imply bad outcomes, and people should be able to see that in advance. Check this list of "reforms," and I think you'll conclude that Transantiago was predictably a choice of planned

---

53 McCarthy, Julie. "In Chile, Commuters Sue City over Transit System" National Public Radio. https://www.npr.org/templates/story/story.php?storyId=15100976?storyId=15100976

54 Walter, Matthew. "Santiago's flawed new bus system takes toll on Chilean economy and president," International Herald Tribune, April 10, 2007. http://www.iht.com/articles/2007/04/10/bloomberg/bxchile-web.php

chaos, rather than orderly market, from the outset.

1. Bus routes that paralleled Metro rail routes were eliminated. Planners ignored the information embedded in those route choices: commuters wanted to travel those routes, and not some other route preferred by the planner.
2. Nearly all the new routes were feeders into, or from, Metro stops. Commuters who had ridden straight from home to work, and back, now had to wait, take one bus to the Metro, wait, board the Metro, wait a third time, and then board another bus to their workplace. Commute times tripled, causing thousands of commuters to drive cars instead. Worst of all, the Metro, which had been near capacity before the reform, was operating at ten to twenty percent above its designed capacity. No money had been allocated for handling this additional load and the maintenance it required. The system barely operated at all at peak rush hour, again leading commuters to use private single-passenger surface transport to avoid being fired from their jobs.
3. The ten companies licensed by the city to operate bought hundreds of huge accordion-hinged "bendy buses" and put them into service on the streets. Each company operated monopoly routes prescribed by the authorities and had no latitude in level of service, frequency of service, or fares. The old competitive system, with many small and nimble buses, was entirely replaced. But the narrow lanes on many roads in the old city and mountain foothills simply could not handle the new behemoths.
4. Drivers were paid hourly, and could be fired if they didn't

keep on schedule. The old system, in which drivers were paid by number of passengers, was proudly scrapped. The new system, rather than 'rewarding greed,' was planned to improve public service. And it should surprise exactly no one that this system was even worse than its predecessor. For one thing, the long hinged buses had four doors. Of course, passengers were supposed to enter at the front door, and to exit through any of the rear three.

But the drivers had no reason to care about the number of paying riders, and it was very time-consuming to go back and throw non-payers off the back of a crowded 30-meter-long bus. So, many drivers would simply drive their routes, operating on something close to the honor system: If you wanted to pay, you got on through the front door, and otherwise you used the rear doors. A dishonor system.

Then, things got even worse. The streets became clogged by increased private traffic, confusing new routes, and huge buses on tight corners that looked big only on planners' maps. The on-time performance of drivers deteriorated. And the drivers recognized that they didn't need to stop at all. Some drivers, by no means all but a disturbingly large number, would simply pass large groups of passengers, some of whom had been waiting for an hour or more.

Any Idiot Can Criticize; What Would Work?

As I noted above, with hindsight anyone can criticize. The question is what should have been done, instead? There were problems, real problems, with the old system. I will take up the "problem" of profits in the next section. But it is true that under the old private system, the buses were poorly maintained and spewed pollution. Drivers raced each other for passengers, sometimes injuring pedestrians or occupants of cars as they "overfished" what was, in effect, a commons of possible passengers and stops. Although Chile had fewer traffic accidents than most Latin American nations, it had a rate of pedestrian injuries and deaths as high as Brazil's or Mexico's, well-known pedestrian death traps. And it's true that the streets were congested.

A remarkable book, *Curb Rights*, by George Mason University Economics Professor Dan Klein and two coauthors (Adrian Moore at Reason and Binyam Reja at the World Bank; hereafter KMR, 1997), analyzes the problem of urban transit more deeply than any other source I have seen. KMR point out that there are two key problems with many private bus services, especially in areas where property rights may not be defined or defensible. The first is the problem of congregation, or coordinating on a stop location where a sufficient number of passengers are conveniently massed. The second problem is timing since no one makes money from a passenger waiting for a bus.

Now, monopoly public bus service "solves" the first problem by having well-defined bus stops, with (in some cases) attractive well-lit shelters. The road can be modified to make a pull-off lane for the bus, in some locations. Public bus systems solve the second problem by having schedules.

KMR point out that there is nothing particularly "public" about either of these solutions. In fact, most public bus systems rely on government enforcement of their monopoly property right, so that no private buses can pick up or drop off passengers at public bus stops. But this would work just as well for private buses, provided government simply enforces private rights to exclusive local pick-up areas. All that is needed for competition is enforceable "curb rights:" If a bus company builds a bus stop and pays for a pull-off lane, then no other bus company can steal the passengers congregating there. Different bus companies, different bus stops, and a "no poaching" enforced by government.

There are other, obvious institutional features of well-functioning private markets in the urban transit setting, and they would flourish if government regulation allowed them to. Bus companies might have two-tiered pricing systems to ensure a reliable supply of customers throughout the city. An ad hoc rider, one who simply catches a ride from one point to another without a consistent pattern (someone going across town to shop for an electronic part, perhaps) might pay a high fare. But "monthly pass" cards give riders a sharply discounted average fare if they pay up front for a whole month. Once a rider purchases a monthly pass, he can ride as many times as he wants for no extra charge on that bus line, whereas he would have to pay on any other line. Monthly pass holders thus form a reliable, constant base of customers that cannot easily be "overfished" by another company. Routes could be run, with high ridership, from the same neighborhoods to the same workplaces on a predictable schedule.

Finally, one cannot emphasize enough the advantages of allowing competition over routes and level of service. The argument that bad service is "fair" because literally everyone suffers places the value of equality over every other public goal, no matter how desirable. In a large, diverse urban area, some people want higher-speed express service, with amenities and perhaps an attendant. Others want rock-bottom prices and are willing to accept more inconvenience and less service. Charging everyone the same price and providing only one state-mandated level of service ensures that nearly everyone actually wants something else, but can't get it.

The Hydra-Headed Beast

Here is the real problem with the "greed is always bad, public provision is always good," perspective. As James Buchanan pointed out in "Politics Without Romance" (1979) it makes no sense to assume that, under some circumstances (private buses), people are greedy, and under others (government buses), people are benevolent. The fact is that in both cases people behave purposively, pursuing their own goals filtered through the incentives and costs the system presents to them. Yet, the idea persists that removing profits and using government planning results in a kind of moral transubstantiation. Many planners think that profits are evil and would prefer a system that eliminates profits, even if it means accepting substantial losses and no improvement in service.

No matter how many times this notion is killed off by experience and evidence, the hydra of planning grows another head, and political leaders trumpet the new reform in public service. Then, when the reform fails, commissions are formed, implementation is blamed, and budgets are raised.

The Transantiago bus reforms took an imperfect private system, operating without public subsidy and serving well over a million people a day, and "publicized" it. The expectation, almost pathetically naïve in retrospective, was that outlawing profits and demotivating drivers would change human nature. Worse, planners believed that they could dictate choices to commuters, who turned back to private automobiles instead. Why don't they ever learn?

8. We Should DO Something!

Shamans of old knew they could bend the credulous to their will (and make a boatload of money) if the shaman could predict something like a storm, or an eclipse. "This very evening, the Night Wolf will devour the Moon Virgin! But if you pay me many coins of silver, I will force Night Wolf to cough the Moon Virgin back up, unharmed!" Humorist and author P.J. O'Rourke used a version of that story 20 years ago, in All the Trouble in the World, to describe fundraising letters from Greenpeace to help solve global warming. But everyone does it now: just substitute global warming, or terrorism, as the problem, and propose a magical solution so that people will give you their money (or their vote).

Parsing this as if it were logical, the argument goes like this:

1. X is a problem.
2. We should do something
3. Z is something.
4. Therefore, we should do Z.
5. If Z does not solve X, it must mean we didn't do enough Z, and we need to do more.
6. If you disagree that we should do more Z, you actually favor X, or else you hate the people suffering from X.

Imagine you have a six-year-old daughter and that she has 'nervous fever,' today known as typhoid. It's 1755, and we don't yet understand germs or fevers very well. Still, you love your daughter, and you can't just sit around. You call the doctor.

Now, if the doctor were honest, he would say, "We don't know much about fevers. It's better if we just try to make her comfortable, cool her head with compresses, and let this run its course." But if he said that, he would be soon be an ex-doctor. You are scared, so you want him to do something.

That something in 1755 was a combination of bleeding and a glyster. A glyster involved the introduction of that new wonder drug, tobacco smoke, into the lower bowel because the medicos thought the chemicals in the smoke would be absorbed faster that way, alleviating the pain more quickly. Yes, that means exactly what you think it means: The doctor filled a bellows with dense tobacco smoke, and then inserted the bellow into the patient's…well, you know. Some of our modern medicos and drug companies do this metaphorically, but in 1755 they just straight up did it, literally.

Then the doctor–the one you hired because he promised to do something–takes out a lancet, and makes a small incision in your daughter's wrist. The theory was that the fever was in the blood itself, and bleeding was the only treatment doctors knew, other than the tobacco smoke thing.

Of course, your daughter doesn't get better; she gets worse. Your daughter's fever is still very high, so the earnest quack takes another half-pint of blood. And another.

Then she dies. And then you blame the doctor, and he blames himself. For not having bled her enough.

What does this story have to do with shamans, fundraising, and contemporary problems? In all of these cases, someone promises to do something to solve a (seemingly) pressing problem. Just read an article by Paul Krugman. It doesn't matter which one; every op-ed Dr. Krugman has ever written follows exactly the same formula.

Unemployment is a problem. We should do something. Stimulus spending (or a fake alien invasion) is something. We should try massive amounts of stimulus spending. If we try it, and it doesn't work, we didn't do enough. And if you object that "stimulus spending" is dumb, and that the multiplier theory[55] is little better than a theory of fevers based on bleeding out poisonous "humors", then you just hate unemployed people! (I have gotten that reaction, verbatim, from people at dinner parties.)

And that's hardly the only example. Poverty is a problem in Africa. We should do something. Foreign assistance, based on huge construction projects, is something. We should build dams and roads. When it doesn't work, it's because we didn't spend enough. What if you object, as New York University economist Bill Easterly (2001) has done repeatedly, that this solution makes things worse by destroying local business and creating a dependency on aid? You are told that you just hate poor people in Africa.

An interesting recent example is the "reform" of restaurant menus. The problem is obesity (we are told it's an "epidemic," though it is not communicable!). We should do something. Requiring expensive reprinting of all menus and food listings to require calorie counts is something. But it turns out that these expensive and cumbersome labeling requirements had no measurable effect.

In other words, we haven't really come so far since the 18th century. We have about the same level of understanding of macroeconomic policy problems now that doctors had about fevers then.

---

55 Shostak, Frank. "Is the Keynesian Multiplier a Real Thing?" *Mises Daily Articles*. Mises Institute. May 12, 2015. https://mises.org/library/keynesian-multiplier-real-thing

The best we can hope for is that the 'treatment' will fail to kill the patient outright. Given our lack of understanding, the best thing to do is often nothing—other than try to make the symptoms a little less painful.

But then what is the solution? Don't focus so much on the fact that the proposed solution won't work. Instead, grant the premise: "Yes, X (poverty, unemployment, poor education) is a problem, you are right. We agree about that. But I think that your solution will do more harm than good. If you really want to solve Problem X, research has shown that we should [Y]."

Of course, that means you'll need to have researched the problem yourself. You'll need examples of how increased liberty, access to markets, and respect for the autonomy and dignity of human beings can actually work.

The point is that you have to avoid getting stuck debating their policy solutions. Instead, you'll need to provide solutions of your own, emphasizing the efficacy of free markets and liberty in eradicating social ills. In my next blog post, I'll try to give some examples. But in the meantime, the thing to remember is this: Stop attacking the dumb solution. Grant the premise that X is a problem. And then change the subject to your solution. You'll actually persuade a lot more people with that approach.

9. The First Rule of Wing-Walking

Wing-walking was the practice of getting out of the cockpit of a biplane (while someone else was flying the thing) and staggering along the wing holding onto struts or wires. It was a thrill show for onlookers at air shows and barnstorming events in the 1920s and 1930s in the U.S.

But for the wing-walker him (and often her) self, the experience was terrifying. It was tempting just to freeze up and hold on. If you were going to move, you had to be careful to make sure you were holding something substantial enough to take your weight in the face of wind blowing nearly 100 miles per hour. The "first rule" of wing-walking, according to observers, went something like this: "Don't let go of what you've got until you get hold of something better."

Earlier, I claimed that there is a bias in public policy debates toward doing *something*, rather than nothing, even if doing nothing might be the right thing to do. But I also promised in a future post—this one!—to say more on the matter. The gist of my earlier post is that people in the liberty movement often lose arguments by simply denying that there is a problem, or by claiming—which amounts to the same thing—that the proposed solution won't work, and therefore "we" should do nothing. Since libertarians often want the state to do nothing (though the "Right Kind of Nothing,"[56] to

56 Munger, Michael C. "The Right Kind of Nothing." *The Chronicle of Higher Education*. January 7, 2010. https://www.chronicle.com/article/The-Right-Kind-of-Nothing/63344/

be sure!), this seems facile.

We can do better, I think, by agreeing with the premise that there is a problem. Often, a small restatement of the problem helps. If someone is upset about inequality, I always wonder what they are really worried about. So, I ask some questions.

> *Isn't the real problem not inequality, but poverty?*
>
> *Rather than taking envy, which is a sin, and trying to raise it to the status of a virtue by calling it social justice, why don't we try to help poor people?*
>
> *Furthermore, if the poor in the U.S. have it so rough, why do genuinely poor people from the rest of the world want so desperately to come to the U.S. and be poor here instead of being poor where they are?*

As you can imagine, hilarity ensues. Still, I actually agree that poverty is a problem. The best cure for poverty is a job, however. If I can get my conversational partner to agree on that, we have a place to start.

The most difficult thing (and I may step on some toes here, so let me apologize in advance) for proponents of libertarian ideas is the propensity to dismiss all candidates for office, on the grounds that they want to run for office. Just the fact that a person is a candidate must mean that the person is evil, or power-hungry, or perhaps just naive.

I understand the sentiment, believe me. When I was running for Governor of North Carolina in 2008, I often found "supporters" who were extremely critical of the fact that I was running, or that I had adopted platforms that might tend to attract votes. The most contentious element of my platform was education vouchers, which I saw as a means of reducing state involvement in education. Right now, the state uses taxes to finance education, and then generally takes those taxes and in addition imposes monopoly state provision of education through public schools. Rather than change everything at once, we could at least break the monopoly on provision, and allow parents to make choices with what is, after all, their own money.

But this was outrageous, in the view of many of my supporters. The fact that the state was involved at all meant that the policy was unacceptable. Yet many voters, persuadable voters who might vote for me, found the proposal intriguing enough to contact me for more information. They recognized enough of the proposal (state funding) to be willing to consider letting go of something (monopoly statc provision). Wing-walkers don't want to let go all at once.

Our experience with the state makes us, perhaps surprisingly, even less willing to let go of things the state promises, because we have been told so many half-truths and outright fibs. But the result is that we fail to accomplish minor improvements that should be within our abilities. People in democracies have, it is fair to say, ambiguous attitudes toward their leaders. An old English tradition is that the reason the faces of leaders were put on postage stamps is that this allows citizens to thumb leaders' noses whilst they lick their hinder parts. The Roman statesman Cicero decried the indignities he saw in elections, saying:

> A most wretched custom, assuredly, is our electioneering and scrambling for office. Concerning this also we find a fine

> thought in Plato: "Those who compete against one another," he says, "to see which of two candidates shall administer the government, are like sailors quarrelling as to which one of them shall do the steering." And he likewise lays down the rule that we should regard only those as adversaries who take up arms against the state, not those who strive to have the government administered according to their convictions. (Section XXV)

There's quite a bit in that one little passage. For one thing, it's heartening in a way that people were disgusted by the behavior of politicians in 44 B.C.E. But maybe that's actually sad, because we are still beset by the same basic problems today. Sailors quarreling over who shall steer assumes that there is a ship, and that it can be steered. You might want to question those claims, but the fact remains that some sailors, and some directions, are better than others given our current system. Abdication to avoid complicity is simply shirking; you can't let go until you actually can grab something better. Wingwalkers can't be too picky.

There is also the definition of "adversaries." I see so many people who consider themselves libertarians spending all their time fighting with other libertarians. To any outsider, the differences over which we fight seem not just inconsequential, but invisible. Yet to "us" these tiny points of doctrine become the very fulcrum of the faith. The problem is that if we spend all our time burning heretics, there won't be many of us left to take on the infidels, the people we actually disagree with.

People are scared. Voters are looking for a new alternative, but whenever we offer them the libertarian alternative they invoke, whether they know it or not, the first rule of wing-walking. They are reluctant to let go of the "solutions" they are used to, of detaching themselves from the hoary terms of debate in which they are used to thinking. When we say that those solutions don't work, that doesn't offer an alternative that they can imagine, even if we are right. No one is going to let go of the familiar policy debates without something solid to grab onto instead.

In times when people are afraid of terrorism, of losing their jobs, and of the kind of life their children will inherit, we need to offer an actual alternative. We've been telling people, "Just let go! You won't fall!" That isn't working very well.

VII

PROBLEMS WITH EXPERTISE AND VOTING IN DEMOCRACY

One of the foundational claims of this book was advanced back in Chapter I: every flaw in consumers is worse in voters. It's perfectly true that consumers may be misled, may want things that are bad for them, and are over-concerned with "free" things, as my Duke colleague Dan Ariely argued in his 2010 book, *Predictably Irrational*.

But so are voters. For one thing, they are the same people. I'm not speaking metaphorically; in a democracy, consumers and voters are the same people. Perhaps more importantly, the incentives in politics are perverse: voters have limited reasons to acquire accurate information, and they may vote for alternatives that make them feel good instead of what they would choose if they were informed and decisive.

By "decisive" I mean, "actually in charge." As one of millions of voters, I know my single vote is unlikely to affect the outcome.

I have preferences over the outcome, mind you. But I also have a preference, possibly a separate and less informed preference, over the vote I cast. If I could actually select the outcome, I would likely research the alternatives, the way private citizens do when they are buying a car or a television. In private settings, the choice I make is the alternative I get, and have to live with.

But in elections, I can vote for the alternative that makes me feel good, without having to worry that my protest or my joke will influence anything. Many Britons likely voted for Brexit thinking they were poking a thumb in the eye of the stodgy establishment. Many Americans likely voted for the 18th Amendment, prohibiting the sale or possession of alcohol, so they could feel good about themselves on Sunday morning. But so many people wanted to feel good about poking David Cameron, or showing their religious virtue, that the aggregate outcome was changed. Voters, too, are predictably irrational.

One possibility would be to take choices out of the hands of citizens and give them to experts. But this is at best an accountable technocracy, and would likely devolve into fascism in short order. Better to accept the flaws of both markets and democracy, and try to evaluate each fairly, identifying the settings where one or the other is likely to perform better.

1. Arthur Pigou Warned of the Failures of Government

Many market advocates, especially public choice scholars, are scornful of Arthur C. Pigou, Cambridge economist. I think the reason is that Ronald Coase, not entirely unfairly, used Pigou as his foil in criticizing the idea that problems with externalities could only be solved by the state.

But as is often the case, the original text is much more nuanced than the work of the followers. Marx, for example, is interesting and worth reading; many self-styled Marxists are not. I have found the same to be true of Pigou. In fact, I'd say that Arthur Pigou founded public choice.

The reason is that Pigou, to his credit, recognized that the concepts of "market failure" and "externality" actually require an investigation of the specific institutions of state intervention. He may have been too optimistic about the prospects for improving state action, but he had no illusions about the problem states faced in acting correctly.

Coase's critique of Pigou is rather strident. In "The Problem of Social Cost" (1960), Coase says that Pigou "deals with divergences between social and private net products which come about because [quoting Pigou] 'one person A, in the course of rendering some service, for which payment is made, to a second person B, incidentally also renders services or disservices to other persons (not producers of like services), of such a sort that payment cannot be exacted from the benefited parties or compensation enforced on behalf of the injured parties.'"

Pigou tells us that his aim in Part II of The Economics of Welfare is

> to ascertain how far the free play of self-interest, acting under the existing legal system, tends to distribute the country's resources in the way most favorable to the production of a large national dividend, and how far it is feasible for State action to improve upon 'natural' tendencies.

To judge from the first part of this statement, Pigou's purpose is to discover whether any improvements could be made in the existing arrangements that determine the use of resources. Pigou concludes:

> But even in the most advanced States there are failures and imperfections [...] There are many obstacles that prevent a community's resources from being distributed [...] in the most efficient way. The study of these constitutes our present problem.... Its purpose is essentially practical. It seeks to bring into clearer light some of the ways in which it now is, or eventually may become, feasible for governments to control the play of economic forces in such wise as to promote the economic welfare, and through that, the total welfare, of their citizens as a whole.

Coase (1960) responds: "Pigou's underlying thought would appear to be: Some have argued that no State action is needed. But the system has performed as well as it has because of State action. Nonetheless, there are still imperfections. What additional State action is required?"

Coase is right, of course. Pigou really did say those things. But he also was careful to note that what later came to be known as the market-failure paradigm should be applied with care. Usually, the logic of Pigouvians goes like this: markets fail (by externalities, asymmetric information, etc.), so the state should act. Of course, that would only be a complete prescription if one is reasonably certain that the actual actions of the state are likely to be an improvement over the actual results obtained from the market.

The main thrust of the public choice movement was to correct this naïve optimism about the state. There are two main types of problems identified in the work of James Buchanan, Gordon Tullock, and the other scholars who developed the public choice critique starting in the 1960s.

The first is information: It may be true that prices do not reflect the full opportunity cost, or "social cost," of resources. But without prices the state is just as blind! The government has an information problem no less profound than market systems'. Knowing the correct level of Pigouvian tax, in the absence of prices, is not just difficult; it's impossible. The dispersed knowledge of value is possessed by no single individual, and no bureaucratic technique can fully solve that problem. The information problem is not solvable by imagining that the state is an omniscient dictator.

The second problem is incentives: there is no reason to expect that those in power are motivated solely, or perhaps even primarily, by the public good. The bureaucrats making guesses about corrective taxation may have their own conception of the public good, of course. Or they may be motivated by some other basis. But the human beings who make up the state are motivated by their own goals; the places where they work are called "agencies," after all.

The principal-agent problem is profound, and not solvable by imagining that the state is a benevolent dictator.

In short, the public choice critique argues that the Pigouvian model, by assuming that the state is an omniscient, benevolent dictator, assumes away all the problems of social choice, information, and incentives that confound actual policy. This is a valid critique of Pigouvians, I believe. Is it an accurate critique of Pigou himself?

It is not. A fair reading of Pigou reveals that he is actually one of the founders of the public choice critique. He should get credit for that. In his 1912 book, Wealth and Welfare, Pigou said:

> It is not sufficient to contrast the imperfect adjustments of unfettered private enterprise with the best adjustments that economists in their studies can imagine. For we cannot expect that any State authority will attain, or even whole-heartedly seek, that ideal. Such authorities are liable alike to ignorance, to sectional pressure, and to personal corruption by private interest. A loud-voiced part of their constituents, if organized for votes, may easily outweigh the whole.

I sometimes give that quote, without the reference, and ask people to identify the source. The most common responses are Hayek or Buchanan. But no, it was Pigou. Notice that he gets both information and incentive problems right here. The state doesn't know what to do, and if it did it might not want to do it. That, in a nutshell, is the origin of public choice.

Later, in "State Action and Laissez-Faire" (1935), Pigou again sounded a note of caution:

> In order to decide whether or not State action is practically desirable, it is not enough to know that a form and degree of it can be conceived, which, if carried through effectively, would benefit the community. We have further to inquire how far, in the particular country in which we are interested and the particular time that concerns us, the government is qualified to select the right form and degree of State action and to carry it through effectively....
>
> High-sounding generalisations on these matters are irrelevant fireworks. They may have a place in political perorations, but they have none in real life. Accumulation of evidence, the balancing of probabilities, judgment of men, by these alone practical problems in this region can be successfully attacked.

I should note that this argument — that Pigou was not really a Pigouvian, and might even be seen as a precursor of public choice — is made in much greater detail by Steve Medema (2014)

My point is just that it strengthens the public choice argument to argue that Pigou himself recognized the problem and admonished followers to pay attention to information and incentives. Naïve followers of statist remedies often forget that part, and being able to cite one of their own in this regard is important.

2. Brexit Illustrates Why Voting Is One of the Worst Ways to Make Decisions

Nearly 25 years ago, two scholars—Geoffrey Brennan and Loren Lomasky—published a book that was proved prescient by the recent "Brexit" vote. The book was called *Democracy and Decision*, and one of its central theses was that "democracy" (if you mean majority rule decisions) is simply not up to the task of making good choices for large groups of citizens.

Now, to be clear, I'm not trying to say that Brexit itself was a bad decision. My point is about majority rule and voting. In this post, I'm going to argue that voting was not the best way to represent the will of the people when the Brexit decision was being made.

Let's dig a bit further into Brennan and Lomasky's argument to illustrate what I mean.

Two Conflicting Sets of Preferences

Brennan and Lomasky argued that the key failure of democracy is that the means of choosing (asking people to register an individual preference, even though each person knows his or her single vote won't affect the outcome) is inconsistent with the ends of choosing (selecting the best outcome for the group or nation).

Citizens of any society, after all, have two sets of preferences:

- The preferences they feel, and act on in private.
- The preferences they feel they should have, and act on in public.

For example, an individual might sometimes drink too much, though he thinks it is morally wrong to get drunk. Or someone might support speed limit laws in theory. That, however, does not stop her from occasionally breaking those laws.

Both sets of preferences are "real." Both have the end goal of making individuals as happy and satisfied as possible.

So why does what we want as individuals often seem to clash with the public good? Why do our feelings and our conscience sometimes fail to match up?

It's not because our preferences are constantly changing or irrational. It's because there's a tension between our primitive instincts and our sense of morality.

Decisions on moralistic policies affect not just the citizen himself, but others as well. Thus, citizens may act paternalistically in decrying behavior in others in which they themselves engage. For our purposes, this means that, though our one citizen may think he can withstand the temptations of alcohol on his own (though he might have a nip on weekends), his "weaker brethren" need more help from the laws and authorities.

Free-Riding on the Responsibility of Others to Make a Statement

The conflict between the two types of preference is particularly severe when political decisions are being made, because citizens (rationally) do not perceive that their own statements have any real influence on the collective outcome.

The probability of any one person's vote, or opinion, determining the outcome weakens as the number of decision-makers grows large, each individual simply accepts the outcome as given and decides what preference they should project to others in their church, community, or other group.

In the case of Brexit, take "Adam from Manchester," who told BBC:

> I'm shocked that we actually have voted to leave. I didn't think that was going to happen. My vote, I didn't think was going to matter too much because I thought we were just going to remain.[57]

To understand how this works, all you need to do is separate the "what I can actually do," and "what I hope actually happens," parts of the public decision.

For many people, such as "Adam from Manchester," there were just two different things that they wanted.

- The first was to be able to put a thumb in the eye of smug blaggers like David Cameron, and vote "Leave." That's the political equivalent of teenage boys toilet-papering a neighbor's tree after he yelled at them to "Get off my lawn, you damned kids!"
- The second was to have everyone wake up the next day and say, "Gosh, there's a lot of anger out there! We'd better listen. Fortunately, Brexit did fail, and so all the problems that come with Brexit are avoided."

---

57 Vesey, Byrne, Joe. "Leave voter regrets voting Leave when he realises it means we're now Leaving." *Indy100.* June 24, 2016. https://www.indy100.com/article/leave-voter-regrets-voting-leave-when-he-realises-it-means-were-now-leaving--Z1btq_FnVW

Send a message, but free ride on the fact that others will behave responsibly. That's what each person wanted.

But as Brennan and Lomasky pointed out, there's a collective problem. If everyone, or even just most people, act that way, the result is that the whole country gets toilet-papered. If everyone indulges their private preference for a protest vote, the bad outcome actually wins.

The result is that people cast votes in ways that do not add up to "the will of the people." Instead, the result can easily be the opposite of what the majority wants, even though that's how the majority voted, one petulant free-rider at a time.

Brexit is just an example. It will happen again, and again, if we rely on mass voting to make choices for all, rather than encouraging the liberty of each to choose for him or herself.

It's a government failure of the first order, and we should be wary of it.

3. The Thing Itself

There ought to be a law!" You've heard it, and you may have thought it. In the United States, we increasingly turn to the power of the state and legislation to rid the world of injustice, nuisance or inconvenience. Alas, we often have no clue whether the proposed law or rule will do what we intend. And then there's enforcement. Once we divide legal from illegal, we have to defend that line as if it had moral meaning, even if it's just an arbitrary line drawn through a political compromise. Putting power in the hands of the state is always a delicate matter.

Down the Down Escalator

Sometimes I wonder what the "state" is. There is this guy, George Bush, who in many ways runs the state, but my statist friends hate him. The state must be something else. It could be Louis XIV, of course, because he said as much: "l'Etat, c'est moi!" But my friends don't really think Louis XIV was the ideal form of government. What is the answer? What is the state?

I am proud to say that I have found the state: It is Cherrail Curry-Hagler, of the DC Transit Police. The story comes from the *Washington Post* (July 30, 2004).[58] The facts, (remarkably) are not in dispute.

---

58 Layton, Lyndsey. "Metro Questions Arrest of Snacker Eating Ban Backed; Strict Policing Not." *Washington Post*. July 31, 2004. http://www.washingtonpost.com/wp-dyn/articles/A28601-2004Jul30.html

About 6:30 p.m. July 16, 2004 Stephanie Willett, EPA scientist, age 45, was riding the escalator down from 11th Street NW to the subway station, and eating a "PayDay" candy bar. Cherrail Curry-Hagler, D.C. transit police woman, was riding up on the other escalator. Officer Curry-Hagler warned Willett to finish the candy before entering the station.

Willett nodded. But she kept chewing the PayDay as she walked through the fare gates. Curry-Hagler, who had turned around and followed Willett, warned her again as she stuffed the last bit into her mouth before throwing the wrapper into the trash can near the station manager's kiosk, according to both Willett and the officer.

Curry-Hagler ordered Willett to stop and show ID. Willett refused, and retorted, "Why don't you go and take care of some real crime?" Admittedly, this may be seen as rude, since her mouth was still half full of the PayDay bar. The scientist rode a second escalator down to catch her Orange Line train.

At this point, according to Willett, the officer grabbed her and searched her, running her hands under Willett's bra and around her waist. She put Willett into the back seat of a police car, took her to the 1st District station, and locked her in a cell. At 9:30 p.m., after she paid a $10 fee, Willett was released to her husband.

Got it? Okay, now consider:

1. Ms. Willett was on a DOWN ESCALATOR. She couldn't turn around.
2. She was already chewing the candy bar. She couldn't spit it out, without littering. I'm a libertarian extremist, but even I think you should be given a ticket if you spit chewed-up food on a public escalator.

3. When Willett got to the bottom of the escalator, she put the last bit into her mouth, threw the wrapper into the trash can, and continued on toward her train.

There is no way that Ms. Willett could have obeyed the instruction not to eat in the station, unless she had run back up the escalator, or spit out the candy bar. The difficult part, for the "let's have the state be our nanny," tribe, is this: Given the laws on the books, Ms. Willett had committed a crime. You can't take food into a station, and you can't eat in the station. It's the law. The officer had not, in fact, abused the system; Ms. Curry-Hagler, and all the other Transit Police in DC, are supposed to keep their gimlet eyes peeled for offenses exactly like these.

You think that's wrong? Fine. But don't blame Cherrail Curry-Hagler, D.C. Transit cop. She was simply doing her job. So is the TSA employee who makes my kid take off his shoes at the airport and who makes me show my boarding pass four times. So is the cop who gives me a speeding ticket for going 38 in a 35 mph zone.

Is there an alternative to these zealous examples of pettiness? Sure. We could give discretion to bureaucrats and the police. And that is a ticket on the train to tyranny, folks. Discretion allows the representative of the state to indulge racism, or sadism, or blankism. That won't fly (and it shouldn't!) in a democracy. So we are stuck with legislation that must be foolishly blunt and mindlessly enforced. It is the nature of law, not a perversion of it.

The Thing Itself

Edmund Burke (1982) had it right when he said, "In vain you tell me that Artificial Government is good, but that I fall out only with the Abuse. The Thing! the Thing itself is the Abuse!" Ludwig von Mises (1944) said it less elegantly, but with a profound analytical understanding:

> Bureaucratic management is management bound to comply with detailed rules and regulations fixed by the authority of a superior body. The task of the bureaucrat is to perform what these rules and regulations order him to do. His discretion to act according to his own best conviction is seriously restricted by them....
>
> It is not the merit of a collector of internal revenue that the residents of his district are richer and pay higher taxes than those of another district. The time and effort required for the administrative handling of an income tax return are not in proportion to the amount of the taxable income it concerns.... This makes it indispensable to operate public offices according to principles entirely different from those applied under the profit motive.... Remember: we do not say that a successful handling of public affairs has no value, but that it has no price on the market.... Bureaucratic management is management of affairs which cannot be checked by economic calculation. (pp. 48-50)

We are always tempted to reform government agencies, to fiddle with organization charts, creating new units and scrapping old ones. We hear the sirens' song: We could do good, things could be better. We simply need good government, good people, and sensible rules. Sure, we have problems now, but things could be good. The rules should be strong, yet flexible. Gravity should be reduced, and friction outlawed completely. (I never liked it, and I think a majority of people agree with me.)

Okay, the last two may seem silly, but they are no less likely than flexible rules or governments motivated by your peculiar and equally flexible conception of the good. If, as von Mises claimed, bureaucracy is the sine qua non of the territorially extensive state, then decrying bureaucracy's rigidity is wrong-headed. We can't make government more efficient, or more like business, because it insulates officials from such pressures by design.

The thing itself, the fundamental reliance ON the state, is at the core of the difficulties we have WITH the state. Attempts to reform through reorganization will generally prove disastrous. Bureaucracy can not be improved, because its very nature is incompatible with a society of free citizens who take responsibility for their own lives and their own choices. The incentives and hierarchies in the two forms are fundamentally different.

To put it most starkly, citizens may say, and believe, that the problem is unresponsive bureaucracy, or corruption, but these are the essential features of the governments of large nations. The solution is a citizenry that understands the economic and political forces that make government inherently incapable of carrying out the tasks we want to assign to it. But the mainstream media, nearly entirely innocent of knowledge of basic economic principles, has no hope of aiding such an understanding, and more often than not contribute to the "we can do better" mindset by carrying sensational stories of corruption inevitably followed by demands for reform.

What about the educational system? As William Niskanen (1971; pp. 7-8) pointed out, von Mises concluded his discussion "with the hope, almost pathetic in retrospect, that a broader education in economics will reduce the popular support for large government and the consequent pervasive bureaucracy." Not much hope lies in that direction, either.

The truth is that education in economics—as opposed to trade studies in business or marketing, or the applied mathematics taught as "economics" in universities—is nearly nonexistent. So, citizens have a correct but inchoate intuition that something is wrong. Since they have no way of perceiving the real problem of unrealistic expectations, we reform endlessly. We spend huge resources appointing task forces and study groups, and trying to get the right people in government to write the right legislation.

The U.S. has criminalized so much behavior, from eating a candy bar in a Metro station to mild drug use to consensual sexual practices, that our prisons are full of people innocent of any real crime. The only reason that I even heard about Ms. Willett is that she was middle class and an employed professional. In poor areas all over the U.S., police harass and beat nameless citizens while trying to enforce unenforceable laws. Those cops, and those bureaucrats try to enforce the tax laws and regulations on transactions and safety standards and a thousand other things. They may or may not be good people, but their failure to do good is a direct consequence of the contradictory, and in fact impossible, job they have been given: enforce injustice.

I expect that Ms. Curry-Hagler took her tin Transit Cop badge, and herself, a little too seriously in handcuffing Ms. Willett. But the personality, the goodness (or not) of the people enforcing the law, is beside the point. We don't fall out only with the abuse. It's the state, the state itself, and its logically inherent mechanisms of control and oppression, that is a hydra-headed monster of legal restrictions on liberty. The thing itself is the abuse.

Alternatives to the Thing Itself

My claim in this piece is that social problems are often made worse by legislative solutions. Such coercive solutions are inherently inflexible or tyrannical. We would be better off relying on a mix of tolerance, common sense and private morality to deal with the fact that the world isn't quite the way we'd like it to be.

At the Munger house, for example, we snack high on the food chain. I don't know if God gave man dominion over the beasts of the field, but She certainly gave me an ATM card and big metal cart for cruising meats at Piggly Wiggly. That beats dominion.

A lot of the beasts of the field, and the forest, and the oceans, and the air…. they land on my stove, and then my plate, sacrifices to my enjoyment. I have a lot of friends who are vegetarians, and they have my greatest respect. They are (mostly) healthier than I am. Further, they are principled: they make a choice, and they stick to it, and they don't berate me when I get a 120 ounce Porterhouse. I likewise try to cater to vegetarian tastes, and make sure I only suggest restaurants with good vegetarian alternatives. At my house I serve vegetarian dishes to guests, without even asking.

This is how most big problems should be handled, locally and without resort to coercive force. We can try to persuade each, but sometimes, we should accept the fact that reasonable people can differ. That's why there is no attractive solution to the abortion debate. Our insistence on trying to solve the problem with a system of law is not just logically doomed, but it is tearing communities apart. Personally, I think abortion is morally wrong, as well as imposing a psychological blot that the woman can never wash away.

I also think that that is my opinion, and I should keep it to myself. If you ask me, I'll tell you: Abortion is evil and harmful; don't do it. But if you don't ask, you'll never hear a peep. And I certainly wouldn't use the coercive powers of the state to force you or your partner to bear a child that isn't wanted.

Rather than try and reform the inescapably blunt and often disastrously implemented power of the state, a civilization has to realize that there are two other ways to solve the problem of actions we don't like. The first is simple forbearance—putting up with disagreement and other points of view is the price of living in a society. The other is recognizing that the reliance on the state as the enforcer of morals and norms displaces real morals and real norms.

Instead of teaching our children to be moral, and to care about social opprobrium, parents and schools abdicate their roles as shapers of minds and rely on the state to punish misbehavior after the fact. Children naturally conclude that if there is no punishment from the state, there must have been no misbehavior. But the state cannot fulfill this function, for reasons of simple competence and resource constraint. And the state would fail to carry out the function correctly, even if it were competent, because power corrupts and breeds malevolence. The abuse and the thing are the same. The conviction that we can harness Leviathan is the most dangerous conceit of our age.

4. Every Flaw in Consumers Is Worse in Voters

I have been making a mistake for most of my life. See, I'm an economist, and one of the things that attracted me to economics is the notion of the "ideal economy."

Of course, there are valid objections to the use of markets. There are people who cheat and commit fraud, and there are problems with information and market power and externalities. Sometimes consumers make mistakes. In fact, some of those mistakes, as my friend and Duke colleague Dan Ariely is fond of telling me, raise questions about the very nature of our "model" of consumption.

In his book *Predictably Irrational*, Dan makes two main points. First, consumers are not "rational," at least not in the sense economists assume. Consumers have trouble choosing among several alternatives; new product prices are arbitrary; and people are seduced by "free" stuff. Second, sellers and marketers know that consumers are predictably irrational, and they take advantage of that weakness by advertising, packaging, and carefully framed comparisons.

So what's the mistake I've been making for most of my life? I've been trying to defend the perfection of markets. I've been sucked in to the notion that markets are "ideal": "Markets aren't so bad!" "Consumers are generally better off!" and so on. Friends, if you have been defending the perfection of markets you have been played for a sap. Stop it.

The simple fact is that people can be hoodwinked. People. Human beings. The results of behavioral economists and psychologists such as Dan Ariely, Richard Thaler, and others are correct, and persuasive. But when someone uses those results to criticize markets – and stops there – they are not playing fair. Because the criticism of markets always has to be in reference to some other system: markets are bad, compared to what?

So if you are confronted with someone who has been reading behavioral economics, I would recommend that you grant their claims. People are not that great at making decisions. But then challenge your friend with this: Every flaw in consumers is worse in voters.

Think about it. Every flaw that people point out in consumer choice is also present, but *much worse*, in political choice!

- Asymmetric information (where producers have more knowledge about the product than consumers) about quality? Check. Consumers can look at ratings or Consumer Reports to learn about product quality. But it's very difficult to know when a politician is lying (unless you buy the old line that it's when her lips are moving).
- Monopoly? Check. Yes, the cable company is pretty bad. But the state is the very definition of monopoly. Your only escape is to move…to some other monopoly. There is never competition, and the bureaucrats down at the Department of Motor Vehicles know that. That's why they treat you so badly.
- Seductive and misleading advertising? Check. Maybe I do buy those new Nike kicks because they promise to make me like Mike, and maybe that Twix bar by the checkout counter is too tempting to resist. But at least I like Twix!

Politicians "place" themselves in ads all over the place like photo bombers from hell, and how often do we really get what we're promised?

- Finally, seduced by free stuff? Check. Ariely notes, rightly, that people will often (irrationally) choose the free alternative, and will fail to understand the other costs of free stuff, like waiting in line or filling out paperwork. Frankly, that sounds to me like a pretty good description of government programs ranging from our new healthcare system ("It's all free!") to recycling programs, which conserve on everything except time, which is the one resource that is truly non-renewable. I've seen people waste 10 minutes, and 50 cents worth of gas, to recycle two plastic soft drink bottles and a cardboard box worth a total of a nickel. But since recycling gives us free resources, it must be worth it!

A number of recent books (including Caplan's *Myth of the Rational Voter*, Somin's *Democracy and Political Ignorance*) have made this point, but for some one reason advocates for liberty don't close the circle very well in debates. Here's the fact: People do a poor job of acquiring information and using it to make decisions in the way that the rational choice model predicts. Here's the conclusion: This has implications for the capacity of consumers to benefit from markets, because consumers are people. But the conclusion also has to be that voters have the same problem, unless you think people are dumb in the supermarket but miraculously smart in the voting booth. It's the same person.

Why are voters even dumber than consumers? Consider this: A consumer who buys a bad television, or pays too much for a coffee-maker, or gets ripped off on an investment, is stuck with the bad TV, and loses her own money on the coffee-maker or the dumb stock buy. It happens, but you learn from your mistake (this is called "market feedback") and make a better decision the next time around.

Voters, on the other hand, have even less information, have no way of getting accurate information, and know that their choices won't determine the outcome anyway. If I spend months learning about the candidates, and then cast my vote for President, it has absolutely zero impact on the outcome. Not small, mind you: zero.

I still vote, of course. I'm a good citizen. But I vote for the candidate who makes me feel good. As Jason Brennan has pointed out in *Ethics of Voting*, this breaks the connection between civic commitment (voting) and desirable outcomes (good government). Ignorant, irrational voters don't just make themselves worse off. They can harm everyone.

People choose badly. But they choose worse as voters than they do as consumers. So unless you believe in suspending democracy, that's a pretty powerful argument for markets.

5. Democracy is a Means, Not an End

Everyone loves democracy. Ask an American if there is a better form of government, and they'll be insulted. You believe in democracy, don't you? And what exactly is it that you believe in? What people mean by "democracy" is some vague combination of good government, protection of individual rights, extremely broad political participation, and widely shared economic prosperity. One might as well throw in an ideal body mass index and a great latke recipe. It's all good, but doesn't mean much, and few people like to think about what democracy really means.

It is fine to celebrate the great achievements of democracies, once they are firmly established. But such celebrations confuse cause and effect. The reason democratic nations have personal liberties, property rights, and rule of law is not that they are democracies. Rather, nations that have those things embody the entire package of the Western tradition of good government. Requiring that government actions hinge on the consent of the governed is the ribbon that holds that bundle together, but it is not the bundle itself. Fareed Zakaria (2007) identified this "bundle" problem perfectly.

> For people in the West, democracy means "liberal democracy": a political system marked not only by free and fair elections but also by the rule of law, a separation of powers, and the protection of basic liberties of speech, assembly, religion, and property. *But this bundle of freedoms—what might be termed "constitutional liberalism"—has nothing intrinsically to do with democracy and the two have not always gone together, even in the West.* After all, Adolf Hitler became chancellor of

> Germany via free elections. (p. 17, emphasis added).

So—just what is democracy? In our mental potpourri, good government leads the list. But then what is 'good government?' A starting point could be voting and majority rule: most people can choose for all of us, and majorities can impose their will on minorities.

Such blanket endorsements of majority rule make me wonder whether democracy is a fraud or just a conceit. As William Riker pointed out in his 1982 book, Liberalism Against Populism, the claim that "fair" processes always, or even often, lead to "good" outcomes ignores much of what is known about institutions and institutional change. If people disagree, and if there are several choices, democracy is manipulable, even dictatorial. For modern political science, this is called the "Arrow Problem," after Kenneth Arrow.[59]

If all we mean by democracy is a civil myth, a conceit, it could be useful. The idea of democracy honors common people, calming the mind and pleasing the agora. If democracy is a fraud, however, then we are in bleaker and more sinister terrain. The pretense that in the multitude we find rectitude is dangerous: many of us would love to impose our "wisdom" on others. Saluting the collective wisdom is simply a way to hold other citizens down whilst we steal their purses, or pack their children off to war.

And it has ever been thus. As Polybius (1889) tells us:

> The Athenian [democracy] is always in the position of a ship

59 "Kenneth Arrow." The Library of Economics and Liberty. https://www.econlib.org/library/Enc/bios/Arrow.html

> without a commander. In such a ship, if fear of the enemy, or the occurrence of a storm induce the crew to be of one mind and to obey the helmsman, everything goes well; but if they recover from this fear, and begin to treat their officers with contempt, and to quarrel with each other because they are no longer all of one mind,—one party wishing to continue the voyage, and the other urging the steersman to bring the ship to anchor; some letting out the sheets, and others hauling them in, and ordering the sails to be furled,—their discord and quarrels make a sorry show to lookers on; and the position of affairs is full of risk to those on board engaged on the same voyage; and the result has often been that, after escaping the dangers of the widest seas, and the most violent storms, they wreck their ship in harbour and close to shore. (Book VI, Chapter 44).

This is not a call for dictatorship, however. The core of the Arrow problem is that societies choose *between* two evils: the tyranny of a Hitler or the potential for incoherence described by Polybius. My thesis is that "democracy" without the safeguards of constitutional liberalism is *both* tyrannical *and* incoherent, the worst system imaginable.

The U.S. is Not a Democracy

None of this was news to the American founders. Elections helped citizens control elected officials, and little more. This early skepticism is plain, as in this passage from Federalist #10:[60]

> ...a pure democracy, by which I mean a society consisting of a small number of citizens, who assemble and administer the government in person, can admit of no cure for the mischiefs of faction. A common passion or interest will, in almost every case, be felt by a majority of the whole; a communication and concert result from the form of government itself; and there is nothing to check the inducements to sacrifice the weaker party or an obnoxious individual. Hence it is that such democracies have ever been spectacles of turbulence and contention; have ever been found incompatible with personal security or the rights of property; and have in general been as short in their lives as they have been violent in their deaths. Theoretic politicians, who have patronized this species of government, have erroneously supposed that by reducing mankind to a perfect equality in their political rights, they would, at the same time, be perfectly equalized and assimilated in their possessions, their opinions, and their passions.

America is a federal republic, with horizontal separation of powers among executive, legislature, and judiciary, and vertical separation of powers between the central government and the states. The Declaration of Independence is straightforward: the American system is based on the claim that all citizens have rights, and "That

---

60 From the Bill of Rights Institute, the text of Federalist #10: https://billofrightsinstitute.org/founding-documents/primary-source-documents/the-federalist-papers/federalist-papers-no-10/

to secure these Rights, Governments are instituted among Men, deriving their just Powers from the Consent of the Governed..." That means that elections are still important. We need elections, literally *depend* on them to make the whole system work. But elections are not the ends of government, just the means by which citizens can withhold consent.

The problem is that the rules, procedures, and the basic "machinery" of electoral choice *as a means* have not kept up with the faith people seem to have in democracy *as an end*. We try to divine the will of the people, their "intent," on complex questions. Who can forget Florida in 2000, where officials held ballots over their heads, trying to see light through partially detached bits of cardstock chads?

Elections cannot work this way, not in a nation four time zones wide (not even counting Alaska or Hawaii). Even though in other aspects of our lives we demand instant information, electoral fairness requires that the states withhold information until all the polls are closed. Voting precincts must sacrifice efficiency (which new paperless voting technologies would appear to offer) for legitimacy, where paper receipts are available and where recounts involve actual physical checks of ballots, one by one.

But you knew about this problem, which is mostly technical. I am trying to argue that there is a different problem, at least as important: *we don't just demand too little of our democratic procedures, we are expecting too much of our democratic process.* The educational system in the U.S. has failed students, because we don't know the limits of unlimited democratic choice. We teach that consensus as a value in itself, even though we know that true consensus appears only in dictatorships or narrowly defined decisions. As James

Buchanan, Kenneth Arrow, and a host of public choice scholars have shown, *groups cannot be thought to have preferences in the same way that individuals do*. To put it another way, it is perfectly possible, and legitimate, for reasonable people to disagree. The role of democracy is not to banish disagreement, but rather to prevent political disagreements from devolving into armed conflict.

But then in what sense does government depend on "the consent of the governed"? The American system seems cumbersome, but it combines the notion of a republic, where policy choice is indirect, with separation of powers of legislation, where an overlapping consensus is required. A majority of the population is required to pass the House, but a majority in a majority of the states is required to pass the Senate. Then the President, whose constituency is the entire nation, must separately consent before the bill becomes law. The result is far removed from "democracy," but the system does ensure the fundamental democratic principle: government can't do things to us unless we the governed give our consent. Elections are a check on tyranny, not a conjuring of the will of the people.

Where Do We Go From Here?

Policy makers must understand the twin anachronisms that complicate the failures of voting institutions and democratic ideologies in the U.S. There really are two distinct anachronisms, each of which requires immediate attention.

First, our technology of democracy is too old, and prone to abuse or at least distrust. We must bring voting technology into the 21st century, because we accept much less than is possible. We must immediately solve the problem of guaranteeing mechanisms for recording and counting votes that are beyond reproach. As the election of 2004 shows, we are nearly out of time.

Second, our ideology of democracy, our notion of what democracy can accomplish, is anachronistic also. But in this case, the anachronism is not out of the past, but out of a utopian science fiction future. So, we must also take voting ideology back to the 19th century, where it belongs. We have come to expect much more than is possible from democracy, and democratic institutions.

This essay may make me sound like an enemy of democracy, some kind of elitist nut. Well, that's not entirely wrong. But describing democracy's flaws is not the same as arguing the virtues of elitism or dictatorship. I just want to foster a humble skepticism about what democracy really is and what it can actually accomplish. Many policy conflicts hinge on whether the public can tell individuals what to do. There is a subtlety that is often missed in policy debate: there is a difference between *public* decisions and *collective* decisions. Public decisions affect everyone by the nature of the choice itself: we can only have one defense budget; polluting rivers befouls not just my water, but yours.

Collective decisions, on the other hand, affect us all only because the majority is empowered to force its will on everyone. There need be no true public aspects to the decision as a policy outcome; we have just chosen to take the decision out of individuals' hands and put the power in the hands of the mob.

Now, it may very well be the case that lots of collective decisions are also public. But we need to see the line dividing private and collective choices, and to defend it fiercely. As P. J. O'Rourke notes, the fact that a majority likes something doesn't mean that the majority should get to choose that something for everyone.

> Now, majority rule is a precious, sacred thing worth dying for. But—like other precious, sacred things, such as the home and the family—it's not only worth dying for; it can make you wish you were dead. Imagine if all of life were determined by majority rule. Every meal would be a pizza. Every pair of pants, even those in a Brooks Brothers suit, would be stone-washed denim. Celebrity diets and exercise books would be the only thing on the shelves at the library. And—since women are a majority of the population, we'd all be married to Mel Gibson. (O'Rourke, 1993, p. 5).

The real key to freedom is to secure people from tyranny by the majority, or freedom from democracy. The problem, then, is what Fareed Zakaria has called "illiberal democracy." The metaphor we use to understand ourselves matters, because it figures in how we try to advise others.

> For much of modern history, what characterized governments in Europe and North America, and differentiated them from those around the world, was not democracy but constitutional liberalism. The "Western model of government" is best symbolized not by the mass plebiscite but the impartial judge. (Zakaria, 2007; p. 20.)

The framers of the U.S. Constitution fully recognized that there is nothing, nothing at all, inherent in democracy that ensures the freedom of persons or property. When we advise other nations about how to devise better systems of government, our own historical skepticism about the power of pure democracy can be neglected only at our peril. When we help a developing nation design its government, we need unashamedly to advocate something like the U.S. model. Thomas Hobbes (1990) said "Covenants, without the Sword, are but words." The modern equivalent might be this: "Democracy, without the Bill of Rights, is but tyranny."

6. Think Globally, Act Irrationally: Recycling

Two empty bottles, still cool from their malty contents. I glance at my lovely wife. And as always after a couple of beers, she looks strikingly attractive… as an audience for an economics lecture.

Her reaction, also as always, is to pretend to focus intently on her book, and probably to wonder how we ever managed to have children.

I press on, though. "These two bottles. Suppose you value earth stewardship, and want to use the fewest resources. What if you want to minimize the negative impact on the environment? With that as your goal… should these bottles be made of recycled glass? Should anything be recycled? How would we know?"

Turning them, I can't tell just from looking if they are made from "cullet," the industry name for ground recycled glass. But I keep talking. "Of course, we don't need to know after the fact; we can predict! Markets price resources by opportunity cost; if recycling is more expensive than using new materials, it can't possibly be efficient. And no producer would choose to use packaging that costs more for the same result. Economics rescues us again!"

I look up from my reverie. Donna seems to have gotten up and gone to bed, a while ago. The easy chair isn't even rocking anymore. Oh, well. Now that certain other options are foreclosed, I can focus on analyzing recycling. Let's think it out together.

Moral Imperatives Rule Out Trade-Offs

Near my own hometown in North Carolina, two recent news items caught my eye. The first was a statement by Greensboro councilman Tom Phillips:

> "The net cost for recycling is more than double the cost for regular garbage collection that will go to the transfer station. (This is after selling the recyclables we can.) A lot of what we recycle winds up at the landfill anyway because of contamination or lack of markets for the recycled material.... While it "feels good" it is too expensive and we must look for better alternatives." (public comment, March 17, 2006)

[61]This made me wonder: how could we *know* if recycling makes sense? What are the standards? Is Mr. Phillips right: should we look at costs?

The second was more remarkable, a parable of the costs of ignoring costs. It happened in Durham, home of Duke University. Here are the facts:

- Durham residents pay $60 per year for separate pick-up of "yard waste" (grass clippings, stumps, tree limbs, etc.) Residents must separate the waste streams, putting yard waste in separate containers. Yard waste is "too valuable," as compost-in-training, to dump in the landfill.
- The city operated a facility that had become clogged with

61 Max Borders, 2008. "State Has Made a Religion out of Recycling." January 13. Civitas Institute. https://www.nccivitas.org/2008/state-has-made-religion-out-recycling/

huge amounts of stumps and rotting vegetable matter. The $60 per year fee didn't come close to covering the extra costs of collection. No one offered to buy the "valuable" yard waste, for some reason.

- The stumps at the yard waste facility caught fire, deep in the huge pile. The fire could not be completely extinguished for weeks, and neighbors for miles downwind complained of the pollution. So the waste that homeowners paid extra for reusing was dumped instead in the main garbage staging facility.
- But the law prohibits disposal of yard waste in landfills in North Carolina.
- So, Durham shipped all its trash, including grass clippings, to a landfill more than 85 miles away, in Lawrenceville, VA.
- The clean-up and the extra hauling charges have already cost Durham an extra $1 million, compared to landfill disposal.

The reaction of the citizens of Durham? We can catch a glimpse in this newspaper story:

> People such as Frank Hyman, a garden designer and former City Council member, *pay for yard waste collection with the understanding that the city is reusing it.*
>
> "That's my expectation, and I think that's the expectation of most people," he said.
>
> "A lot of people may be angry when they hear the city is

shipping the yard waste to the landfill."[62]

Reuse it? *For what?* The city is desperate to save money, and would surely use the stuff if they could. A question for Mr. Hyman: If yard waste is so useful, why do you have to pay the city to take it away?

There is a simple test for determining whether something is a resource (something valuable) or just garbage (something you want to dispose of at the lowest possible cost, including costs to the environment). If someone will pay you for the item, it's a resource. Or, if you can use the item to make something else people want, and do it at a lower price or higher quality than you could without that item, then the item is also a resource. But if you have to pay someone to take the item away, or if other things made with that item cost more or have lower quality, then the item is garbage.

If yard waste were a resource, then trucks would drive up and down streets in your neighborhood, bidding up the price of your bagged grass clippings. That doesn't happen. *Ipso facto*, yard waste is garbage. No amount of wishful thinking, or worship of nature as a goddess, can change this basic calculus. Let's go back to the problem of recycling glass bottles.

Clear as Glass: If Recycling is Expensive, It's Not A Resource

One of most interesting treatments of the problem of markets

62 Quoted in Michael Munger, 2013. Cato Unbound. https://www.cato-unbound.org/2013/06/03/michael-c-munger/recycling-can-it-be-wrong-when-it-feels-so-right

and waste disposal is by an old friend of mine, Peter VanDoren. He writes:[63]

> Some policy analysts justify government intervention in refuse collection by invoking market-failure arguments in the collection of recyclables. Why don't free markets for recycling work? Well, in some circumstances they do. Scrap yards, for example, recycle iron and steel. The growth segment in the U.S. steel industry is the so-called "minimill" whose raw material is recycled. Recycling markets work fine in this sector of the economy because making steel from virgin iron and coal is more expensive than making it from recycled raw materials. In other areas of the economy involving glass, paper, and plastic, for example, the discrepancy between recycled and virgin prices often does not justify the development of markets for recycling.... [S]upport for recycling is more religious than economic in nature.

Markets can handle lots of things that look like "recycling." We reuse copper, even stripping it from old homes before they are torn down. When I'm traveling on business, I never buy a car. Instead, I rent a car at Hervis, and take it back two days later so someone else can use it. And when I finish with the turkey at Thanksgiving, or the ham at Easter, I always boil the bones to make soup. That soup is much cheaper, and better, as a result of recycling the bones. None

63 Peter van Doren, 1999. "Time to Trash Government Intervention in Garbage Service."
Cato Policy Analysis. https://object.cato.org/pubs/pas/pa331.pdf

of these things is mandatory; we do them automatically, because they make economic sense.

What VanDoren means by "religious" is that the claims for recycling rest on an assumed, if not always articulated, moral imperative rather than on trade-offs or costs. But underlying this claim, for many people at least, is some murky idea that recycling "uses up" fewer resources than making things from scratch. Or, in the case of glass, making bottles from sand. As one earnest young staffer at a public works department in the northeast told me, "Recycling is cheaper, no matter how much it costs!" You can believe, if you want, that there is some mystical quality of products that make them valuable, and that price is the wrong measure of value. But if prices matter, lots of recycling we now do is irrational.

The difference between cullet (glass ground up by machines, using electricity) and sand (rocks ground up by nature) is clear: most cullet is full of additives, contaminants, and impurities. These contaminants are trapped in the cullet, inert and harmless. But if someone melts the cullet, an important step for making new glass, the contaminants can become toxic releases into the atmosphere, water, or soil. The impurities introduced by even small amounts of merged colors or types of glass in waste streams make mixed cullet nearly useless.

Sand, by contrast, is cheap and can be made into glass without extra steps, extra expense, or extra danger to the environment.

So why do we recycle glass? Why is it against the law, in many cities and counties, to dispose of glass as garbage? *The fact that glass made from cullet is much more expensive than glass made from sand should be a hint that recycling uses more resources and more energy.*

Interestingly, in many cities, the answer to the "why recycle glass?" question is, "We don't!" Green glass, in particular, is so plentiful, and the cullet market so overwhelmed by excess supply, that disposal of green glass through recycling is prohibitively expensive. A number of cities have tried to delete green glass from the list of recyclable materials, but they face a political veto from recycling enthusiasts. And, interestingly, the political opposition comes precisely from those people who will end up paying more for the inefficiency of the recycling they insist they want. Taxpayers, citizens, the folks who take their garbage out to the street, want to ask the city to put green glass back on the recyclable list, regardless of the cost.

Incredibly, the pressures have been strong enough that some municipal systems have caved in, and either continued, or have restarted, accepting green glass. In a number of areas, private companies under contract with the city collect the green glass as recyclable, and then under direction from the city simply put the green glass back into the garbage waste stream. Given the resource costs of recycling, treating green glass as garbage is the environmentally responsible thing to do.

Save Resources, Recycle at All Costs

Let me close this essay by focusing on "contaminants," another example of good intentions gone badly wrong. Two of the sources of contaminants in cullet that make it less valuable, or even useless, are (a) mixed types and colors of glass, and (b) food residues that remain on glass surfaces.

The first problem was discussed in a news story in 2006 in the

Arizona Republic.[64] Here's the interesting part:

> Nearly one-quarter of everything tossed into Phoenix's blue [recycling] barrels shouldn't be there. Removing all that non-recyclable trash costs the city nearly $1 million each year....
>
> For residents who treat their recycling barrel like a garbage bin, the fact is sometimes lost that other people will eventually have to rummage through their cast-offs. "The question that I always ask children and adults alike is, '*Would you want to sort this stuff?*'" said Sheree Sepulveda, Chandler's environmental programs education coordinator. "It really puts a different perspective on it." (Purtill, 2006; emphasis added)

My mouth gaped when I read this. "Would you want to sort this stuff?" That's *exactly* what recycling zealots want us to do. Sort by color, sort by type, store separately, carry to facility and deal out your garbage in half a dozen little cubby holes. It's as if time, our most precious resource, the one thing we can't make more of, has no value whatsoever.

Here's my perspective, which is rather different: does it make more sense for (a) a few workers, and specialized equipment, to separate waste streams, or for (b) all the rest of us, with far more valuable uses of our time, to spend time, gas, and effort separating "recyclable" materials and feeling good about ourselves by putting them in little separate slots in some expensive facility dedicated to this purpose?

---

64 https://www.newspapers.com/newspage/126214201/

Trick question! The answer is: *Neither*. It makes no sense for either the waste worker, or the homeowner, to separate waste streams, because the price system is telling us this is an inefficient and wasteful activity. If recycling were efficient, someone would pay you to do it. Disguising the costs by forcing citizens to do the labor, instead of paid government employees, changes nothing. It just reduces the explicit budget of the recycling program, and raises implicit taxes on the people.

And that brings us the second type of contamination, food residues. Now, I have long heard of people running their mayonnaise or spaghetti sauce jars through the dishwasher before recycling them. But I had assumed this was an urban legend, since no rational person could justify the time and hot water needed to run garbage through the dishwasher.

To my surprise, it is actually easy to find examples of cities encouraging this lunacy. I found two examples very quickly; one from Beverly, MA, and one from Mason City, IL. But it is surprisingly common all over the U.S., in towns large and small.

Why would a city do this? Two reasons, and both of them are bad. The first we have already discussed: any costs imposed on citizens is avoided by city budgets strained by the irrational insistence on "recycle at all costs." Cleaner glass is worth more as cullet, and citizens' time and effort cost the city nothing.

The second reason is more disturbing. A generation of Americans has been indoctrinated into a "save resources, recycle at all costs," mindset. "Recycle!" is used as a moral bludgeon. This is different from "Don't Litter!" Littering is a collective action problem, a genuine social dilemma: cheaper for me to throw that cup out the window. But I myself would prefer a world where no one throws cups out of windows over a world where everyone does. "Don't litter" is an attempt to solve a real problem.

"Recycle, regardless of cost!" doesn't solve a problem; it creates one. Laws requiring recycling harm me, the environment, and everyone else. We have to take prices into account, because prices are telling us that we can't save resources by wasting resources.

Well, it's late, and it's time I head upstairs. I put the glass bottles in the recycle container. They are brown glass, and though their "value" is negative, at least they can be recycled at nominal cost. Besides, it makes me feel good. I'm saving the Earth, one piece of expensive garbage at a time.

7. Why Population Predictions Bomb

One of the central "policy problems" faced in modern societies is population growth. I used the scare quotes because it's not clear that population is a state issue at all, much less a problem.

Population, after all, is the sum of the consequences of millions of individual actions, some of them choices and some just actions. A woman has a certain number of children, for complex reasons. If we add up the results within a nation, the result is the growth overall in the population. Or, in many nations, decline.

The reasons vary substantially across the individuals involved: availability of contraception, social norms, family pressures, or sexual violence and the problems of political stability all play a role. Thinking of the aggregate as a single variable factor—"population"—something that can be manipulated by changing policies—is a strange conceit of central planners.

There has been a lot of famously breathless worrying about population growth. One of the first, of course, was Thomas Malthus, whose views were actually more complex than the "population crisis" claim we find in his followers.

Bad Predictions

Perhaps the most famous Malthusian doomsayer is Paul Ehrlich, who famously said, "The battle to feed all of humanity is over. In the 1970's and 1980's hundreds of millions of people will starve to death in spite of any crash programs embarked upon now." That was in his extremely influential 1968 book, *The Population Bomb*. Ehrlich went on to predict that

> At this late date nothing can prevent a substantial increase in the world death rate…The train of events leading to the dissolution of India as a viable nation is already in motion... If I were a gambler, I would take even money that England will not exist in the year 2000.

That's some serious hogwash, there. The population of India was 530 million when this "prediction" was made; India has more than 1.34 billion in 2018, and there is less poverty, not more.

Further, readers may recall that Ehrlich *was* a gambler; he foolishly took Julian Simon's famous bet on commodity prices. Ehrlich lost, of course, but never came close to admitting that he was in any way mistaken.

In 1969 Ehrlich predicted that life expectancy in the U.S. life "will drop to 42 years by 1980 due to cancer epidemics." I could go on; there are hundreds more very specific predictions about disaster that have been not only wrong, but qualitatively in the wrong direction.

Every time Ehrlich and other population alarmists have said "down" the actual result was "up": Population has increased without causing major problems; the biggest problems of poverty in most countries are obesity, not starvation; and the world is less polluted and the air is cleaner (for everything except carbon dioxide, a problem Ehrlich never mentioned even once) than it was in the 1960s. Things are better, not worse, and things are better most of all for the poor.

In a sense, Ehrlich has been consistent: every ten years or so he just adds another decade to his fatuous "predictions" and barfs up a new batch of nonsense. And he has managed to get paid a fortune to do it. The point is that it's not surprising that a seller of ideological snake oil would continue to sell the same useless concoction of nonsense, as long as people want to line up to buy it. But that raises the real question: why would anyone buy this nonsense? How could a fake scientist continue to be listened to, and even respected, when not one of his specific predictions are even in the correct direction?

I have an answer. And I have to admit I hope I'm wrong, because if I'm right it's a pretty horrible indictment of the moral impoverishment of the population alarmists. But hear me out, and see what you think.

Population is a Problem, Unless You Have Capitalism

The answer to population growth is capitalism. Commodifying labor. Yes, I went there. Full on accepting the worst-case characterization of the left. Not "market system." Capitalism. Let's own it.

The reason that capitalism solves the population problem requires a little explanation, though it's not really very complicated. Every society that has adopted a capitalist system has seen wages for labor rise sharply. As Benjamin Powell shows in his remarkable 2014 book, *Out of Poverty*, countries that start out with poverty and out-of-control population growth see those problems solved, in just two or three generations. If you line countries up in "event time"—so that you are comparing countries at the point they adopt capitalism, even if that happened centuries apart—a striking parallel emerges. Wages rise, poverty falls, and population growth shrinks to replacement.

It happened in northern Europe by 1975; it happened in Japan in 1970; in Korea and Taiwan in 1980; and in several Latin American nations, the end of population growth has been seen in the past two decades. Some nations are still growing, but much of that growth is from immigration rather than births above the replacement rate.

When do nations see their fertility rates, defined as births per woman, fall? When labor is priced; that's what capitalism does, putting a price on labor. If a woman is educated and allowed to work, the opportunity cost of her time skyrockets, and she becomes far more valuable to the society—and to herself—to have a child every 18 months or two years.

Nations that develop capitalist institutions see the median age of first children rise, and the total number of children fall dramatically. China's birthrate had fallen below replacement by 1995 (though the "one-child" policy was a big part of the cause), and India's fertility fell from nearly 6 in 1960 to 2.3, or just above replacement, in 1015.

Since becoming wealthy also decreases infant mortality rates, and increases life expectancy, it's actually surprising that the number of nations at or below replacement fertility is growing so rapidly. If more children survive, and people live longer, the replacement rate falls. But nonetheless, it's true: population growth is disappearing all over the world in nations that start to use the price system.

This shows the real underlying problem with the "analysis" of Ehrlich and his acolytes. Ehrlich, to his credit, is quite clear about this, writing in 1969: "We've already had too much economic growth in the US. Economic growth in rich countries like ours is the disease, not the cure."

Hating Prosperity

The alarmists' real concern is not the growth of population; it's prosperity. Their concern is that the resources of the earth will be used up, and that humanity has to prepare by becoming fewer and poorer. But all the evidence points in the opposite direction.

The solution to the population problem is also the right thing to do, morally. In countries without capitalist institutions patriarchal institutions oppress women and relegate them to reproductive slavery. This means that the opportunity cost of women's time is too low. Only capitalism values women, and only capitalism can end the population crisis.

The solution is deceptively simple: develop capitalism, and educate the female population to enable them to join the workforce. All the countries in the world that educated female populations and market institutions have fertility rates right around replacement. There is no population problem; there is only a "not enough capitalism—yet!" problem.

VIII

THE FUTURE, AND MAKING THINGS WORK

In this final section, I step back and consider some problems from a broader perspective. We live in a time of rapid change, and a number of these changes will influence the way we think about markets, about the state, and about ourselves.

The most difficult problems for analysis and prediction are understanding changing technology and accounting for innovation. It can be difficult for a nation to change directions, but adaptability is one of the central features of success in complex systems. Regulations should not block innovations, but government officials must also resist the temptation to "play favorites," as has happened in many countries with bureaucratic guessing about the "alternative" energy source that should be subsidized.

As has been discussed repeatedly in earlier sections of this book, people are terrible at predicting what products or processes will best serve consumers. And the folks who work for government are people. The search, or "discovery" process in capitalism is the profit test, using the prices of inputs as signals of the opportunity costs of making a product, and the prices consumers are willing to pay as the value of making that product. If the value of the product exceeds the costs of making the product, profits result.

It seems as if it should be possible for central planning and technocrats to do as well, or better, in making such judgements and predictions. But there are no examples of countries--no examples, as in none--managing to make this work. And some countries, as culturally diverse as Sweden and China, have turned away from central planning toward capitalism when they (re)discovered the painful truth that social planning is a poor substitute for the profit test.

I try to explain how adaptation to a future we can't predict might work. One recurrent theme in economic history is the centrality of "platforms," or integrated systems that reduce transaction costs for decentralized, impersonal exchange. The Souq in Aleppo was a platform; so was the Sears Catalog. Today, Amazon, Uber, and Wikipedia are all platforms. As I argue in the section called "Two Steves and One Soichiro," platform innovation may be very difficult to see, much less foresee. Markets and the profit test operate at the margin, starting small and expanding if the idea works. Products and services that once were the sole province of the very rich quickly become available to the common folk.

Politics doesn't work like that. For something to win approval in politics, the new platform would have to appeal to the center, the "median" voter. That's okay for making things such as rules, because there is an inherent conservatism and privileging of the status quo in making or changing. But for trying new products or searching for new ways to cooperate and serve each other, we need the openness and flexibility of markets.

1. Capitalism Saved Sweden

Josh Billings famously diagnosed a problem with beliefs: "I honestly believe it is better to know nothing than to know what ain't so." I am astonished at how many students, and for that matter adults, in the U.S. honestly believe that the U.S. should model itself after Sweden because Sweden has shown that socialism works.

I will leave aside the question of whether the U.S. should try to "be like" Sweden; they are very different countries, with different histories and different institutions. But it is important to refute, using simple and widely available empirical evidence, the claim that Sweden is "socialist." It is not. In fact, Sweden is one of the most robustly capitalist nations on earth.

By socialism, I mean a system that relies on state ownership and control of the means of production, state direction of production decisions, and direct state control of education and employment decisions of individuals. If one does not mean those things, then that would require a little more thinking about what "socialism" means. If by "socialism" you mean prosperity and rule of law, then you are confused.

There are several important issues to discuss, to understand the differences between capitalism and socialism.

First, ownership. Ownership solves the problem of the commons. In capitalism, ownership is (largely) private; under socialism, the state owns and controls the major productive resources of the society. It is sometimes noted that private ownership has a "short time horizon," as owners focus on profits. But in fact private ownership tends toward valuing the future, because investment now can earn profits in the future.

In fact, it is political incentives that force a short-run perspective. If we are talking about "democratic socialism" (few socialists actually favor Stalinism), then the time horizon of officials does not extend beyond the next election. In the U.S., that means that there is a two-year window, and that is in November of even-numbered years, before every member of the House of Representatives has to stand for reelection. As Marian Tupy wrote:

> Historically speaking, environmental damage emanating from socialist production was vastly greater than environmental damage emanating from capitalist production. All and I repeat all academic studies done in the aftermath of the collapse of the Soviet empire found the quality of the environment in the formerly socialist countries to be inferior to those in capitalist countries.[65]

Private ownership provides better information about future values, and better incentives to value the future, than democratic socialism.

Second, opportunity costs. Using prices gives useful signals about relative scarcity, and incentives for decentralized, emergent, but highly organized individual action. A socialist system sets prices, rather than allowing prices to adjust to reflect the dynamics of fast-moving events.

---

65 Tupy, Marian. "There Is Nothing Green about Socialism." Foundation for Economic Education. December 8, 2017. https://fee.org/articles/there-is-nothing-green-about-socialism

The problem seems like a narrow technical obstacle, but in fact it is fundamental. Top-down social planning is not just difficult; it's literally impossible. No individual or group can collect information quickly enough, and design incentives persuasive enough, to solve the problem, at scale. And by "scale" I mean somewhere around 10,000 total individuals. Clearly, it is possible to organize groups smaller than that using "command" networks, because (as R.H. Coase pointed out in 1937) that's why there are firms embedded in markets.

For large groups, where individuals operate independently, the knowledge possessed by one person is not communicated to other individuals. That means that the opportunity costs of resources are not represented in the decision process of participants. More simply, you do one thing when you should do something else; I use one resource when I should share or send that resource to someone else who needs it more.

Socialism operates without prices, either because the state is one big firm, with no mechanism for communicating opportunity costs internally, or because the democratic process determines what prices "should" be based on voting, rather than the reconciliation of diverse plans and purposes achieved by market processes.

Third, coercion. Without prices, we must either rely on desires of individual dictators, or state control expressed through majority rule. Without prices in the form of salaries, there is no way to direct people toward job shortages except coercive force. That means that when there is a shortage of one kind of worker, especially in an occupation where there is little social prestige or intrinsic benefit, the state must use the threat of violence to induce people to work.

And where there is a surplus of another kind of worker, especially in an occupation with lots of social prestige and great intrinsic benefits, the state must ration available positions by setting up some kind of wasteful rent-seeking contest. More simply, the only way to get sanitation workers in a socialist system is conscription; the only way to select among the many applicants for teaching positions is to use excessive educational licensing, or favoritism by the authorities.

How do market systems solve this problem? By adjusting the prices we call "wages." In some cases, that means garbage collectors make more than teachers. Is that "fair"? In a market system, the wages that send signals to people choosing careers are means of directing people voluntarily, rather than coercively. Ideas about how much people "should" make, based on political preferences, are simply disconnected from the economic problem of occupational choice. Socialist systems must, by definition, direct workers into occupations they would not choose voluntarily.

Scandinavia: A World Center of Capitalism

Now that I have discussed the differences between capitalism and socialism, let's consider the question I started out with: is Sweden socialist? I often participate in debates on capitalism vs. socialism, and students often give Sweden as an example of how socialism "works." Well, yes, Sweden works, that's true. But it works because it is one of the most capitalistic nations in the world! It became capitalist after trying socialism, and reaching the (correct) conclusion that socialism just doesn't work.

If you think Sweden is socialist, then you know something that just ain't so. As has been documented repeatedly by popular treatments[66] and more scholarly discussions,[67] any use of the actual measures of economic freedom that constitute capitalism show Sweden is solidly in the camp of fully market-oriented economies. As Andreas Bergh points out in his 2016 book, *Sweden and the Revival of the Capitalist Welfare State*, it is inconceivable to think of the Sweden of the current decade as being anything other than a capitalistic, and in fact libertarian, country.

It is fair to say that Sweden was socialist, at least in terms of temperament and the direction of public policy. In 1975, Sweden's state owned well over half of the productive resources in the country, and directed prices in much of the rest. It subsidized debt, in part paradoxically by having enormously high tax rates with generous deductions for borrowers. Its attempts at "Keynesian" policy interventions were clumsy, mistimed, and created disastrous uncertainty in investment returns even in the portions of the economy that were still market-oriented.

The state taxed successful industries heavily, and used the proceeds to subsidize industries that were inefficient, corrupt, and failing. This meant that interest rates on capital were prohibitive, especially when you tack on double-digit inflation.

To protect workers, the state required that wages could not be cut, and also enforced a panoply of restrictions on firing, layoffs, and other means of adjusting hours. Swedish products shot up in

---

66 Stossel, John. Stossel: Sweden Is Not a Socialist Success." *Reason*. Video file. October 23, 2018. https://reason.com/video/stossel-sweden-not-a-socialist-success

67 Gwartney, James, et. al. Economic Freedom of the World: 2018 Annual Report. Fraser Institute. September 25, 2018.

price, and the government was forced into a series of devaluations of the krona that made purchases of imported products beyond the reach of much of the middle class.

The electorate took a dim view of all of this. The tax system was a Rube Goldberg mechanism, with a level of complexity and arbitrary favoritism that encouraged distortion of investment into whatever happened to be taxed less, rather than whatever might produce useful products. Gunnar Myrdal, hardly a conservative, famously asked in 1978 whether Swedes "had turned into a people of swindlers."

Fortunately for its citizens, but unfortunately for those who think Sweden is still socialist, the Swedish government, more or less by universal consensus, turned sharply back toward capitalism beginning in about 1995. It deregulated domestic industry, privatized its education and pension systems, and opened the economy to international trade and competition. The reason it did this is precisely because capitalism, wherever it is practiced seriously in a system with rule of law and protection for property rights, always creates prosperity.

As Harvard's Torben Iversen put it, in his 2005 book *Capitalism, Democracy, and Welfare*:

> Labor-intensive, low-productivity jobs do not thrive in the context of high social protection and intensive labor-market regulation, and without international trade countries cannot specialize in high value-added services. Lack of international trade and competition, therefore, not the growth of these, is the cause of current employment problems in high protection countries. (p. 74)

In 2018, Sweden was the 18th most capitalist country in the world, measured based on property rights, trade openness, and freedom to use stock to create new corporations. In fact, Sweden is in the top 15 most capitalistic nations in terms of property rights, financial freedom, and business freedom. Most sectors are largely unregulated, and the freedom to move capital makes Sweden a bastion of markets and capitalism.

As the figure below shows, this change was sharp, and intentional. Between 1999 and 2001, Sweden deregulated most of its economy, sold off most of its dinosaur-slow state-owned enterprises, and converted substantial parts of its welfare commitments into private systems.

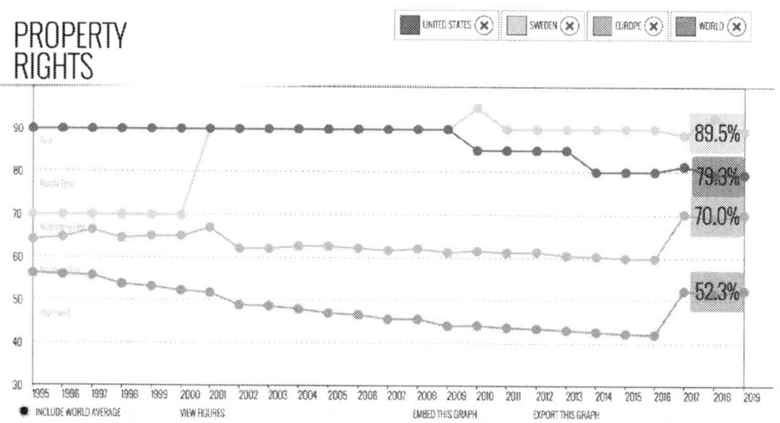

(Generated from the 2019 Heritage Foundation Index of Economic Freedom)

As a result, at present Sweden is the 6th most protective of private property rights, of all the nations in the world. By comparison, the U.S. is 25th most protective, our Fifth Amendment notwithstanding. If a nation has powerful protections for private property, even if the ownership protected is of the means of production, that is not socialism, no matter what you think you know.

- Sweden fully privatized its pension system, moving from "defined benefit" to "defined contribution." Yes, there is a means-tested add-on guaranteed pension top-up for the least well off, but the first-line system is personal pension accounts, invested in one of 700 private index funds, managed by private fund managers. It is the most privatized pension system, by far, in all of Europe.
- Sweden has a 100 percent universal voucher system for education. There are questions about whether Sweden's educational system works as well as it should, but it is one of the most private (and not socialist) education systems in the world.

Sweden is not alone in rejecting socialism and embracing capitalism. If you look at the general trend in the countries of Northern Europe, it has become much more capitalistic in the past 25 years, after its own failed experiments with socialism. In particular, on the measures I have discussed, Denmark, Finland, and Norway are all three even more capitalistic than Sweden.

You may recall that in 2016 a number of Bernie Sanders supporters held up Denmark as the example of the kind of "socialism" they envisioned for the U.S. Speaking at Harvard's Kennedy School, Denmark's prime minister (Lars Løkke Rasmussen) told students, "[I have] absolutely no wish to interfere in the presidential debate in the US," but politely told them that what they thought they knew about Denmark just ain't so:

> I know that some people in the US associate the Nordic model with some sort of socialism. Therefore I would like to make one thing clear. Denmark is far from a socialist planned economy. Denmark is a market economy.... The Nordic model is an expanded welfare state which provides a high level of security for its citizens, but it is also a successful market economy with much freedom to pursue your dreams and live your life as you wish.

In terms of deregulation of business freedoms, measured in the Fraser Institute's "Index of Economic Freedom," Denmark, Finland, and Norway are the 7th, 8th, and 9th most free; Sweden is 12th.[68]

The U.S.? It is 15th. The U.S. is rapidly regulating new industries, and further restricting old ones, at the state level in particular. The expansion of professional "licensing" rules, supposedly for the benefit of consumers but in fact in support of organized corporate interests, is making the U.S. less capitalistic every day.

My own view is that the U.S. still has strong institutions of its own, and that we simply need to restore business and investor confidence in our economy. But those of you who prefer the Swedish system, where robust capitalism is used to create prosperity and then redistribution is used to support welfare programs, are entitled to those beliefs.

Just please, please don't call Sweden "socialist." 'Cause it ain't so.

---

68 https://www.fraserinstitute.org/studies/economic-freedom

2. Why We Can't Break Up With Our Stuff — Yet

Fifty years from now, people will look back on the turn of the century and wonder about us. They will wonder why we were so wasteful, so selfish. Why we had closets, garages, and rental storage units, all under lock and key so we could keep other people from using the stuff that we weren't using, either.

I can't brag that I'm not part of the problem. I have a shiny, black BMW 330i with a six-speed transmission. The BMW has its own special shrine, with a door that magically — well, electronically — opens when I approach. My car takes up quite a bit of space. In fact, it "lives" better, in a clean, well-lit garage, than at least a quarter of the world's human population.[69]

Sometimes I drive it to work, where I park it on a very expensive piece of real estate called a parking lot. I've taught at Duke for a long time, so I have the "parking spot of God," near the buildings.

I drive my car about 45 minutes a day, four days a week, less when I'm traveling, as I often am. I'm writing this article in Sydney, Australia, and my car is sitting, unused, in a parking lot at the airport, behind barbed wire. When I'm in town, I also use my car for errands — I might use it another five hours a week. That's 163 hours a week that the car is unused, and while it is unused, it actually takes up two parking spaces, in the sense that both my garage and

---

69 https://www.learnliberty.org/blog/why-my-pit-bull-lives-like-a-king/

work parking are reserved for me alone.

Why We Own Too Much Stuff

As I recounted at the beginning of this book, one of my grad school advisers was Douglass North, who won a Nobel Prize in 1993 for arguing that transaction costs were the central concept in modern economics. It didn't matter what the question was; the answer is always transaction costs.

If you want to make a trade, you have to spend time and other resources finding the right person to trade with and then arranging and enforcing the exchange. That cost is the transaction cost.

Why do I pay to store my car rather than let other people use it and collect rent? Transaction costs. Why don't more people hitchhike? Transaction costs. Why, more generally, do we own things rather than rent them? The answer, as Doug North said, is transaction costs.

But we are living in the beginning of a pivotal era that will transform our relationship to "stuff" (we'll need less of it) and to each other (we'll share more). For all of human history until about 1995, the desire to reduce transaction costs was tied to the desire to sell a particular product. Now, entrepreneurs are combining three things — mobile platforms, software apps, and internet connections — to sell reductions in transaction costs with no product attached. And that combination will change everything.

You already know about Uber, of course. If I have a car and a few minutes, and you need a ride, it's unlikely we could solve the transaction costs problem on our own. We'd face problems of triangulation (finding each other), transfer (arranging the delivery of the service and negotiating payment), and trust (being sure I won't rob you and you won't assault me, though Uber hasn't been flawless in that regard). Those three categories — triangulation, transfer, and trust — are the reasons that we own so much stuff and pay to store it all.

But there is an enormous and largely unused amount of excess capacity in the system now, just waiting for a reduction in transaction costs to make it available. Consider hitchhiking: almost no one in the United States hitchhikes. If you stand on a bridge over an interstate highway, you'll notice that most cars, and almost all the trucks, have a single passenger. Why aren't there more people in all those vehicles?

How BlaBlaCar Is Solving the Transaction Costs Problem

The answer is transaction costs. But a company called BlaBlaCar figured out a way to sell reductions in those costs.

Unlike many other software platforms, BlaBlaCar offers pure sharing. The software provides key pieces of information: (1) the passenger's location, (2) the passenger's destination, and (3) the time the passenger wants to leave. Someone who has an extra seat in their car or truck and who is traveling that route at about that time is matched with the passenger. The passenger pays part of the cost of the trip that the driver is going to take anyway. The result is a pure efficiency gain with close to zero marginal cost to the system but benefits to both, or all, participants.

The software platform's name comes from a fourth piece of information: desired "chattiness." If you prefer a quiet ride (if you are the passenger) or drive (if you are the operator), then you check "bla." But if you love to talk the whole trip, you can select "bla-bla-bla." The name of the company is the middle setting, "bla-bla"

("Enjoys a natter," on the software), as the way to represent the service overall.

As of this writing, BlaBlaCar has well over 25 million "members" in 22 countries. At least 10 million trips are arranged per quarter, and of course each "trip" requires at least two members. In fact, the average car occupancy is 2.8 in a BlaBlaCar ride, compared to 1.6 to 1.8 (depending on the country) for car trips in general. BlaBlaCar estimates a reduction of CO2 emissions on the order of more than 1 million tons per year, but of course that estimate assumes that all riders would have taken their own trips solo, rather than take a train or simply not travel, if the service were not available.

What Sharing Economy Services Really Sell

Notice that BlaBlaCar does not sell rides, or transportation, or anything remotely like a physical service. What BlaBlaCar sells is a reduction in transaction costs. And that's the unifying theme of the new sharing economy: for the first time in human history, entrepreneurs can make money just by selling reductions in transaction costs. We have plenty of stuff; it's just in the wrong place. The only thing keeping stuff in the wrong place is transaction costs.

Portable platforms (mostly smartphones) using software (often modular, self-contained apps) and connecting over the internet mean that transaction costs are plummeting. Uber doesn't sell taxi rides; Airbnb doesn't rent hotel rooms. These companies, and a thousand others, "sell" reductions in transaction costs.

We'll need a lot less stuff and a lot fewer parking spaces if we can take better advantage of what we already have. And cities will have a lot more space once we aren't paying the costs of storing cars in parking lots and loads of equipment and clothing in self-storage facilities.

3. Two Steves and One Soichiro: Why Politicians Can't Judge Innovation

The Cold War turned on a race to produce more weapons and wealth, a race run between markets and central planners. Khrushchev's famous 1956 warning, "History is on our side! We will bury you…" evoked an old idea. Marxists believed that the empowered proletariat is the undertaker of capitalism, and they also believed that economic planning would empower the proletariat.

In the 1970s, even most of the non-socialist world wondered whether any system of private, decentralized innovation and development could stand up to the planning and market direction of the Japanese juggernaut. Central planning, whether of the socialist (U.S.S.R) or corporatist (Japan, Sweden) flavors, seemed to many to be the more powerful economic engine.

How times have changed! Nobody (well, nobody outside of college English departments) still believes that socialism outperforms markets, of course. And Japan has gone into the same muddy tank that Sweden has wallowed in for years. Even Alfred Kahn, Jimmy Carter's inflation guru, said by the end of the '70s that we should "Cast a skeptical eye on glib references to the alleged success of government interventions in other countries in picking and supporting industrial winners."

But we still face the same basic problem. The boundary we fight over today divides what is decided collectively *for all of us* from what is decided *by each of us*. You might think of it as a property line, dividing *what is mine* from *what is ours*. And all along that property line is a contested frontier in a war of ideas and rhetoric.

For political decisions, "good" simply means what *most people* think is good, and everyone has to accept the same thing. In markets, the good is decided by *individuals*, and we each get what we choose. This matters more than you might think. I don't just mean that in markets you need money and in politics you need good hair and an entourage. Rather, the very nature of choices, and who chooses, is different in the two settings. P.J. O'Rourke has a nice illustration of the way that democracies choose.

> Imagine if all of life were determined by majority rule. Every meal would be a pizza. Every pair of pants, even those in a Brooks Brothers suit, would be stone-washed denim. Celebrity diets and exercise books would be the only thing on the shelves at the library. And—since women are a majority of the population, we'd all be married to Mel Gibson. (O'Rourke, 1993; p. 5).

O'Rourke was writing in 1993. Today, we might all be married to Ashton Kutcher, instead. But you get the idea: Politics makes the middle the master. The average person chooses not just for herself, but for everyone else, too. Let's see why.

Politics: We All Have to Want the Median

Imagine five people have to choose a road salt budget for their hamlet. Mr. A doesn't drive, but has azaleas; he wants zero salt. Mr. B would spend enough to clear the main road. Mr. C would spend a little more, salting the side roads a bit. Mr. D advocates a "clear roads for all" budget, and Mr. E wants clear roads and also sidewalks (he hates azaleas).

So, their diverse goals look something like this:

Person	Salt Budget Preference
A	$0
B	$100
C	$10,000
D	$12,000
E	$20,000

One of the achievements of modern public choice theory (beginning with Black, 1958) is to show definitively that, if anyone can make proposals, the middle preference must win. So Mr. C, and the town, get a budget of $10,000 for salt next year. Mr. A has more azaleas killed, and Mr. E sees more azaleas survive, than either would prefer. And this makes sense: the town has just one road salt budget, and the choice is a compromise.

And we know exactly where the compromise lies: it's the median, not the average. In our example, the average is $8,420, and it is easy to see that this budget is not possible for the town. All that would be necessary is for Mr. C to propose $10,000, and a majority (C, D, and E) would all vote for it, preferring $10,000 to $8,420. Only

A and B would prefer the $8,420 average, and they would lose out. The bottom line is that $10,000 beats any other budget, by the same logic, by a vote of 3-2 or more.

This approach to decision making resists change or new ideas from individuals. Suppose that Mr. E decides not only that he doesn't like azaleas, but that ice itself is immoral. He demands that no ice be allowed to form on any surface in the city limits. Mr. E estimates that this would require a 1/4 inch coating of salt, dropped from rented crop dusters. The total cost would be $2,500,000. He puts up a banner at the town meeting: "E: Ending Ice as We Know It." After Mr. E tells the other voters of his insights on icicular immorality, we can present the revised goals of our citizens this way:

Person	Salt Budget Preference
A	$0
B	$100
C	$10,000
D	$12,000
E	$2,500,000

The effect on the median and on our town's road salt budget is... nothing, even though Mr. E changed the average desired salt budget to more than $500,000. Nobody has to talk E out of it; the town still chooses $10,000, because the median is unchanged by movements at the extremes. Large democracies are inherently, and in many ways intentionally, resistant to changes in the ideas of just a few individuals. And that can be a good thing, since a lot of towns have a Mr. E.

But what if we asked citizens to make one-size-fits-all choices on everything? For example, instead of a proposal to "end ice as we know it," suppose we asked the middle guy (call him "Median Joe") what he thinks of personal computers? And to make it more interesting, let's go back before personal computers even existed; how would Median Joe have reacted to that new idea? Is that a decision that the middle sort person would have made better than someone at the extremes? Let's take a look.

Two Smart Steves

In 1976, there were two Steves, in a garage. One worked for Hewlett-Packard, and the other for Atari, in California. The Atari guy, Steve Jobs, had the garage, and the two Steves worked on a revolutionary machine. Or so they hoped. Near the end of 1976 the Steves, Jobs and Wozniak (the HP guy), released into the market a metal box attached to a TV screen, and tried to charge $666.66 for each one. The contraptions were called Apple I's.

Suppose we had taken a vote at that point on this "personal computer" thing. Most people would have guessed that there was no future in these silly, overpriced boxes. ($666.66 is more than a satanic pricing point; it is also $2,350 in 2006 dollars. This for a paper weight with no fixed memory and 16k of RAM.) No government agency would have funded the thing, unless Messrs. Jobs and Wozniak were also big campaign contributors. And it is unlikely that there would have been a grass roots wave of support, since no one even knew who the Steves were or what they were trying to accomplish.

But Jobs and Wozniak were out at the extreme of opinions about computers and the future. They moved out of the garage in 1976, and in 1980 they rolled out the $3,495 Apple III (that's about $9,000 today!). Clearly, this company had no future. Of course, they had not received, or risked, any public money, so it was no one's problem but theirs. Their hunch, their money, their loss.

Then, the Steves held a public stock offering of stock later in 1980. And against all expectations, they became instant millionaires, selling 4.6 million shares. That's a lot of shares; is Median Joe a risk taker, after all? Not really; suppose that each sale was for just one share, to 4.6 million people. That would still mean that more than 97% of the U.S. population thought the stock was a bowzcr. And in fact just a few people bought any shares at all, though these few oddballs bought heavily, making a "yes" bet when everyone else was betting "no."

And who wouldn't bet against the overpriced boxes? The business editor at Prentice Hall said, in 1957: ""I have traveled the length and breadth of this country and talked with the best people, and I can assure you that data processing is a fad that won't last out the year." Later, when the microchip was invented, an engineer at IBM's Advanced Computing Systems was puzzled: "But what … is it good for?" And in 1977, Ken Olson, founder of computer giant DEC, sniffed that "There is no reason anyone would want a computer in their home."

Let's give DEC's Olson his due: *He was right, in a very unimportant way*. For years, few did want home computers. If we had put it to a vote, computers would have lost, with more than 95% of population voting "no." But we didn't vote. We left it up to the individuals at the extremes. By 1985, only 5% of American households had voted "yes," with people having some kind of access to personal computers. For a political comparison, Ross Perot got 19% of the vote in 1992, and that was after he announced (accurately, if you have seen a picture) that he was "all ears."

By 2005, a majority of "we the people" had changed their minds. Just over 60% of households had at least one computer, with even more having access at work or libraries. Those who bet "yes" on personal computers early on, won. And eventually most of the rest of us came along, free riding on the correct guess. None of the skeptics had to risk anything on the success of the computer, and were free to wait until all the up-front costs of development were paid by others. And had PCs flopped, none of the skeptics would have lost any money. It would just have been "I told you so!" time.

One Fast Soichiro

Sometimes, the person saying "I told you so" gets to say it to the government, or to the political process. In the late 1950s, MITI (the Japanese Ministry of International Trade and Industry) decided to rationalize and streamline the Japanese automobile industry. The goal was to realize economies of scale in design and production, and increase the number of cars that Japanese companies would export to the U.S. and elsewhere.

It was decided that just two auto companies (Toyota and Nissan) would get government financial support. All other companies were told that they should direct their energies to motorcycles, or blenders, or perhaps those new televisions. Costs would fall as each company produced more cars. The logic was undeniable: fewer producers, lower costs.

But there was one strange loner, named Soichiro. He was an odd prickly person, and wouldn't listen to MITI, or anyone else. Soichiro's company sold excellent high-performance motorcycles, and he thought his engines and manufacturing procedures would work well in automobiles. In 1959, in spite of the bleating of MITI, Soichiro's company introduced the S360 sports car.

Today, you have likely heard of the company led by an oddball, a guy who refused to comply with the dictates of the central authority. By the mid 1950s, the company had come to be known by Soichiro's last name, Honda. If the policy had prevailed, Honda would be… well, it wouldn't be. But because Soichiro Honda refused to give in, consumers all over the world got one more choice of automobiles.[70] And millions of them choose Honda, a car that now appeals to the comfy median very well indeed.

Final Words: A Glock, If You Want One

On many kinds of policy, where one unique alternative must be selected from among many, and the legitimacy of that choice is at least as important as the choice itself, democracy has no equal. One defense budget, one speed limit on any one stretch of road, one standard width for railways, and one choice (left side or right side?) for driving automobiles.

But many choices aren't like that. There may not be a "we" that

70 Fioriani, Sam. 12/30/2001. "The Automotive Century: Most Influential People—Soichiro Honda."Auto History On-Line. http://www.autohistory.org/feature_7.html

has to choose at all, imposing the median view on everyone. Instead, individuals can make their own choices. This is particularly true for innovations, or new ideas cooked up by some oddball. Some (in fact, most) of those ideas will fail, but we can't tell the winners from the losers in advance. The most significant innovations and advances in human history have been the result of the efforts of men and women too determined, or maybe just too strange and isolated, to know that the whole world was betting against them.

Think back to the ice-hating Mr. E in our road salt budgeting example. He wanted to impose his choice on everyone, not just himself. And he wanted everyone to pony up 1/5 of the costs of his strangely salty utopia. Democracies are stable in part because they deny any effective voice to the extremes, unless many other citizens are also persuaded. If the choice is one-size-fits-all, and the new guy wants to play with house money, it pays to say "no" most of the time.

That's why there are such important differences in our examples of the two Steves, or the one Soichiro. For one thing, even though their ideas were nearly as wild as Mr. E's, their proposal for innovation was but one of many alternatives, not one-size-fits-all. And for another, they were betting their own money, not the taxpayers'. If they went all in and lost, Uncle Sam (or Cousin MITI) didn't have to raise taxes to make up the shortfall.

And that brings me to my final two points, the really key points I want the reader to take away from this essay. The first one is this: The conventional wisdom rejects innovation, and is usually right; that's why it's conventional. But the reason Median Joe is right to be skeptical is that most innovations are just balloon juice.

Still, a pessimist would then point out (and be right!) the flip side: the conventional wisdom is *nearly always wrong*, at least at first, about innovations that work. If you always say no, you do turn down all the bad ideas, but you turn down all the good ideas as well. Only if the innovation gets its chance, probably to fail but possibly to succeed, on its own merits and unconstrained by the views of Median Joe, will we find out what works and what doesn't.

Second, and no less important, this problem, this choice between collective and individual judgments, is at least as vital today as it was when Khrushchev was threatening burial, or Honda was nearly getting run off the road, or even when the two Steves were noodling in their garage. True, no one wants to return to a Soviet system, or an industrial policy with an agency of experts who make national investment decisions. But we still face the same basic problem: can I decide, and risk *just my money*, for great reward if *I'm* right? Or will *we* decide, and risk *our* whole future budget, on things we *aren't very good at deciding*?

The examples come thick and fast: should we have a uniform ethanol standard in all gasoline, or should we let gas stations (or individuals) concoct their own fuel mix formulas? Should the government subsidize hydrogen fuel cell cars, or let people at the extremes, perhaps two Mikes in some garage, work on the problem? Why not allow terminally ill, or even mildly ill, people to use whatever drugs they want, regardless of whether Median Joe (working through his stone-faced employee, the FDA) thinks that drug has five chances in a million of giving you a stroke?

Markets, and market processes, are themselves a pretty important innovation, one not always approved or understood by Median Joe. Why not let the market work at an even more radical level, one that many people might think goes too far? Imagine that airlines could compete based on the level of security they provide. Let passengers choose their own security, along with a mix of price and inconvenience that some entrepreneur thinks would increase profits.

And we could go further: imagine a security line at the airport where the guard looks at your boarding pass and asks, “Are you carrying any weapons?” When you say no, he gives you one, a 9mm Glock. “All passengers are required to carry these, sir. Airline policy.” Not all airlines, mind you; only “Glock Air” (motto: “We just flew in from Cleveland, and boy are our arms locked and loaded!”). You might choose to fly Glock. They have never had a terrorist incident, and if you push the flight attendant call button the guy comes *running*.

Or, you might not fly Glock. You don’t have to. You might choose some other airline with a unique combination of services, safety, and schedule. In the current regulatory environment, too many decisions are one-size-fits-all, because we don’t recognize the possibility that it could be different.

We have become too accepting of the views of the middle, in too many aspects of our lives. Worse, we have fallen victim to a soft but encroaching political paternalism. In many cases, it isn’t even the median citizen who enforces his views on everyone. Instead, special interests and “public” lobbyists dominate the making of rules and decisions that force all of us to act as if we all had the same views on risk, taste, and service.

The thing to keep in mind is that market processes, working through diverse private choice and individual responsibility, are a social choice process at least as powerful as voting. And markets are often more accurate in delivering not just satisfaction, but safety. We simply don’t recognize the power of the market’s commands on our behalf. As Ludwig von Mises (1958) famously said, in *Liberty and Property*, "The market process is a daily repeated plebiscite, and it ejects inevitably from the ranks of profitable people those who do not employ their property according to the orders given by the public."

4. Permissionless Innovation: The Fuzzy Idea that Rules Our Lives

People sometimes ask me, "What is the most important concept in political economy?" The answer is easy, but subtle: permissionless innovation, a strong presumption in favor of allowing experimentation with new technologies and with new business platforms that use those technologies. A lot has been written about why this vague concept is so powerful (my own go-to source is Adam Theirer's *Permissionless Innovation*, 2014).

It's at the core of what Friedrich Schiller, the German philosopher and poet, wrote about in a letter to a friend in 1793 where he describes the beauty of the "Englische Tanze" (English dance):

> I know of no better image for the ideal of a beautiful society than a well executed English dance, composed of many complicated figures and turns. A spectator located on the balcony observes an infinite variety of criss-crossing motions which keep decisively but arbitrarily changing directions without ever colliding with each other. Everything has been arranged in such a manner that each dancer has already vacated his position by the time the other arrives. Everything fits so skillfully, yet so spontaneously, that everyone seems to be following his own lead, without ever getting in anyone's way. Such a dance is the perfect symbol of one's own individually asserted freedom as well as of one's respect for the freedom of the other.(Schiller, 1967; p. 163)

This passage contains a fundamental insight, because the first sentence shows that Schiller intends more than admiration for the lovely order that emerges from the free expression of individuals' dances within a set of rules that coordinate the whole. He intends this "image" to be a metaphor for human society.

[71]Barriers to permissionless innovation

Permissionless innovation may seem like common sense, but it isn't. For decades, the Bell telephone network refused to connect any phones except those it licensed. The claim was that the phones might not be safe; the effect was to arrest progress at the stage of rotary phones attached by wires to walls. The problem went far beyond phone sets, though: economist Tom Hazlett's 2017 piece in Reason describes how requiring permission set back communications in the United States for decades.

There are two kinds of obstacles to permissionless innovation: requiring permission from regulators and requiring permission from competitors.

The first type of obstacle, needing permission from regulators, seems more innocuous. But it isn't. The delays in processing "applications" for permission to experiment sharply curtail the types and frequency of experiments that are possible. Worse, attempts by regulators to pick winners and losers can pose obstacles of their own. Suppose the authorities do not require licenses for technological experiments, but they do offer subsidies for the kinds of work that seems "promising." Consider the massive government

71 My thanks to J. Fred Giertz of the University of Illinois for suggesting the citation, and interpretation.

"incentives" that subsidize solar power in the USA.[72] That's not to say that policies are irrelevant — as a 2017 BBC podcast illustrates, deregulation is the way to foster solar power — but rather that market processes of discovery are better than bureaucrats at picking the precise form innovation will take.

The second type of obstacle seems absurd, since by definition most innovations harm competitors; that's what makes them innovations. But there are many such requirements, as John Stossel recently pointed out, also for *Reason*.[73]

Of course, the nature of innovation means that it is often the least "promising" technologies — in the view of experts — that turn out to be the most important. A Yale management professor famously told student Fred Smith, the founder of FedEx, "The concept is interesting and well-formed, but in order to earn better than a C, the idea must be feasible."[74] The idea of Federal Express may have gotten a C from Yale, but it got an A+ from the market once it was implemented.

In that instance, the "permission of competitors" and "permission of regulators" came down to the same body: the US Postal Service. FedEx was allowed to slip through only because there was a loophole for "extremely urgent" letters and parcels; that's why "Extremely Urgent" still appears on every envelope FedEx delivers.

---

72 http://www.learnliberty.org/blog/solar-energy-cant-survive-without-massive-subsidies/

73 http://reason.com/blog/2017/08/01/stossel-stop-you-need-a-license-for-that

74 https://www.entrepreneur.com/article/197542

How Twitter exemplifies the golden age of permissionless innovation

We live in the golden age of permissionless innovation. The Internet offers an infrastructure where a bewildering variety of innovations can be tried out, and (almost) all of these experiments can be conducted without getting anyone's permission. Think for a second what a dumb idea Twitter was. Surely, nobody was going to spend time writing clumsy haikus, and even fewer people were going to read them. Here's what cofounder Ev Williams told Inc. in 2013, shortly before taking Twitter public was expected to make him a billionaire:[75]

> With Twitter, it wasn't clear what it was. They called it a social network, they called it microblogging, but it was hard to define, because it didn't replace anything. There was this path of discovery with something like that, where over time you figure out what it is. Twitter actually changed from what we thought it was in the beginning, which we described as status updates and a social utility. It is that, in part, but the insight we eventually came to was Twitter was really more of an information network than it is a social network.

I don't want to get too "meta" here, but the point is this: Access to the Internet spawned an innovation called Twitter, but no one knew what it was for. A beautiful social media version of the English dance happened, though. It just happened. People figured out a use for Twitter, because once it was there, they could experiment without asking for anyone's permission. No one, not even Twitter's own founders, understood what would make it useful.

---

75 https://www.inc.com/issie-lapowsky/ev-williams-twitter-early-years.html?cid=em01011week40day04b

As Schiller might put it if he were on Twitter today:

> A spectator following a hashtag observes an infinite variety of criss-crossing tweets which keep decisively but arbitrarily changing directions without ever censoring each other. Everything fits so skillfully, yet so spontaneously, that everyone seems to be following his own lead, but the thread builds into an informative whole without any guidance or central direction. Such an app is the perfect symbol of one's own individually asserted freedom to convey useful truths, as well as of one's respect for the freedom of the other to post random cat videos.

Permissionless innovation allows us to create truly new things for each other to enjoy — things the experts may not understand or approve of, but that nonetheless hold the potential to transform the world.

5. Will Reducing Transaction Costs Be the End of Retail?

Ronald Coase, a Nobel Prize–winning (1991) economist, was best known as a scholar who asked a simple question and then spent decades trying to give an ever-deeper answer.

The question was simple: why do we see the particular arrangements that appear in the economic world, rather than other arrangements? And the answer was also simple, though that simplicity was and is deceptive. The answer is "transaction costs."

In my book *Tomorrow 3.0* (Munger, 2018), I claimed that all costs are transaction costs, at least to the consumer. If we divide transaction costs into triangulation (buyers and sellers finding each other, agreeing on a price, and making an agreement), transfer (arranging for delivery, and making payment), and trust (ensuring that the product, the payment, and the parties are all safe from fraud or theft), that suggests that transactions are quite expensive. But of course that was Coase's point all along, beginning with his 1937 article, "The Theory of the Firm": using markets is expensive.

In the early 1930s, Coase toured the U.S. and parts of Europe, asking the same question of anyone who would sit still long enough to listen. The question was: "If markets are so great, why are there firms?" After all, workers don't come home at the end of a long day and complain, "Man, prices were ordering me around a lot today." Instead, everyone complains about their boss. Even bosses complain about their bosses.

In an economics class, students learn about how prices direct people in a market economy. But in the real world, most people work in little "command economies" called firms. The reason is that the transaction costs of using markets are high. Imagine that a worker on an assembly line puts some bolts into an auto chassis. She doesn't then go look for a buyer for that partial car, or sell the thing on eBay. Instead, the assembly line just moves the chassis on to the next worker, who adds a fender. And so on, worker after worker, task after task, until the car is ready to be sold.

Prices Matter

Prices matter, of course. The price of the car will likely determine how many such cars are sold, and how quickly. The comparison of price to the cost of making the car registers as profit or loss, and signals to other producers whether they should ramp up their own car-making activities. But firms mostly operate internally using hierarchy and command.

Coase noticed that this margin, the point where it is cheaper to use the market than to use a firm to internalize the costs of organizing a transaction, is highly variable. The size of the firm, then, depends crucially on the cost of using the market.

Every firm faces what we now think of as the "make or buy" decision. An auto company may own the steel company that supplies the metal used to make the cars. It probably does not own the iron mine where the ore to make the steel is dug out. And almost certainly, the auto company does not own the wheat farm where the grain used to make bread for sandwiches in the employee cafeteria is grown. If it is cheaper to buy, the firm shrinks; if it is cheaper to make, the firm grows.

Much of the cost of using the market and price mechanism is

transaction costs. You have to be able to find, obtain, and reliably depend on the quality of what you can buy, if you decide not to make that item yourself.

That raises the question of whether there have to be firms at all, if transaction costs fall far enough. I explored that idea earlier in this book when I claimed "Bosses Don't Wear Bunny Slippers." In that account, the bosses discover that they can't rely on outside contracts alone, and need some employees.

But I wrote that 10 years ago. In 2008, Sears was still a reasonably strong company, and Amazon mostly sold books. In 2018, buying almost anything and making or selling only your core product at least seems possible.

Will large, vertically integrated firms as we have known them disappear?

"Vertically integrated" means owning some of the "upstream" supply chain or some of the "downstream" retail space where consumers actually buy things. That control over the supply chain, and the consequent cost saving, was actually the explanation for the growth of the integrated big-box stores, most particularly Sears in the early 20th century, and Walmart, Best Buy, and Barnes and Noble in the late 20th and early 21st centuries.

Being able to buy in large quantities and guarantee an output market for small producers was an excellent way to bring down transaction costs of finding products to sell, and the big-box stores could sell at a lower final price as a result. They drove many smaller firms out of business because their supply-chain dominance was unstoppable.

But, as economist Herbert Stein famously observed, "If something cannot go on forever, it will stop." The new "platform economy" is built around using apps to sell reductions in transaction costs, enabling peer-to-peer transactions and sharing of many products. Sears and Barnes and Noble have for all practical purposes disappeared as viable enterprises. Best Buy and Walmart are both surviving, but they are doing that at least in part by expanding their online presence, becoming more like Amazon.

One big expense for retailers is a brick-and-mortar location where consumers can "interact with" (usually, but not always, meaning "try on") merchandise. The problem is that a new store location or a new product may generate attention and foot traffic for a few weeks, only for the retailer to see the interest die down quickly. This has led to a number of large commercial spaces — especially, but not only, shopping malls — to encourage "pop-up" stores.

Malls need to cover their average costs, on average, but many times of the year they are happy to cover their marginal costs with short-term leases if the alternative is for the space simply to be vacant. After all, foot traffic and the visual appeal of colorful signs and interesting displays make all the other stores look a little less drab. As Melissa Wylie put it in the November 2017 Bizwomen:

> Pop-up stores allow online brands to interact with shoppers and reach new people without breaking the bank on a retail lease, TechCrunch reports. Simon Malls recently launched The Edit to give e-commerce startups a place to set up shop, and to attract shoppers looking for fresh retail options.
>
> Simon, which operates more than 300 malls in the U.S., opened The Edit's first location last week at Roosevelt Field shopping mall in New York, TechCrunch reported. The Edit provides a pop-up retail space on a one- to six-month basis.

> The Edit offers fixtures and displays, security, marketing and background music for as little as $500 a month, per TechCrunch. Brands now showing at Roosevelt Field include Beltology, Thursday Boot Co. and donut shop Cuzin's Duzin.[76]

This can all get pretty meta. "The Edit" at Long Island's Roosevelt Field mall, which Wylie refers to in the article, styles itself as "a curated space for revolving brands, products & trends ready to shop, share & experience." Thus, The Edit rents a relatively large space, giving the mall a reliable source of revenue. Then The Edit provides the retail equivalent of WeWork, only instead of a work desk and printer the user rents display space and a cash register. A few weeks of physical display and retail location and the current "tenant" moves out, having spent only a few hundred dollars, increased its brand recognition, and risked very little.

By renting rather than owning retail space, and ensuring that there is always something different and interesting to see, The Edit hopes to make evanescence a permanent feature. The Edit presents itself as the "first scalable turnkey retail platform." The firms that use The Edit space can have far fewer employees, and a far smaller footprint, because they only rent, and briefly at that, their consumer-facing physical space. You can imagine that six firms use just one physical retail space over the course of a year, taking turns using the space for two months each.

76 https://www.bizjournals.com/bizwomen/news/latest-news/2017/11/are-pop-ups-the-future-of-retail.html

Why Not Rent?

Which is why I think that if Coase were alive today, he would ask a different question: why do so many firms own, when they could rent? The answer, though, would be the same: transaction costs. But as new forms and platforms are created, we see a dramatic decline in firm size and the physical presence of retailers. Those empty Sears, Penney's, and other large retailer stores at your local mall may soon be repurposed as flexible retail platforms where online sellers can let people interact with their products at very low cost. Firms may become dramatically smaller, as other systems for controlling transaction costs replace them. Stores will act like miniature malls, renting space, not selling products.

Richard Sears was originally a railroad man; he vertically integrated into retail through his famous Sears Catalogue as a way to ensure business for his railroad. Later, the company paid a fortune for retail space, which it owned and operated at a high volume.

We are moving back toward a "catalogue" setting, where people can find things online. But folks still want to touch, to feel, and to try on. Renting space and sharing it with other retailers in a "curated" setting is not really new. It's just a different way of reducing transaction costs.

6. The Revolutionary Economic Achievement of Platforms

Sometimes we share things; sometimes we buy things and pay to store them. When economists see two different ways of organizing an activity in a social setting, they have learned to think that the first explanation of the puzzle of why both ways are employed is a hidden trade-off.

In the case of most goods and services, identifying the hidden trade-off reveals that sharing and storing are substitutes, and that the relevant "price" that separates the activities is "transaction costs." I have claimed that transaction costs can be divided into three categories:

1. Triangulation: The name comes from the old practice of locating a point on the surface of the earth using geometry. The transaction costs of locating opportunities for mutually beneficial exchange or cooperation involve finding information and organizing a space in which people can interact with the specific partners who can benefit. Most blackboard examples of economics start with one person who has a widget and needs money, and another who has money and needs a widget. But triangulation is not automatic, and it's not cheap.
2. Transfer: Once the possibility of exchange is identified, there remain many obstacles. The negotiation of a price, the defeating of the tyranny of distance, the problem of packaging, and the process of delivery and payment all stand in the way.

3. Trust: In a way, trust interacts with both triangulation and transfer because trust reflects the expectation that promises will be carried out and that no other harms will be dealt by theft or violence. But it makes sense to conceive of trust as a separate category because solutions to the trust problem involve reputation, the expectation of repeat business, or the posting of some kind of bond or other depreciable asset as a "hostage" to ensure compliance.

Any arrangement for fostering cooperation that solves all three problems is called a "platform." Platforms are systems that operate as meta-markets; it is on or in a platform that what we usually think of as markets operate. What I mean is that platforms are places, virtual or physical, where buyers and sellers make markets in specific items.

Perhaps the oldest platforms of this sort were the markets, or "souqs," in what is now eastern Syria and southern Iraq. Think about it: if the usual model of greed absent transaction costs were operating, where would a seller want to operate? No one would say, "Let's go to a giant market full of competitors, where we have to rent space." Instead, each seller would locate away from the rest to avoid competition.

But that ignores transaction costs. Sellers gathered in souqs because buyers knew that was where they could find sellers. It was easier to provide security over a concentrated area, and it was possible to compare prices and arrange financing, through (say) exchange of goods for different metals or currencies, because of the scale of operation. And it was possible to identify and expel merchants who tried to sell adulterated products or sell products fraudulently.

None of these solutions were perfect, of course, and transport costs, in particular, were prohibitive, but these early platforms created a setting where an enormous variety of products and services could be sold.

Clumsy Physical Platforms

Some version of the souq, the bazaar, the kermis, or the market served reasonably well for thousands of years. But a number of entrepreneurs realized they could sell even more products by selling reductions in transaction costs.

Physical souqs are clumsy platforms because by definition sellers must take goods to the market and then buyers must transport them home or wherever they are to be sent. If the triangulation and transfer steps could be integrated with transport and efficient clearing of transactions, the costs to consumers could be cut dramatically.

To consumers, all costs are transaction costs. It doesn't matter much whether the costs of purchase are monetary price, costs of queuing to obtain the product, or risk of robbery; a reduction in any of those margins will cause consumers to buy more.

There were several kinds of innovations along these lines, but perhaps the most famous, at least in the United States, was the Sears catalog. Sears provided a viable platform, with information about what could be purchased and how much it cost; reliable delivery services with guarantees of safe arrival; procedures for clearing transactions, including credit for buyers; and rental "space" for third-party sellers.

Sears also had a guarantee, with money back for consumers who were not happy with the quality of their purchase. And the name

"Sears" came to be associated with honest and reliable service, so that word of mouth became an outsourced, distributed source of trust.

The point is that large collections of people, even those who don't know each other well and who may not trust each other, may be able to devise decentralized institutions that overcome this problem. Should the government solve the problem, or should people be left to solve it on their own? And how would we know which sort of "solution" is better?

In the next section I offer my own solution: *directional* libertarianism.

7. Directionalism vs. Destinationism

I'm a "directional" libertarian. That means that if a proposed new policy or reform of an existing policy cuts spending or increases liberty, I'm for it, even if it isn't a "real" libertarian policy.

Directionalism infuriates the "destinationists." Destinationists have a notion of the ideal outcome, the perfect solution. Any policy that is not acceptable in the imaginary destinationist world is not acceptable in the present world of realized institutions.

For example, consider "public" education. In most states, we finance education through tax revenues, and the state also retains the monopoly provision of education services. One policy, "vouchers," uncouples financing and provision. Parents could send their children to state-operated schools, or privately-operated schools. And they can switch, a threat that eliminates the worst schools through competition.

Many destinationists hate vouchers. The state is still involved in the collection of funding through taxes and in licensing and permitting schools that qualify to receive vouchers. When I was running for governor in 2008, as a Libertarian in North Carolina, quite a few destinationist libertarians became so angry at me for supporting vouchers that they withdrew their support entirely.

Because "we" want the state to do nothing.

The Full Loaf

I agree with that bottom line, as far as it goes. But I want the state to the right kind of nothing.

Let me give an illustration. In 2009 I was living in the small city of Erlangen, in southern Germany. I didn't speak German, and often found that I got in trouble simply because I didn't understand what the culture expected of me. There are ways to behave, and not to behave. And I didn't know which was which. Problems arose in settings where I thought I knew what to do.

Like in a grocery store.

In the southern U.S., if you see an elderly woman pushing an empty shopping cart back toward the store, and you are heading in to the store, you might take the cart so she won't have to push it.

I saw just that situation one day, and thought I knew what to do. Except that in Europe, groceries have cart deposits. You put a Euro in a slot to unchain your cart. Return the cart, chain it back up, get your Euro back.

Consequently, when I tried to pantomime to an old woman one day in Erlangen that I was willing to do her the favor of pushing her cart back, her reaction surprised me: she scowled, and then cut hard left. But I had on more sensible shoes, so I cut off the angle.

She dodged right, but I was younger and faster and was able to grab her cart. Her reaction surprised me again: she started screaming. She had pretty good lungs for an old lady, but an underground parking garage has good acoustics.

The acoustics were good enough, in fact, that we immediately attracted the attention of a large, and apparently angry, German policeman. Understand: German policemen are not angry. You are a boring insect, unworthy of their interest.

This policeman, though, was very interested in me. And he was running. German policemen don't run. This was not good. He started yelling at me while he was still ten meters away. I tried to explain that I didn't speak German. He shouted (his English was excellent): "WHAT are you DOIN'?" The little old lady rammed the cart into the rack, chained it, got her Euro, and held it high, a glistering gloat of victory over American imperialism.

The Explanation

I explained that I didn't know about the deposit, because in the U.S. our grocery carts are free range. As I talked, and handed over my ID, I could see the cop was calming down. He had been to the U.S., and knew the carts were different. After a few minutes, half-smiling (German cops don't smile; their faces might break), he said: "She's still watching, isn't she?" I glanced over; Oma was indeed peering at us from behind a post. I nodded.

And the policeman said, "Okay, then." Unexpectedly, he started yelling loudly, right up in my face, and thumping my chest with his finger: "I don't think she speaks English. So if you just look scared and sorry, I think this will end our time together here today!"

The cop walked away. The woman gave me a decisive, scornful head snap, and marched back to her car. I went shopping, put the groceries in my backpack, and then went straight home to hide in my bathtub. Still, I was grateful to the policeman. He had done exactly the right kind of nothing.

The Right Kind of Nothing

Now, the cop could have done other kinds of nothing. For example, he could have sat with his partner in the car, and just looked around when they heard the old lady screaming. They could have said, "Oh, old lady getting robbed. You want to get some doughnuts, bro?" Nobody thinks that's the right kind of nothing.

Alternatively, he could have done something. He could have arrested me for trying to steal a euro from an old lady, which in a way I was trying to do. That would have been the dumb kind of something that many police have been doing more of lately.

Instead, he figured out the perfect immediate solution, and went on to look for other, more pressing problems.

That's the argument, as I see it, for directionalism. We can often make progress by pressing for improvement, rather than holding out for perfection. Sometimes, just the right kind of nothing is good enough.

IX

CONCLUSION

This book is a collection of essays, written between 2005 and 2019. The essays have been adapted and updated, and they take up many different subjects.

But the essential themes of the work are consistent. It is worth summarizing those themes one more time, in closing.

A. Two ugly pigs. Markets aren't perfect, and models that set up perfect markets as a goal are misleading and probably destructive. The only realistic alternative to markets, or the only one consistent with any kind of human flourishing and liberty, is democracy. And democracy isn't perfect, either. And in fact the problems with consumers are also the problems with voters, because they are the same people. We all like free stuff, and will pay anything to get it. We have inconsistent preferences--economists call these trade-offs--and we can be manipulated into making choices by presentation, context, or emotional appeals. The argument for markets rests on the fact that markets generate opportunity cost signals about resources, and those price signals are the result of anonymous, decentralized, impersonal processes that are harder to manipulate than elections. In many industries, there are barriers to entry, but these are dwarfed by the barriers to entry facing political outsiders. It's a mistake for either "side" simply to point out the other side's model has flaws, and thus to conclude "Therefore, [my ideal system]." It just doesn't work that way.

B. Markets work in large measure because capitalism enables the fast and flexible mobilization of liquid capital. It is easy to get hung up on the "seen" effects, which are sharp increases in inequality in financial wealth. But the "unseen" (to paraphrase Bastiat) effects are easy to miss: the equalization of consumer surplus. In 1700, the difference in education, life span, clothing, housing, and mode of transport between the top and bottom 10% of the human population was enormous. Today, at least in developed nations, the poor person lives in an apartment, has a microwave and cable television, a car, and a cell phone. Those things are not as nice as the wealthy person has, but we all have them. And we can all use the machinery of creation and delivery of products and services that is operating in the background. We can all use Twitter, Facebook, Wikipedia, Instagram, and other "apps," essentially for free. Because of capitalism, there is more equality among people than at any previous period in human history.

C. Entrepreneurs and "middlemen" are the moving parts of

> the system, the restless, questing motors of capitalism. It is tempting to think that such folks do not really "deserve" the wealth they have. Certainly, my academic colleagues, many of whom have always worked hard and gotten the best grades, from the best universities, are upset by this. How can that car salesman or that plastic toy manufacturer make more money than I, smart university professor, gets paid? It's not fair! We should redistribute that money to the poor! There are two big problems with this "social justice" argument.

First, if you only look at the winners, you miss the reason why the profit system exists. Many people have tried many different things, and they were motivated to start that search for profit because they were trying to create consumer surplus. Most failed, and went bankrupt. A few succeeded, and created enormous value for society. Some commentators complain about the profits of the Apple corporation. But consider the consumer surplus, the difference between the price paid by consumers and the value received by consumers, for Apple products. Many people would pay $2,000 for a new iPhone, and it only costs $900. The problem is that profits sit out in the open, in fancy houses or bank accounts, where consumer surplus is just enjoyed by the consumer. But the winners in this process are those who successfully created great products and delivered the largest benefits to society.

Second, the very notion of "deserve" is nonsensical as a necessary condition for inequality. Remember when Frodo, upset at Gollum's perfidy, says Gollum does not deserve to live? The conversation went like this:

(FRODO) "Now at any rate [Gollum] is as bad as an Orc, and just an enemy. He deserves death."

(GANDALF) "Deserves it! I daresay he does. Many that live deserve death. And some that die deserve life. Can you give it to them? Then do not be too eager to deal out death in judgement. For even the very wise cannot see all ends."

Yes, exactly. Gandalf isn't thinking about central planning here, but this is a very Hayekian perspective on "social justice." Life isn't fair. Bad things happen to good people. Some not very nice people amass large fortunes. Perhaps they don't deserve that wealth, in a strict moral sense. But even the very wise, the most powerful central planner, cannot see all ends, or the new products and services that will benefit consumers most. In our system middlemen and entrepreneurs are entitled, and actually fully entitled, to that wealth because of the value that the system creates for consumers. No system of redistribution or social welfare payments can come close to matching the benefits to the poor that come from having a decent job and access to a WalMart.

I suppose that's the message I want to close with. The concern for inequality is sincere, and there are problems in democratic systems where concentrations of economic power metastasize into concentrated political power. But if our concern is with poverty, and the welfare of the poor in an absolute sense, we live in a golden age. More people have broken out of poverty in the last 50 years than in the previous 500 years. The reason is capitalism; there is no other explanation.

So I would answer the question posed in the title of this book in a cautious affirmative: I hope so. Capitalism faces dangers, from within and without. Externally, forces of envy and hunger for power lead demagogues to direct howling mobs at the very institutions that have led to our unprecedented prosperity. Internally, the temptations to enlist the powers of the state to "help" powerful corporations maintain their central positions by blocking competition seem irresistible.

In fact, the turn toward cronyism means that the very strength of capitalist innovation and the drive to profits are being perverted and corrupted toward destroying the system that created them. Karl Marx was right: there is a "contradiction" in capitalism. Not the contradiction of exploited labor value, leading to a political revolution, but the contradiction of a drive for rents enabled by a corrupting state, a siren's song of safety and protection from competition.

If capitalism is to be sustainable, we require a new consensus, an agreement that the state will not offer such blandishments and that entrepreneurs and corporations will not seek them. This will require a reconceptualization of the role of ethics and profit in the corporation. I cannot easily foresee how this thing is to be accomplished. But I know that if we fail the end for capitalism is like that foreseen in Hosea (8:7): "For they have sown the wind, and they shall reap the whirlwind: it hath no stalk: the bud shall yield no meal: if so be it yield, the strangers shall swallow it up."

REFERENCES

Alchian, Armen A., and Demsetz Harold. (1972)., "Production, Information Costs, and Economic Organization", *American Economic Review*, Vol. 62, No. 5., pp. 777-795, 1972.

Ariely, Dan. (2010). *Predictably Irrational, Revised and Expanded Edition: The Hidden Forces That Shape Our Decisions*. 2nd Edition. New York: Harper.

Aristotle. N.d. *Politics*. The Internet Classics Archivc. http://classics.mit.edu/Aristotle/politics.html (accessed February 2013).

Backhouse, Roger E. and Medema, Steven G. (2012). "Economists and the analysis of government failure: fallacies in the Chicago and Virginia interpretations of Cambridge welfare economics. *Cambridge Journal of Economics*, 36(4): 981–994. https://doi.org/10.1093/cje/ber047.

Bastiat, Frederic. (1850). "What is Seen and Not Seen." In *Economic Sophisms*. Indianapolis: Liberty Fund. https://www.econlib.org/library/Bastiat/basEss.html?chapter_num=4#book-reader

Baumol, William. (1990). Entrepreneurship: Productive, Unproductive, and Destructive. *Journal of Political Economy*. 98(5): 893-921.

BBC World Service. August 28, (2017). "The Texan Energy Revolution.“ Podcast audio. https://www.bbc.co.uk/programmes/w3cstwy9

Benn, Stanley. (1988), *A Theory of Freedom*, Cambridge: Cambridge University Press.

Bergh, Andreas. (2016). *Sweden and the Revival of the Capitalist Welfare State*. Edward Elgar.

Bernstein, Ross. (2006). *The Code: The Unwritten Rules of Fighting and Retaliation in the NHL*. Triumph Books: Chicago.

Biasca N, Wirth S, Tegner Y. (2002). "The avoidability of head and neck injuries in ice hockey: an historical review." *British Journal of Sports Medicine* 2002; 36: 410-427. https://bjsm.bmj.com/content/36/6/410.full

Black. Duncan. 2001 (1958). *Theory of Committees and Elections*. Springer.

Boettke, Peter. (2001). *Calculation and Coordination Essays on socialism and transitional political economy*. New York: Routledge.

Boettke, Peter. (2013). "Boettke on Living Economics." EconTalk. Jan 28. http://www.econtalk.org/boettke-on-living-economics/#audio-highlights

Brennan, G. And J. Buchanan (1985) *Reason of Rules: Constitutional Political Economy*. New York: Cambridge University press.

Brennan, G., & Lomasky, L. (1997). *Democracy and decision: The pure theory of electoral preference*. New York: Cambridge University Press.

Brennan, Geoffrey, and Philip Petit. (2004). *The Economy of Esteem: An Essay on Civil and Political Society*. Cambridge University Press.

Brennan, Jason. (2012). *The Ethics of Voting*. Princeton, NJ: Princeton University Press.

(von) Böhm-Bawerk, Eugen. (1891). *The Positive Theory of Capital.* Indianapolis: Liberty Fund. https://www.econlib.org/library/BohmBawerk/bbPTC.html

Buchanan, James. (1975). *The Limits of Liberty: Between Anarchy and Leviathan*. Chicago: University of Chicago Press.

Buchanan, James. (1979). "Politics without Romance: A Sketch of Positive Public Choice Theory and Its Normative Implications," Inaugural Lecture, Institute for Advanced Studies, Vienna, Austria, IHS-Journal, Zeitschrift des Instituts für Höhere Studien, Wien 3 (1979): B1-B11.

Buchanan, James. (2001). *Cost and Choice: The Collected Works of James M.* Buchanan. Indianapolis: Liberty Fund. https://www.econlib.org/library/Buchanan/buchCv6toc.html#Cost%20and%20Choice:%20An%20Inquiry%20in%20Economic%20Theory

Buchanan, James M. and Gordon Tullock. (1962). *The Calculus of Consent*. Ann Arbor: University of Michigan Press.

Buchanan, James, and W. C. Stubblebine. (1962)., "Externality," *Economica*. 29: 371-84.

Buchanan, James, Robert Tollison, and Gordon Tullock (eds). (1980). *Towards a Theory of the Rent Seeking Society*. College Station, TX: Texas A&M University Press.

Burke, Edmund. (1756 / 1982). *A Vindication of Natural Society: or, a View of the Miseries and Evils arising to Mankind from every Species of Artificial Society. In a Letter to Lord *** by a Late Noble Writer,* * ed. Frank N. Pagano (Indianapolis: Liberty Fund, Inc.)

Candela, Rosolino A. and Vincent J. Geloso. (2018). "The lightship in economics." *Public Choice*. 176(3–4): 479–506 https://doi.org/10.1007/s11127-018-0573-x.

Caplan, Bryan. (2008). *The Myth of the Rational Voter: Why Democracies Choose Bad Policies*. Princeton, NJ: Princeton University.

Chandler, Alfred. (1993). *The Visible Hand: The Managerial Revolution in American Business*. New York: Belknap. (2nd edition).

Carden, Art. (2009). *A Note on Profit, Loss, and Social Responsibility*. New Perspectives on Political Economy. 5(1): 1 – 8.

Carter Crockett, Alistair R. Anderson, (2004) "The Added Value of Virtue", *Journal of Research in Marketing and Entrepreneurship,* 6(1): 5 – 17.

Cheung, Steven N. S. (1973). "The Fable of the Bees: An Economic Investigation." *Journal of Law and Economics*. 16: 11-33.

Cicero, Marcus Tullius. (1991). *On Duties*. Cambridge Texts in the History of Political Thought. E. M. Atkins (Editor), and M. T. Griffin (Translator). New York: Cambridge University Press.

Coase, Ronald H. (1937), "The Nature of the Firm", *Economica,* 4: 386-405.

Coase, R. H. (1960) The problem of social cost. J*ournal of Law and Economics*. 3: 1-44.

Coase, R. H. (1974). "The Lighthouse in Economics." *Journal of Law and Economics*. 17(2): 357-376.

Coase, R. H. (1988) *The firm, the market, and the law*. Chicago: University of Chicago Press.

Cornuelle, Richard. (1999). *Reclaiming the American Dream: The Role of Private Individuals and Voluntary Associations*. New York: Transaction Publishers.

Couyoumdjian, Juan Pablo, and Michael C. Munger. (2016). "The Entrepreneurial Virtues," with J. P. Couyoumdjian. In Iskra Fileva (ed), *Philosophy of Character*, Oxford University Press.

Easterly, William. (2001). *The Elusive Quest for Growth: Economists' Adventures and Misadventures in the Tropics*. Cambridge, MA: MIT Press.

Ehrlich, Paul R. (1968). *The Population Bomb*. New York: Ballantine Books.

Fisher, Kenneth L. (2007). *100 Minds That Made the Market*. Fisher Investments Press / Wiley.

Folsom, Burton W. (1987). *Entrepreneurs vs. The State: A New Look at the Rise of Big Business in America*, 1840 – 1920. Reston, VA: Young Americas Foundation.

Fox, Eleanor. (2002). "What is harm to competition? – Exclusionary practices and anticompetitive effect." *Antitrust Law Journal* 70: 371-411.

Gilder, George. N.d. "Computer Industry." Concise Encyclopedia of Economics." Library of Economics and Liberty. (Indianapolis, IN: Liberty Fund) https://www.econlib.org/library/

Enc/ComputerIndustry.html

Guevara, Che. (1965). *Man and Socialism in Cuba*. Reprint Edition, 2009. Pathfinder Press.

Guzman, Ricardo, and Michael Munger. (2019). A Theory of Just Market Exchange. *Journal of Value Inquiry*.

Hayek, Friedrich. (1945). "The Use of Knowledge in Society", Library of Economics and Liberty. Edition: *American Economic Review*, XXXV, No. 4; pp. 519-30. https://www.econlib.org/library/Essays/hykKnw1.html

Hayek, F. A. (1948). *Individualism and Economic Order*. Chicago: University of Chicago Press.

Hayek, F. A. (1952). *The Counter-Revolution of Science*. University of Chicago Press.

Hayek, F. A. (1978). "Competition as a Discovery Procedure." *New Studies in Philosophy, Politics and Economics*. Chicago: University of Chicago Press.

Hayek, F.A. (1991). *The Fatal Conceit*. University of Chicago Press: 1991.

Hayek, F.A. (1998). *Law, Legislation, and Liberty*. 2nd Reprint Edition. New York: Routledge.

Hayek, F.A. (2011). *The Constitution of Liberty*. Chicago: University of Chicago Press.

Hazlett, Tom. (2017). "We Could Have Had Cellphones Four Decades Earlier." *Reason*. July.
https://reason.com/2017/06/11/we-could-have-had-cellphones-f

Hicks, Stephen. (2009). The Kevin O'Connor Interview: Venture capital and entrepreneurship. *Kaizen: The Newsletter of the Center for Ethics and Entrepreneurship at Rockford College*. April, Issue 6.

Hinich, Melvin, and Munger, Michael. (1997). *Analytical Politics*. New York: Cambridge University Press.

Hobbes, Thomas. (1651/ 1990). *Leviathan*. Hackett Publishers

Hogan, Lawrence D., and Jules Tygiel. (2006). *Shades of Glory: The Negro Leagues and the Story of African-American Baseball*. New York: National Geographic.

Hume, David. (1978). *A Treatise of Human Nature*. New York: Oxford University Press.

Iversen, Torben. (2005). *Capitalism, Democracy, and Welfare*. New York: Cambridge University Press.

Kahneman, Daniel; Tversky, Amos (1979). "Prospect Theory: An Analysis of Decision under Risk." *Econometrica*. 47 (2): 263–291.

Keech, William, and Michael Munger. (2015). "The Anatomy of Government Failure." *Public Choice*. 164(1): 1-42.

Kirzner, Israel. (1978). "Economics and Error," in L. Spadaro, ed., *New Directions in Austrian Economics* Kansas City: Sheed, Andrews, and McMeel.

Klein, Benjamin, Robert Crawford, and Armen Alchian. (1978). "Vertical Integration, Appropriable Rents, and the Competitive Contracting Process." *Journal of Law and Economics.*

Klein, Dan, Adrian Moore and Binyam Reja. (1997). *Curb Rights: A Foundation for Free Enterprise in Urban Transit*. Brookings Institution.

Kraemer, C.C. (2003). "In Defense of Price Gouging." TechCentralStation, September 23.
http://www.techcentralstation.com/092303F.html

Krueger, Anne. (1974). "The Political Economy of the Rent Seeking Society." *American Economic Review*. 64: 291-303.
http://links.jstor.org/sici?sici=0002-8282%28197406%2964%3A3%3C291%3ATPEOTR%3E2.0.CO%3B2-W

Lawson, Robert, and G. Dirk Mateer. (1995). "The Thrill of Victory, The Agony of Defeat." *Public Choice* 83: 305-312.

Leeson, Peter T. (2007). "One More Time with Feeling: The Law Merchant, Arbitration, and International Trade." *Indian Journal of Economics and Business*. https://www.peterleeson.com/One_More_Time_with_Feeling.pdf

Lewis, David, (1969). *Convention: A Philosophical Study*. Cambridge: Harvard University Press.

MacKenzie, Richard. N.d. "Industrial Policy."*Concise Encyclopedia of Economics*. Library of Economics and Liberty (Indianapolis, IN: Liberty Fund) https://www.econlib.org/library/Enc/IndustrialPolicy.html

Maugham, Somerset. (2014). *The Great Novels and Short Stories of Somerset Maugham*. Skyhorse Publishing.

McKeon, Richard. (1947). *Introduction to Aristotle*: Nicomachean Ethics. Translated by W.D. Ross. Modern Library.

Meade, J.E. (1952). "External Economies and Diseconomies in a Competitive Situation." *Economic Journal*, 62, 51-69.

Medema, Steven G. (2014). Economics and Institutions: Lessons from the Coase Theorem. *Revue économique* 65(2): 243-261. https://www.jstor.org/stable/42771815?

Mencken, H.L. (1927). *Notes on Democracy*. Reprinted in *A Mencken Chrestomathy*, Vintage Books, 1982.

Mitchell, William, and Michael Munger. (1993). "Doing Well While Intending Good: Exploitation and the Pareto Criterion," *Journal of Theoretical Politics* 5:34-79.

Milgrom, Paul R., North, Douglass C., and Weingast, Barry R. (1990). "The Role of Institutions in the Revival of Trade: The Law Merchant, Private Judges, and the Champagne Fairs." *Economics and Politics*, 2(1).
https://onlinelibrary.wiley.com/doi/pdf/10.1111/j.1468-0343.1990.tb00020.x

Mill, J.S. (1848 / 2004). *The Principles of Political Economy*. Prometheus Press.

Mises, Ludwig von. 1944/1969. Bureaucracy. Auburn, AL: Ludwig von Mises Institute.
https://mises.org/library/bureaucracy

Mises, Ludwig (von). (2002). "Competition as a Discovery Procedure." Translated by Marcellus Snowe. *Quarterly Journal of Austrian Economics*. 5(3): 9–23.

Mises, Ludwig (von). (2008). *Profit and Loss*. Auburn: Ludwig von Mises Institute.
https://mises.org/library/profit-and-loss-0/html.

Mises, Ludwig (von). (1958). *Liberty and Property*. Auburn: Ludwig von Mises Institute.
https://mises.org/library/liberty-and-property/html/c/212

Munger, M. (n.d.). “Division of Labor.” *Concise Encyclopedia of Economics*. Indianapolis: Liberty Fund. https://www.econlib.org/library/Enc/DivisionofLabor.html

Munger, M. (2011). Euvoluntary or not, exchange is just. *Social Philosophy and Policy* 28(2): 192–211.

Munger, Michael. (2018). *Tomorrow 3.0: Transaction Costs and the Sharing Economy*. New York: Cambridge University Press.

Munger, Michael. (2019). “Tullock and the Welfare Costs of Corruption: There IS a “Political Coase Theorem.” *Public Choice*. 181(1–2): 83–100.

Munger, Michael, and Mario Villarreal-Diaz. (2019). “The Road to Crony Capitalism,” *The Independent Review* 23(3): 331-344. https://www.independent.org/publications/tir/toc.asp?issueID=96.

Murphy, Robert P. “Subjective-Value Theory.” (2011). Ludwig von Mises Institute. May 30.
https://mises.org/library/subjective-value-theory.

“N.C. Senator Works To End Price-Gouging After Natural Disasters: Bill Targets Sales Of Emergency Supplies,” (2003). *News and Observer*, May 9, P. A1.

Niskanan, William. (1971). *Bureaucracy and Representative Government*. Chicago: Aldine-Atherton Press.

North, Douglass. (1981). *Structure and Change in Economic History*. New York: Norton.

North, Douglass. (1990). I*nstitutions, Institutional Change, and Economic History*. New York: Cambridge University Press.

North, Douglass. (1991). "Institutions." *Journal of Economic Perspectives*. 5(1): 97-112.

North, Douglass C. (1994). "Economic Performance through Time," *American Economic Review* 84(3).

North, Douglass. (2006). "Cognitive science and the study of the 'rules of the game' in a world of uncertainty." In Drobak, JN (ed) *Norms and the law*. Cambridge University Press, Cambridgc, pp 48–56.

Olsaretti, Serena. (2004). *Liberty, Desert, and the Market*. Cambridge University Press.

O'Rourke, P. J. (2003). *Parliament of Whores: A Lone Humorist Attempts to Explain the Entire U.S. Government*. New York: Grove Press.

Ostrom E (1990) *Governing the Commons: The Evolution of Institutions for Collective Action*. Cambridge, UK: Cambridge University Press.

Ostrom E (2000) Collective action and the evolution of social norms. *Journal of Economic Perspectives* 14(3): 137–158.

Otteson, James. (2002). *Adam Smith's Marketplace of Life*. Cambridge University Press.

Peden, Margie, Richard Scurfield, David Sleet, Dinesh Mohan, Adnan A. Hyder, Eva Jarawan and Colin Mathers. (2004). World report on road traffic injury prevention, Geneva, Switzerland: World Health Organization.

Peltzman, S. (1975). The effects of automobile safety regulation. *Journal of Political Economy*. 83: 677-726.

Pigou, A. C. (1912). *Wealth and welfare*. London: Macmillan.

Pigou, A. C. (1920). *The economics of welfare*. London: Macmillan.

Pigou, A. C. (1935). State action and laissez-faire. In *Economics in practice: Six lectures on current issues*. London: Macmillan and Co. 107-128.

Polybius, (1889). *Histories*. Translated by Evelyn S. Shuckburgh, 1889.

Pope, Adam, and Robert Tollison. (2010). "'Rubbin' Is Racin'": Evidence of the Peltzman Effect from NASCAR." *Public Choice*, 142(3/4): 507-513.

Potter, Chris. (2006) ."I'm still wondering about the Pittsburgh Left. No one can tell me where it comes from." *PIttsburgh City Paper*. June. 22, https://www.pghcitypaper.com/pittsburgh/im-still-wondering-about-the-pittsburgh-left-no-one-can-tell-me-where-it-comes-from/Content?oid=1334231

Powell, Benjamin. (2014). *Out of Poverty: Sweatshops In The Global Economy*. New York: Cambridge.

Prigg, Mark. (2014). "Will overpopulation drive us to eat our own DEAD? Controversial academic claims humanity is moving towards cannibalism at 'ridiculous speed.'" *Daily Mail.* May 22. Accessed June 17, 2019.
https://www.dailymail.co.uk/sciencetech/article 2636845/Will-overpopulation-drive-CANNIBALISM-Controversial-academic-claims-humanity-moving-issue-ridiculous-speed.html

Prinzo, Zita Weise. (2009). "Pellagra and its prevention and control in major emergencies." World Health Organization.
https://www.who.int/nutrition/publications/en/pellagra_prevention_control.pdf.

Radford, R. A. (1945). The Economic Organisation of a P.O.W. Camp. *Economica*, 12(48): 189-201.

Rehmke, Gregory. (2013). " From Poland to Peru: Black Markets, Parallel Societies." *Economic Thinking.*
http://economicthinking.org/from-poland-to-peru-black-markets/

Ridgeway, James. (1990). "Environmental Devastation in the Soviet Union." *The Multinational Monitor* 11(9). https://www.multinationalmonitor.org/hyper/issues/1990/09/index.html

Robinson, Jackie, and Alfred Duckett. (2003). *I Never Had It Made: An Autobiography of Jackie Robinson*. Harper.

Rosenblatt, Aaron. (1967). Negroes in baseball: The failure of success. *Society*. 4(9): 51–53.

Rowley, Charles, and Robert D. Tollison. 1988. *The Political Economy of Rent-Seeking*. Kluwer Academic Press.

Paul Sabin. (2013). *The Bet: Paul Ehrlich, Julian Simon, and Our Gamble over Earth's Future*. Yale University Press.

Sandel, M. (1998). *What money can't buy: The moral limits of markets. The Tanner Lectures on Human Values*, delivered at Brasenose College, Oxford, May 11 and 12, 1998.

Say, J.B. (1834). *A Treatise on Political Economy. Or, the Production*, Distribution, and Consumption of Wealth. Reprinted 2007, Ludwig von Mises Institute.

Schiller, Friedrich. (1967). Letters on the Aesthetic Education of Man, translated by E. Wilkinson and L. A. Willoughby (Oxford: Clarendon Press).

Schumpeter, Joseph. (1934). "The Nature and Necessity of a Price System", *Economic Reconstruction*.

Schwartz, Richard. (2006). *John Harvey Kellogg, M.D.: Pioneering Health Reformer.* Review and Herald Publication Association.

Sidgwick, Henry. The Principles of Political Economy, (1883). New York: MacMillan and Company.

Simmons, Katie. (2014). "China's government may be communist, but its people embrace capitalism." *Fact Tank.* Pew Research Center. October 10.
https://www.pewresearch.org/fact-tank/2014/10/10/chinas-government-may-be-communist-but-its-people-embrace-capitalism/

Simon, Julian. (1981). *The Ultimate Resource.* Princeton University Press.

Smith, Adam (1982/1759), *The Theory of Moral Sentiments.* Indianapolis: Liberty Fund.

Smith, Adam (1976/1776), *An Inquiry into the Nature and Causes of the Wealth of Nations*, Chicago: University of Chicago Press.

Somin, Ilya. (2013).. *Democracy and Political Ignorance: Why Smaller Government Is Smarter. Palo Alto,* CA: Stanford University Press.

Sproul, R.C. Jr. (1994). "A Profit Without Honor." New York: Foundation for Economic Education.
http://www.fee.org/publications/the-freeman/article.asp?aid=3103

Stringham, Edward P. (2015). *Private Governance: Creating Order in Economic and Social Life*. New York: Oxford University Press.

Theirer, Adam. (2014). *Permissionless Innovation: The Continuing Case for Comprehensive Technological Freedom.* Mercatus Center at George Mason University. 2014.

Tocqueville, Alexis de. (1835/2002). *Democracy in America.* Harvey C. Mansfield and Delba Winthrop (Translators). University of Chicago Press.

Tollison, Robert. (1982). Rent Seeking: A Survey. *Kyklos*. 4: 575 602.

Tomasi, J. (2012). *Free Market Fairness*. Princeton: Princeton University Press.

"Transantiago's Underlying Problem", (2007), Libertad Desarollo, No. 852, December 2007. http://www.lyd.com/LYD/Controls/Neochannels/Neo_CH3988/deploy/TP-852-El%20problema%20de%20fondo%20del%20Transantiago-28-12-2007_ingles2.pdf

Tullock, Gordon. (1967). The welfare costs of tariffs, monopolies, and theft. *Western Economic Journal*. 5: 224-232.

Tullock, Gordon. (1980). Efficient rent-seeking, in J.M. Buchanan, R.D. Tollison and G. Tullock (Eds.), *Toward a theory of rent-seeking society.* College Station: Texas A.&M. University Press.

Tullock, Gordon. (2005). *The Rent-Seeking Society*. In The Selected Works of Gordon Tullock series, V. 5 edited by Charles K. Rowley. Indianapolis, IN: Liberty Fund.

Turner, Sharon. (1840). *The History of the Anglo-Saxons from the Earliest Period to the Norman Conquest*. Pont de Arts, Paris: Baudry's European Library, Printed by Fain and Thunot. Obtained as a digital facsimile document of the 6th Edition.

Tversky, A. and D. Kahneman. (1992). Advances in Prospect Theory: Cumulative Representation of Uncertainty. *Journal of Risk* and Uncertainty 5: 297-323.

Williamson, Oliver E. (1975). *Markets and Hierarchies: Analysis and Antitrust Implications*, NY: The Free Press.

Williamson, Oliver E. (2007). "Transaction Cost Economics: An Introduction." *Economics Discussion Papers*. March 1.

Zakaria, Fareed. (2007). *The Future of Freedom: Illiberal Democracy at Home and Abroad.* New York: W.W. Norton and Company.

ABOUT THE AUTHOR

Michael Munger is a Professor of Political Science, Economics, and Public Policy at Duke University. His Economics PhD was awarded from Washington University in St. Louis in 1984. He worked as a Staff Economist for Dr. Wendy Gramm at the Federal Trade Commission in the first Reagan Administration, and has had academic appointments at Dartmouth College, University of Texas-Austin, and University of North Carolina-Chapel Hill. He directed the MPA Program at UNC, and chaired the Political Science Department at Duke from 2000 to 2010. He currently directs the interdisciplinary Philosophy, Politics, and Economics Program at Duke.

His research interests include regulation, political institutions, and political economy. His most recent book was *Tomorrow 3.0: Transaction Costs and the Sharing Economy*, published by Cambridge University Press in 2018. Munger is a Senior Fellow of the Independent Institute and the AIER, and is a former President of the Public Choice Society (1996-1998). He served as an editor of *Public Choice* (2005-2010) and *Independent Review* (2015 to present). He lives in Raleigh, North Carolina with wife Donna Gingerella and loyal dogs Murphy and Skippy Squirrelbane.

ABOUT AIER

The American Institute for Economic Research in Great Barrington, Massachusetts, was founded in 1933 as the first independent voice for sound economics in the United States. Today it publishes ongoing research, hosts educational programs, publishes books, sponsors interns and scholars, and is home to the world-renowned Bastiat Society and the highly respected Sound Money Project. The American Institute for Economic Research is a 501c3 public charity.

O

P

Made in the USA
Middletown, DE
15 December 2019